IMAGES
of America

INDIANAPOLIS ITALIANS

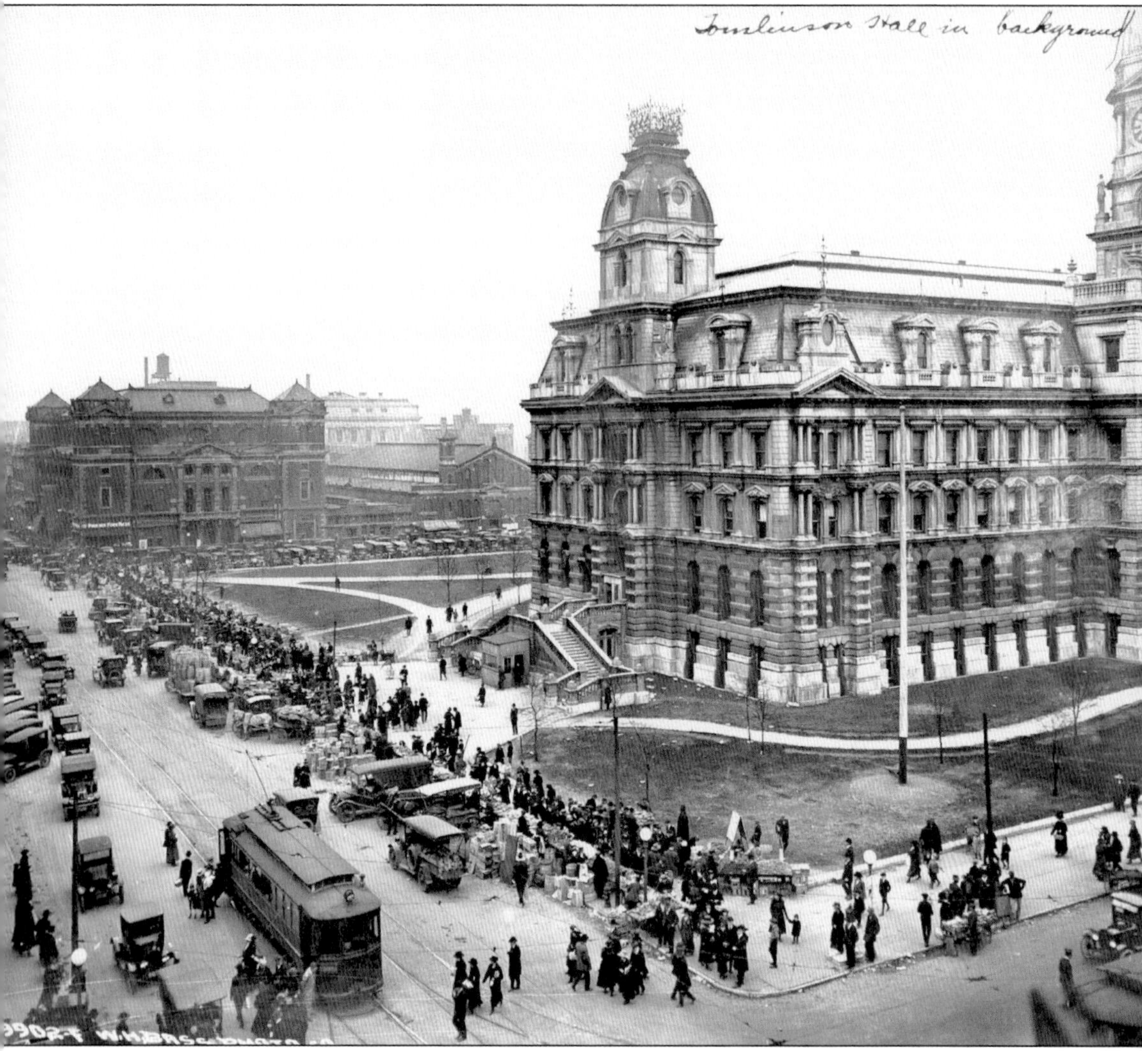

Italian immigrants and Hoosier farmers operated a thriving market in fruits and vegetables along the sidewalks and in the buildings around the Marion County Courthouse in 1920. Located north on Delaware Street is Tomlinson Hall, the city's largest public auditorium (upper left). To its right is City Market, where many stand holders were Italian. (Courtesy Indiana Historical Society.)

On the cover: Several parades passed through downtown Indianapolis to stir patriotic support for the war against the Central Powers in 1918. A parade up Meridian Street just after the signing of the armistice on November 11, 1918, included an Italian float. In this photograph, Italian schoolchildren, community leaders, and the pastor of Holy Rosary Church appear with the float. Support was easily given since Royal Italy was an ally of the United States. (Courtesy Ninfa Gatto DeHilt.)

IMAGES
of America

INDIANAPOLIS ITALIANS

James J. Divita

ARCADIA
PUBLISHING

ISBN 978-0-7385-4095-5

Published by Arcadia Publishing
Charleston, South Carolina

Printed in the United States of America

Library of Congress Catalog Card Number: 2006927645

For all general information contact Arcadia Publishing at:
Telephone 843-853-2070
Fax 843-853-0044
E-mail sales@arcadiapublishing.com
For customer service and orders:
Toll-Free 1-888-313-2665

Visit us on the Internet at www.arcadiapublishing.com

CONTENTS

Acknowledgments 6

Introduction 7

Prologue 9

1. The First Families: Foundation Builders 11

2. A New People: Italian Americans 37

3. Revival: Italian-born in the Community 63

4. Business and Sports: Community Economics and Athletics 73

5. Politics: Local Political Participation 87

6. Religion: Community Church Life 91

7. Monuments: Material Culture 111

8. Organizations: Preserving Heritage 117

Epilogue 123

Bibliography 125

Index 126

Acknowledgments

The author acknowledges his debt and expresses his gratitude to the following who lent treasured family photographs, as well as historical materials, to reveal a pictorial history of the Italian community in Indianapolis. These include Freda Buennagel, Tom Burke, Tony Burrello, Michele Caporale, Pete Cavallaro, Paul and Lisa Cento, Mary Jo Vespo Chandler, Thomas Cortese Jr., MD, Erna Santarossa De Cecco, Phil De Fabis, Ninfa "Ann" Gatto DeHilt, Charles Farah, Pietro and Silvana Ferri, Loretta Guedelhoefer, Matthew and Sandy Iaria, Dominic Iozzo, Angelina Navarra Kramer, Rosemary Annarino Logan, Margaret Murello LaGrotto, Joanna Milto-Bergin, Mary Sansone Mascari, Al and Ida Caito Meyer, Aldo and Ada Maestri Mina, Steve Montani, Nino Morone, David and Rosemary Spicuzza Page, Sol Petruzzi, Rina Piga, Frederico and Antonietta Cento Pizzi, Ray Povinelli, Ray and Mascari, Inc., Paul Jerry Roland, Gus and Ruthann Stinnett, and Joann Faenzi Wilson.

I copied photographs that I had collected for the Indiana Historical Society Ethnic History Collection 20 years ago. I appreciate the assistance that Cenveo provided in preparing images for publication.

Lastly, I express my gratitude to my German American wife, Mary Frances Beckmeyer Divita, for her editorial assistance and enlightened criticism during the completion of this project.

INTRODUCTION

Not to know what happened before we were born is to remain perpetual children. All who see these assembled images and read of those pictured—whether bearing a name like Tortorella, Corsaro, or Divita or not a single drop of Italian blood—will see the striking expressions of sadness and of exhilaration, emotions so unmistakable in the Italian character.

Our Italian ancestors who traveled mostly by ship to the ports of New York, Philadelphia, Baltimore, and even New Orleans, and then on to the railroads, mines, and mills of Pennsylvania, brought with them more than the aspiration to labor in those pursuits. Rather, they sought to exercise the entrepreneurial skills already, for the most part, honed in their homeland. The transition from laborer to entrepreneur was swift. No longer was the immigrant working for someone else.

The musical Montani family, the artistic Gioscios, the produce sellers, Frank Mascari, the brothers Caito and Povinelli, Bova Conti, and the tailors, cobblers, barbers, and cooks dotted the early landscape of a small Indianapolis. They joined churches, formed clubs and societies, and gathered together for festivals in order to laugh, love, and celebrate their heritage—and they bore children by the hundreds. With the Depression came a malaise, however, and community members retreated to their families.

Together with the children of early immigrants, those who came to Indianapolis just before and soon after World War II invigorated the Italian American community. The revival of Italian ethnicity led by Dr. Tom Cortese Sr. and the spirit and drive of Pietro Ferri and many others made it fashionable for the Indianapolis citizenry to talk about their desire to visit Italy, and then upon their return to speak glowingly about anything Italian.

Naturally, this evolution in Indianapolis brought the medical doctors, lawyers, professors, judges, and politicians to center stage. We remember Harry Gasper, Anthony Maio, deputy mayor Mike De Fabis, Judge Mercuri, and elected office holders like Paul Jerry Roland, David Page, and Frank Short.

The Italian community celebrated its religious heritage with the groundbreaking for a new church led by Father Priori. Holy Rosary became, and remains, the epicenter of it all. Due to the hard work of a volunteer group led by Matthew Iaria and David Page, the Italian Street Festival held in June of each year brings thousands of celebrants to Holy Rosary. Even the nearby bocce courts, built by the loving hands of Angelo Piga and the sharp eyes of Joe Giacoletti, can no longer accommodate all who want to play.

In these changing times, family stability is still highly prized by Italian Americans. Because of this core value in the Indianapolis community, people of Italian ancestry have found a place in the fabric of today's city. They can be found taking part in the arts, music, sports, the professions, and business. Jim Divita has collected a historical, vibrant display of *la bella vita*, which we have all come to realize is the indomitable Italian spirit.

Paul Jerry Roland
Indianapolis attorney
Honorary vice-consul Republic of Italy, Indiana (retired)

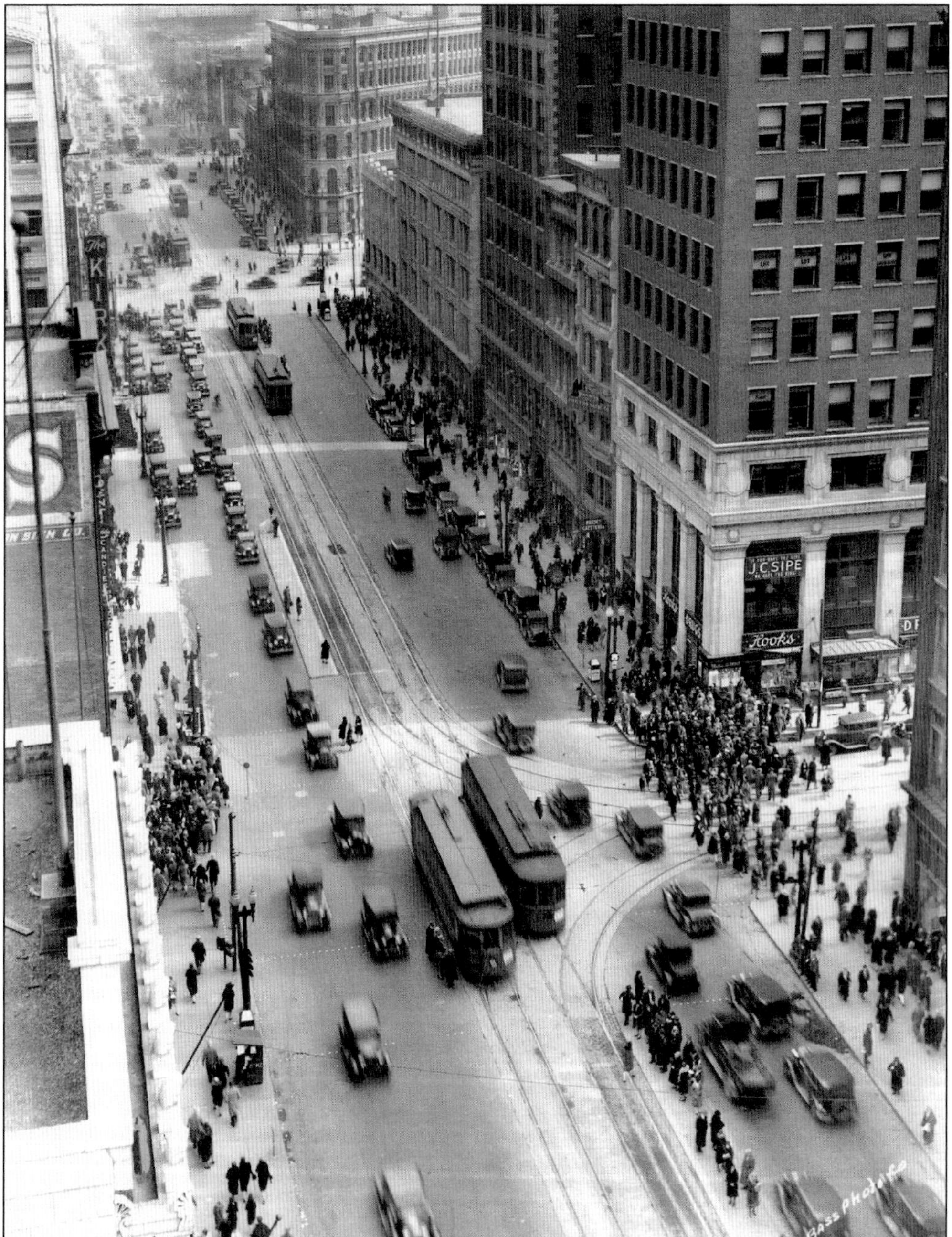

Meridian Street meets Washington Street in Indianapolis's downtown in 1930. (Courtesy Indiana Historical Society.)

PROLOGUE

The heart of Indianapolis in 1930 was the intersection of Washington and Meridian Streets, just a half-block from Monument Circle. At this intersection, the city's addresses divide, north from south, east from west. Here was the National Road, which brought settlers from the east, and the Michigan Road, which crossed the National Road and brought settlers from the south. Because of this, Indianapolis's native white population originated in Ohio, Pennsylvania, or Kentucky and its African American population in Louisiana and the Upper South.

Following the arrival of the railroad in 1847, Indianapolis became the "Crossroads of America." Immigrants from Germany and Ireland began to arrive before the Civil War, while Italians and other southern and eastern Europeans came in the years between the Civil War and World War I. The city's population, 48,000 in 1870, had grown to 234,000 by 1910.

The city's growth resulted in the efficient public transportation system seen in 1930. Streetcars passed along Washington and Meridian every few moments, carrying serious shoppers to the great stores and the employees of government, commerce, and industry to their homes in outlying areas. Downtown shopping made Italian immigrants very much part of the city. At first they lived in the blocks south of Washington and east of Meridian—close to the railroad lines and their produce displays along Delaware Street or in City Market. When they moved to residential streets farther southeast, the streetcar continued to keep jobs and shopping accessible. And if feeling particularly adventurous, residents could board the streetcar clanging down Washington Street, accessing parks and open air at the far corners of the city.

The photograph of 1930 (appearing on the opposite page) also presages the future. The automobile appears here, though it must have only been used to pass through the city or supplement the streetcar. Few parking spaces are evident. Then parking lots and garages began to replace downtown businesses, and as the immigrant generation disappeared so did downtown shopping. In 1960, the city's population reached 476,000, and the commercial significance of the Washington and Meridian intersection declined as shopping malls began to decentralize the commercial activity. By then, even the old Italian neighborhood was in decline, as descendants of Italian immigrants and recently arrived Italians settled into new homes some miles away.

In 1900, the United States Census reported that 1,137 Italians and descendants populated Indianapolis. In 2000, the census takers estimated that 17,442 residents of Marion County, or 2.2 percent of the total population, were of Italian heritage. Through information and nostalgia, this work aims to become a new heart for Indianapolis Italians, much as Washington and Meridian was the heart of the city in bygone days.

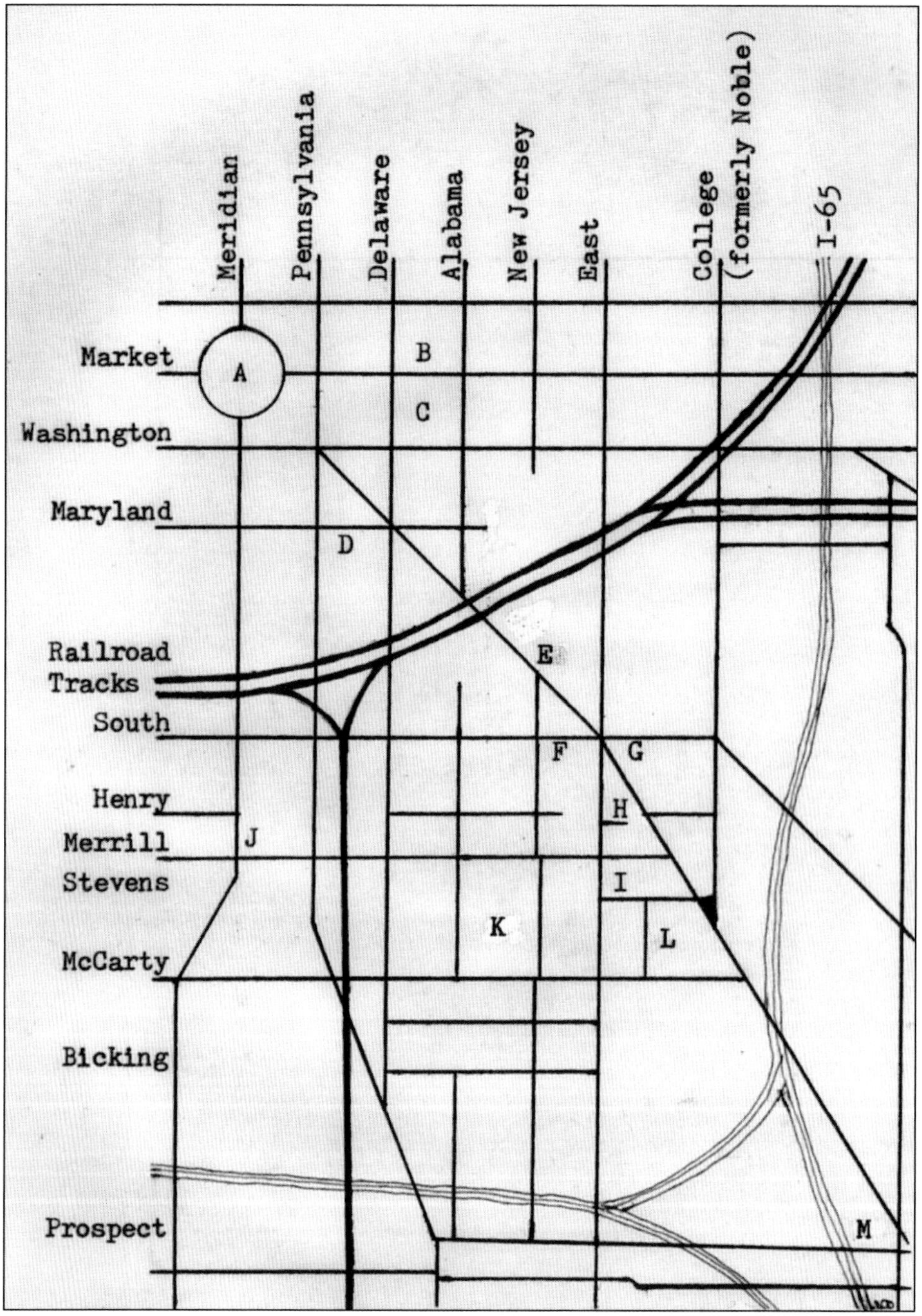

In 1986, Indianapolis's near southeast side, including the Virginia-East Triangle, featured the following sites important to the Italian American community: Monument Circle (A), City Market (B), site of Marion County Courthouse (C), site of the first St. Mary Church (D), Virginia Avenue (E), Farmers Market (F), former Fletcher Place Methodist Church (G), Warsaw Street (H), Holy Rosary Church (I), former Harry E. Wood High School (J), Eli Lilly and Company (planning expansion from South to Interstate 70, Delaware to East) (K), Greer Street (L), and St. Patrick Church (M). (Prepared by Lawrence C. Divita.)

One

THE FIRST FAMILIES
FOUNDATION BUILDERS

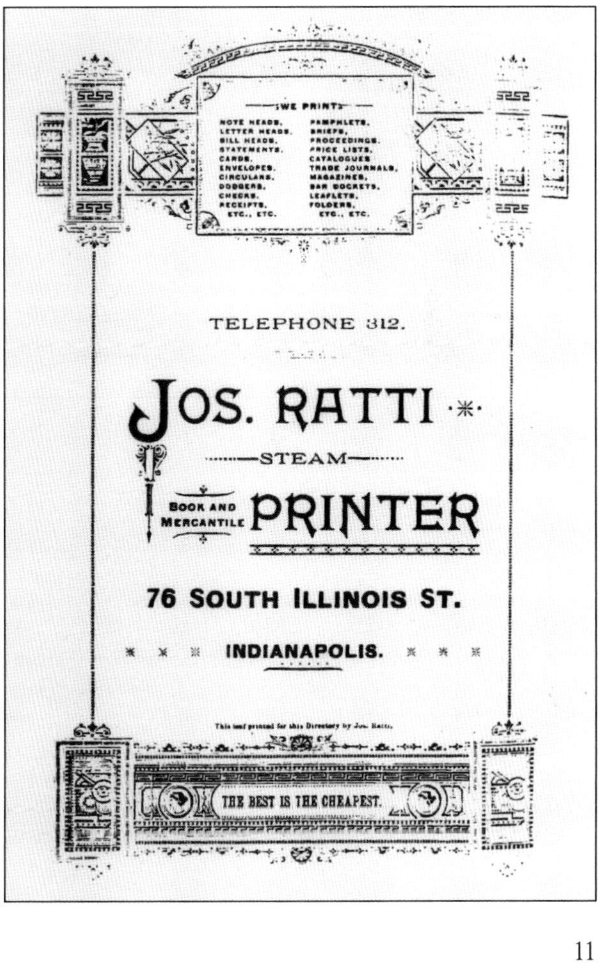

The earliest, continuous name of Italian origin in this city appears to be Ratti. Peddler Francis Anthony Ratti (1797–1879), born in Garbagnate Monastero, provincia di Lecco (Lombardy), and his sons Francis A. (1836–1872), pressman for the *Sentinel*, and Joseph (1840–1913), compositor for the *Daily Citizen*, appear in the 1858 and 1860 city directories, when Indianapolis's population was around 18,000. By 1890, printer Joseph Ratti was advertising his own company. The Ratti building, constructed in 1911, housed his firm at 234–238 South Meridian until the 1960s.

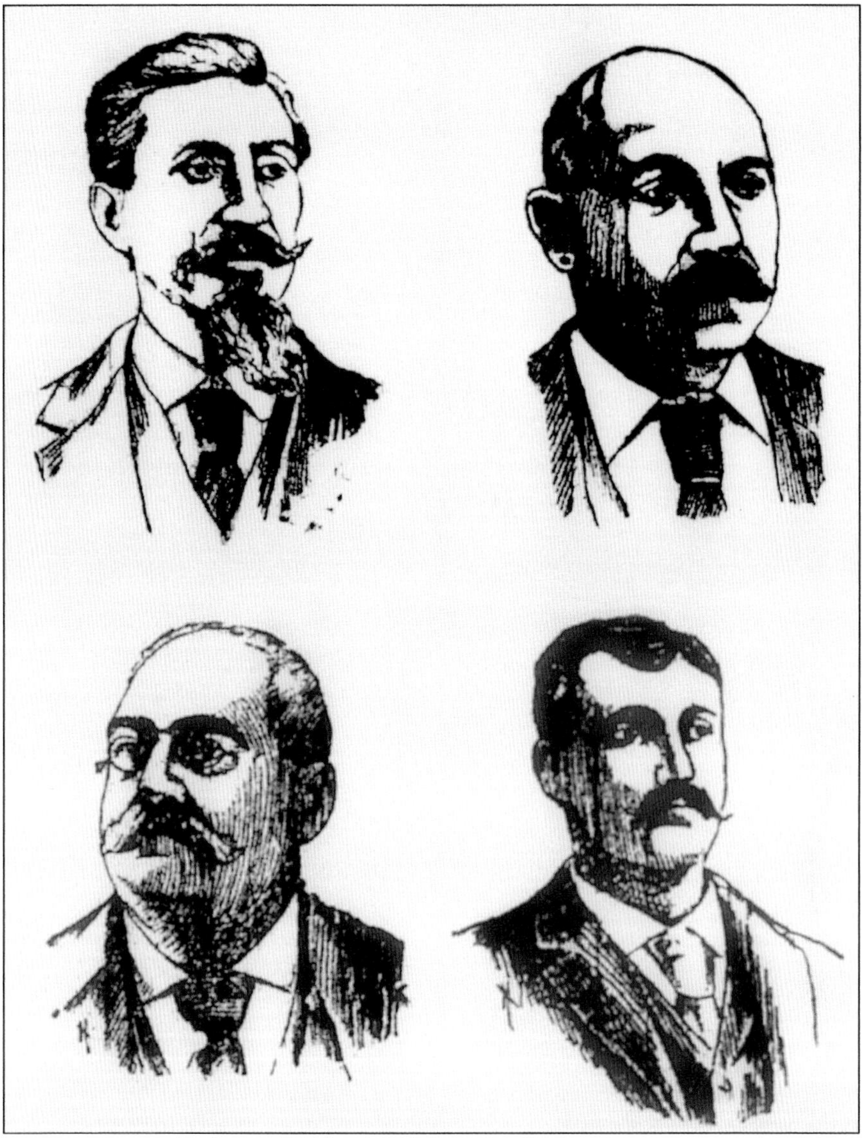

In 1892, the *Indianapolis News* commemorated the 400th anniversary of Columbus's discovery of America by publishing its first article on Indianapolis Italians. Judiciously, the article featured four northern Italians and four southern Italians (including two Sicilians). Nicholas Catalano (above left) was born at Vaglio Basilicata in 1837. He arrived in America in 1870, after eight years in the Italian army. A stone cutter, he settled in Indianapolis in 1878 to labor on the Indiana State House. In 1892, he was in the fruit business. Peter Corsi (above right) was born at Barga, provincia di Lucca (Tuscany), in 1835. He painted in Providence, Rhode Island, and Philadelphia before settling in Indianapolis in 1876. John Foppiano (below left) was a Genoese who arrived in America in 1855. He cooked in fashionable New York restaurants, and then entered the fruit business in Washington, Cincinnati, and Memphis. He moved to Indianapolis to escape the yellow fever epidemic in 1876. Joseph Giuliano (below right) was born in Termini Imerese, provincia di Palermo (Sicily), landed in New Orleans in 1881, and settled in Indianapolis in 1886. A brother-in-law of Frank Mascari, he was president of the Umberto Primo Italian Benevolent Society in 1892.

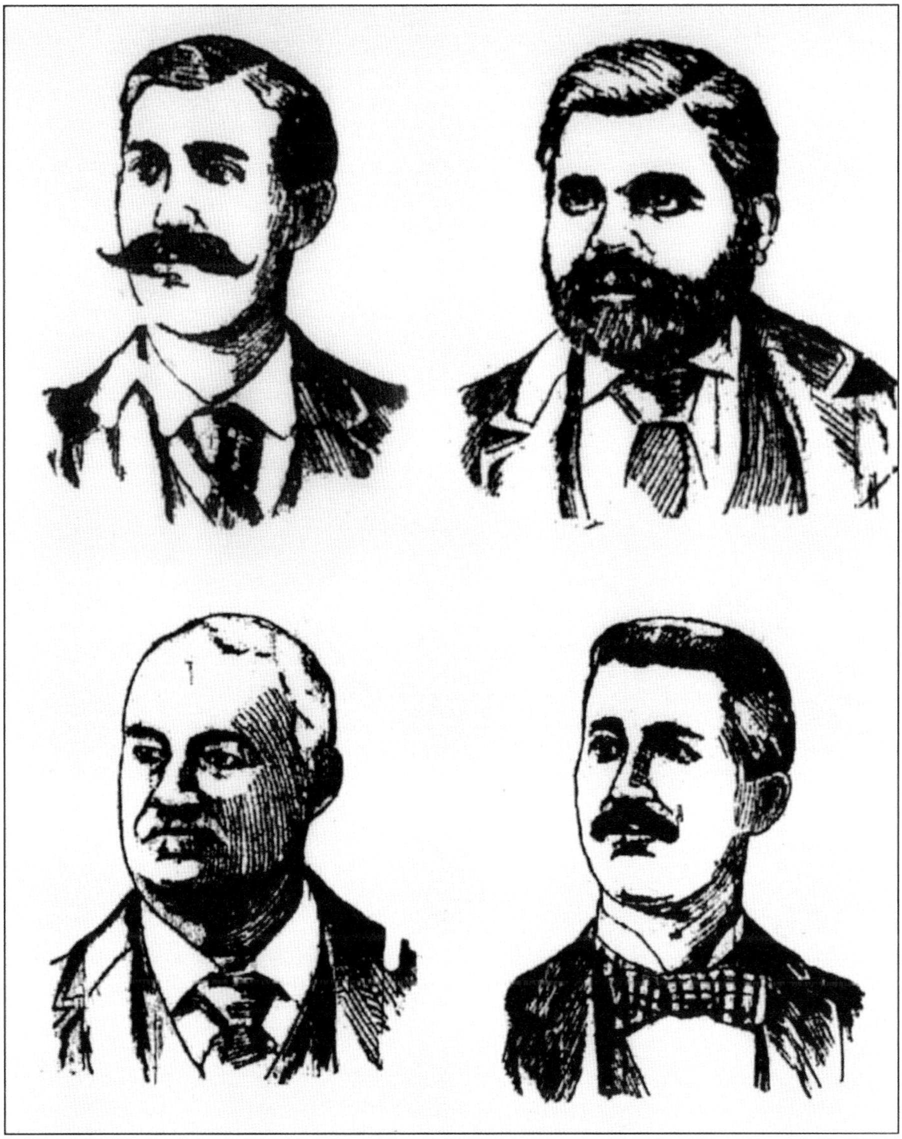

Fisherman Frank Mascari (above left) traveled to New Orleans from Termini Imerese, provincia di Palermo (Sicily), in 1882. According to tradition, finding too much job competition among Sicilians in the Crescent City, Mascari departed for cities to the north. After visiting Memphis and Louisville, he found that rapidly developing Indianapolis was just the right place. In 1888, he lived on East Maryland Street and operated a fruit store on Virginia Avenue. Ferdinando Montani (above right) was born in 1839 in Laurenzana, provincia di Potenza (Basilicata). He arrived in America in 1872 and worked in Utica, New York, among several places. One day he produced a map of the United States and informed family members that they were moving to Indianapolis. So many rail lines crossed there, he declared, that surely this was a city of economic opportunity. Angelo and John Rosasco (below left and right, respectively) were natives of Gattorna, provincia di Genova (Liguria). Angelo, born in 1836, had engaged in the furniture sales and fruit business in other American cities before settling here. Angelo arrived in the United States in 1871, and John, born in 1863, joined Angelo in 1872. Both came to Indianapolis in 1874.

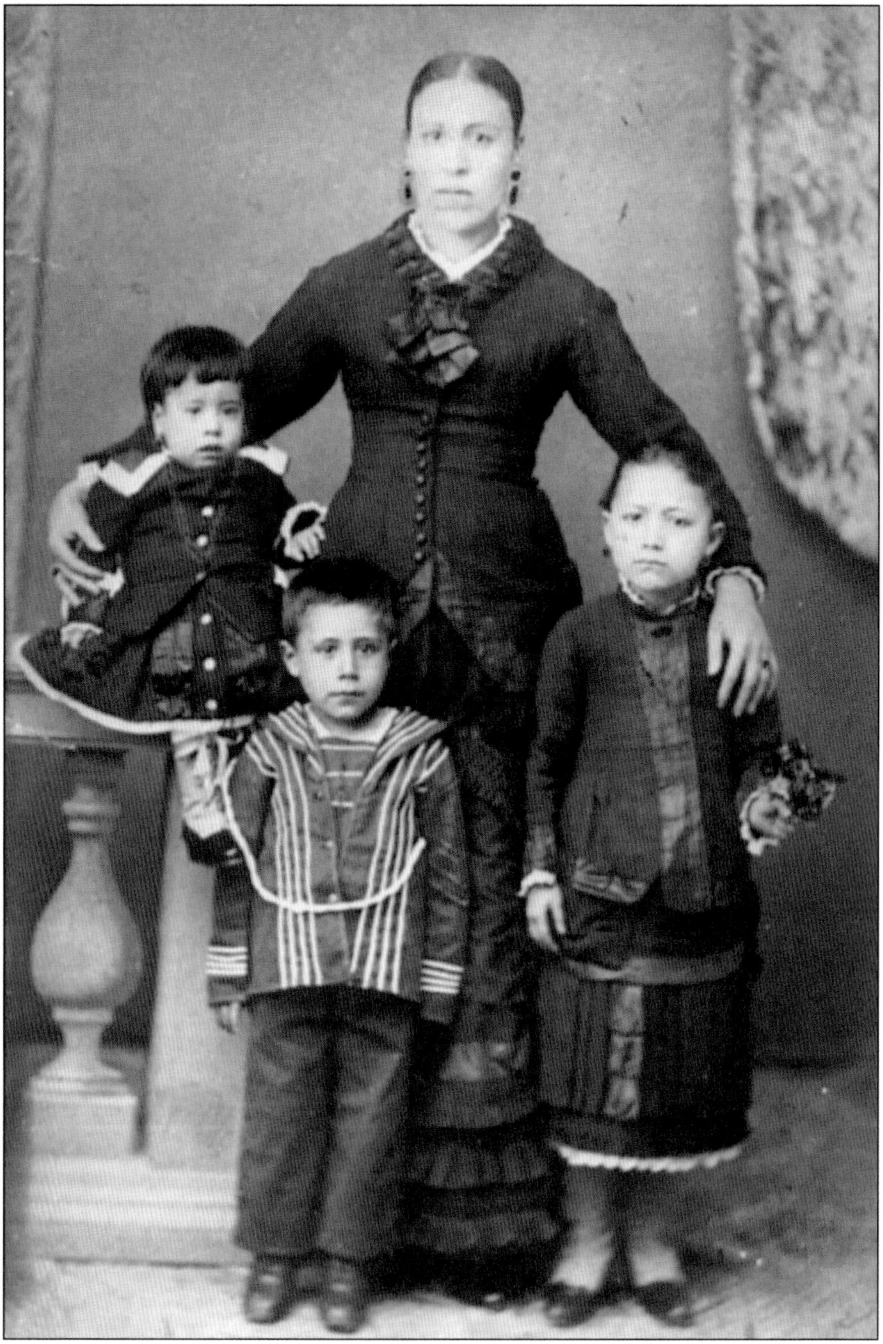

Ordinarily, the first Italians to arrive in America were young, able-bodied men seeking jobs that would pay better than any work available in their own hometowns. If married and willing to remain in a foreign land for the economic advantage, they saved enough to buy boat tickets to bring their families over. This photograph of Ninfa Cacagna Miceli with children, from left to right, Annie, Philip, and Josephine reminded a new immigrant that family members remained in Sicily. By 1895, several families in Indianapolis had been reunited and were occupying new homes in the Virginia-East Triangle south of the Market District.

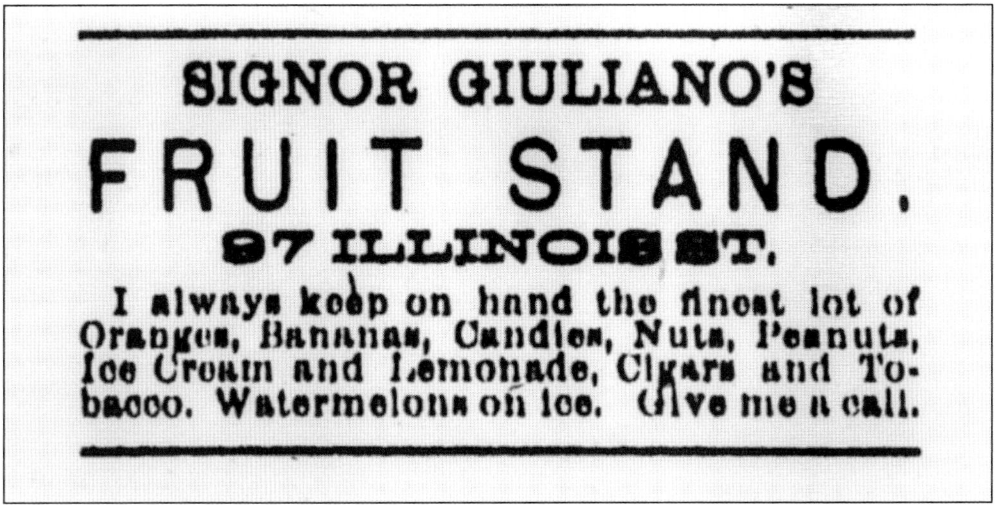

SIGNOR GIULIANO'S

FRUIT STAND.

97 ILLINOIS ST.

I always keep on hand the finest lot of Oranges, Bananas, Candies, Nuts, Peanuts, Ice Cream and Lemonade, Cigars and Tobacco. Watermelons on Ice. Give me a call.

Interestingly, Joseph Giuliano refers to himself as "Signor," thus emphasizing his foreign origin, in this August 1891 newspaper advertisement for his fruit stand. Note that bananas are available at this early date.

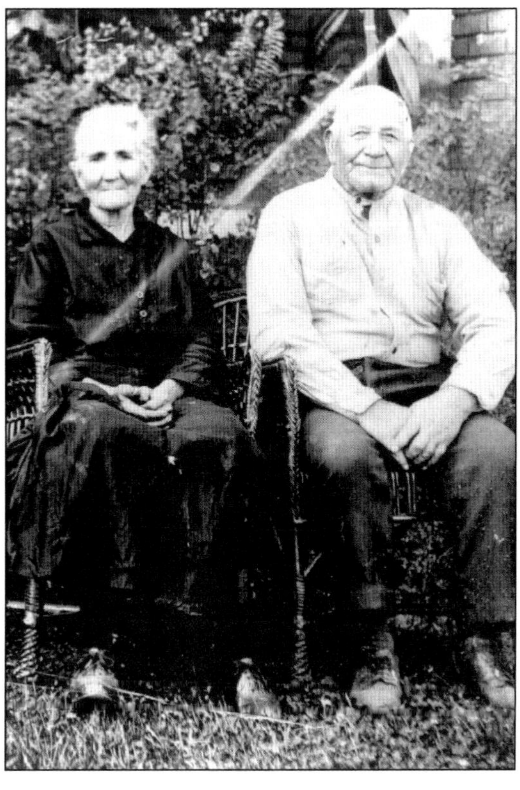

The Caito family has played a major role in Indianapolis's produce business since Michelina Miceli Caito and Filippo Ardizzone Caito arrived here from Termini in the 1890s. Reportedly introducing the banana to this area, they arranged for the Illinois Central Railroad to transport Central American fruit from New Orleans to Indianapolis. They and their descendants were known for their frugality, hard work, and strong sense of business competition. Three of their five sons married Mercurio sisters from Columbus, Ohio, and their daughter to a Mercurio brother. (Courtesy Al Meyer.)

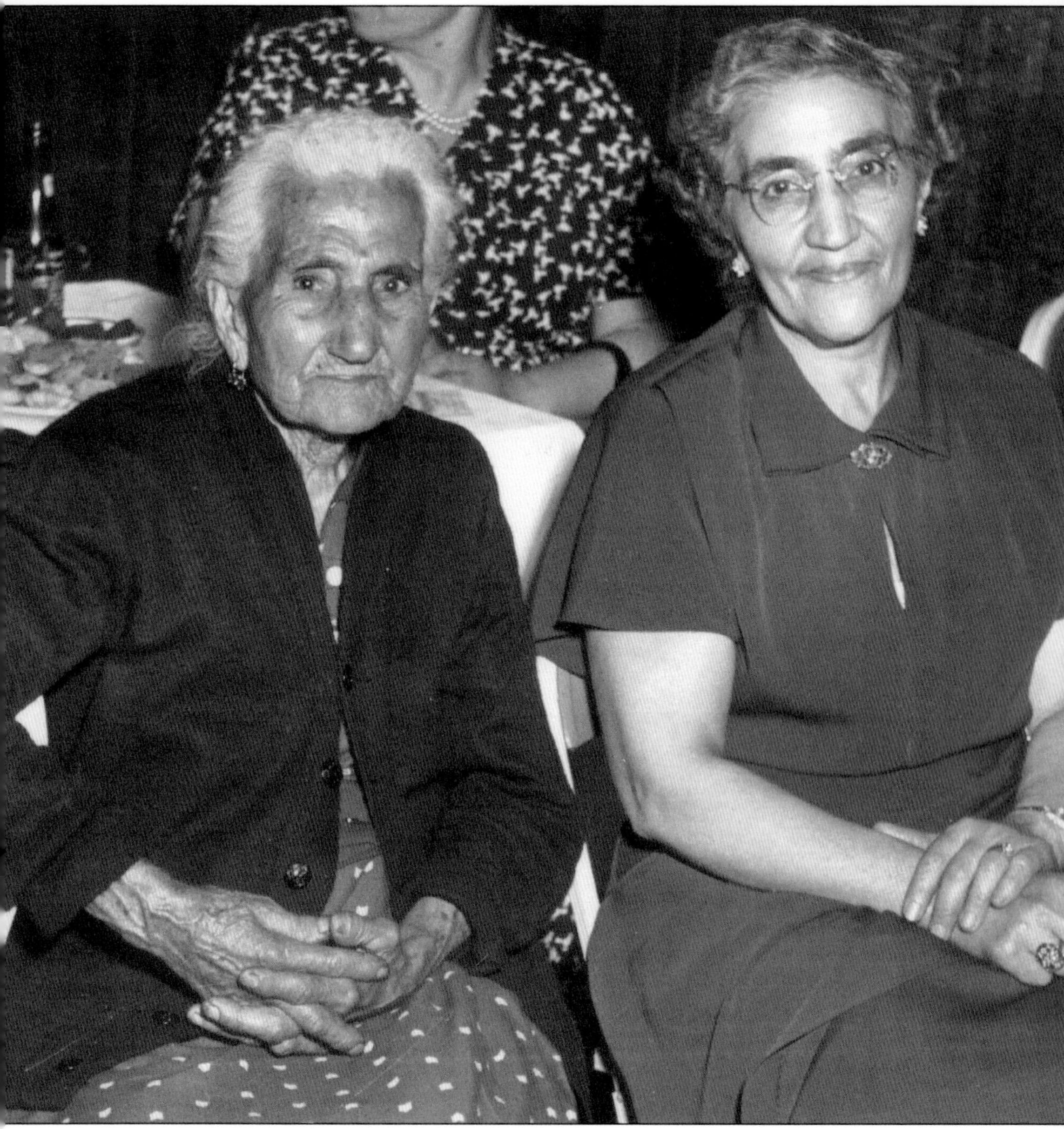

Michelina Caito (left), matriarch of the family, attended a social gathering later in lide with her daughter-in-law Mary Ann Mercurio Caito. Michelina died later in 1954 at age 93. (Courtesy Joanna Milto-Bergin.)

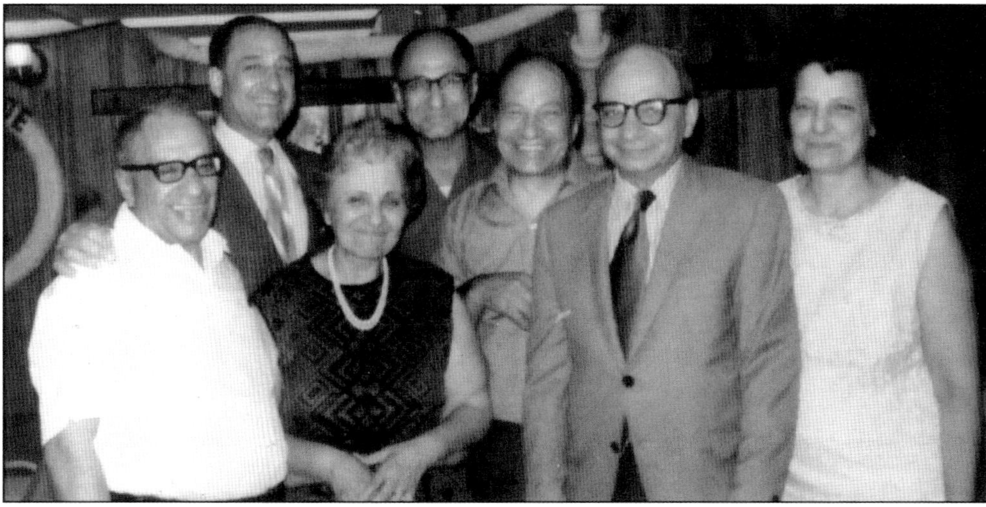

Paolo "Little Jim" and Concetta Tortorella Corsaro came from Reggio Calabria in 1910. He worked in a Pennsylvania mill, then opened a fruit stand in Indianapolis's City Market in 1914. Over 200 Corsaro descendants claim to be the city's second largest Italian-American family after the Caitos. Seven of Little Jim and Concetta's offspring are, from left, Frank operated the Indiana News Bookstore and fathered attorney Paul Jerry Roland; Peter founded Cash and Carry Paper Company; Antonia "Thona" Constantino raised her eight children and her five Page nieces and nephews; Danny fathered lawyer Paul Corsaro; Joe operates Indianapolis Fruit Company with Danny and Mike Mascari; Tony; and Lucile (Nunzia) Feld operated a restaurant on Court Street. (Courtesy Paul Jerry Roland.)

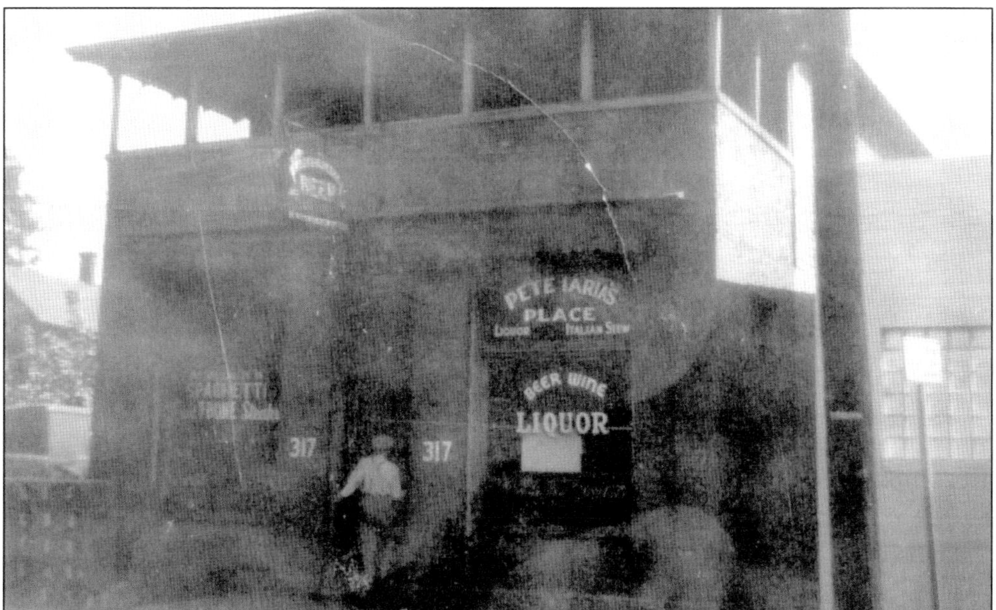

Pietro and Antonia Sgro Iaria arrived from Roccaforte del Greco, provincia di Reggio Calabria, and settled at 317 South Noble Street (now College Avenue). Antonia took in boarders and became so well known for her cooking that, in 1912, the couple opened a grocery that prepared lunch for employees of U.S. Rubber, located across the street. Their business evolved into a restaurant and bowling alley, built on the original site in the 1950s. (Courtesy Matthew Iaria.)

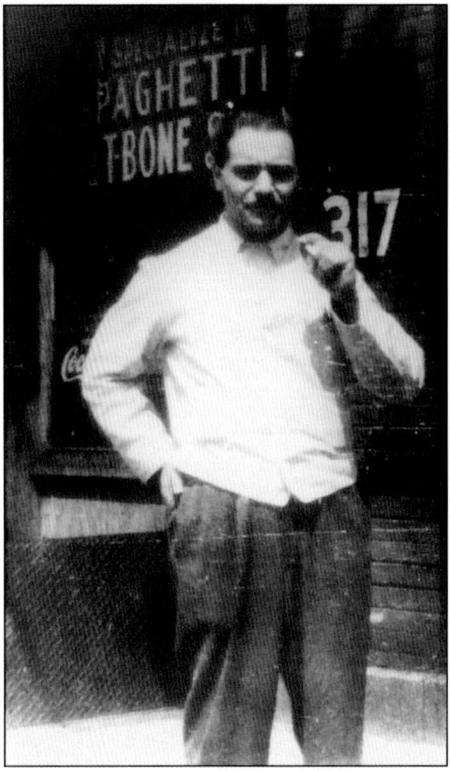

From the signage in this photograph, all it took to become an Italian restaurant was to serve spaghetti. Mate was a son of the elder Iarias. Today, Mate's son Matthew operates likely the oldest continuous Italian restaurant in the city. (Courtesy Matthew Iaria.)

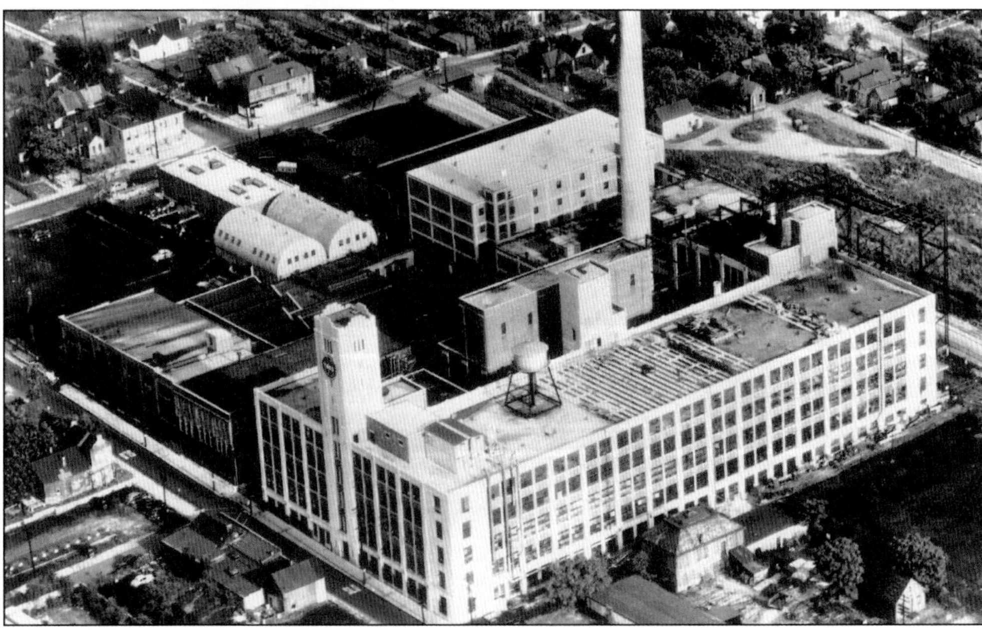

In the foreground is the United States Rubber plant, near Georgia and South East Streets, in the 1940s. Two of the city's oldest *ristoranti* began serving sandwiches and making lunch for U.S. Rubber employees. These eateries are located in the upper left quadrant of the image on Noble Street (now College Avenue). The building on the left is Milano Inn, and on the right is Iaria's. (Courtesy Indiana Historical Society.)

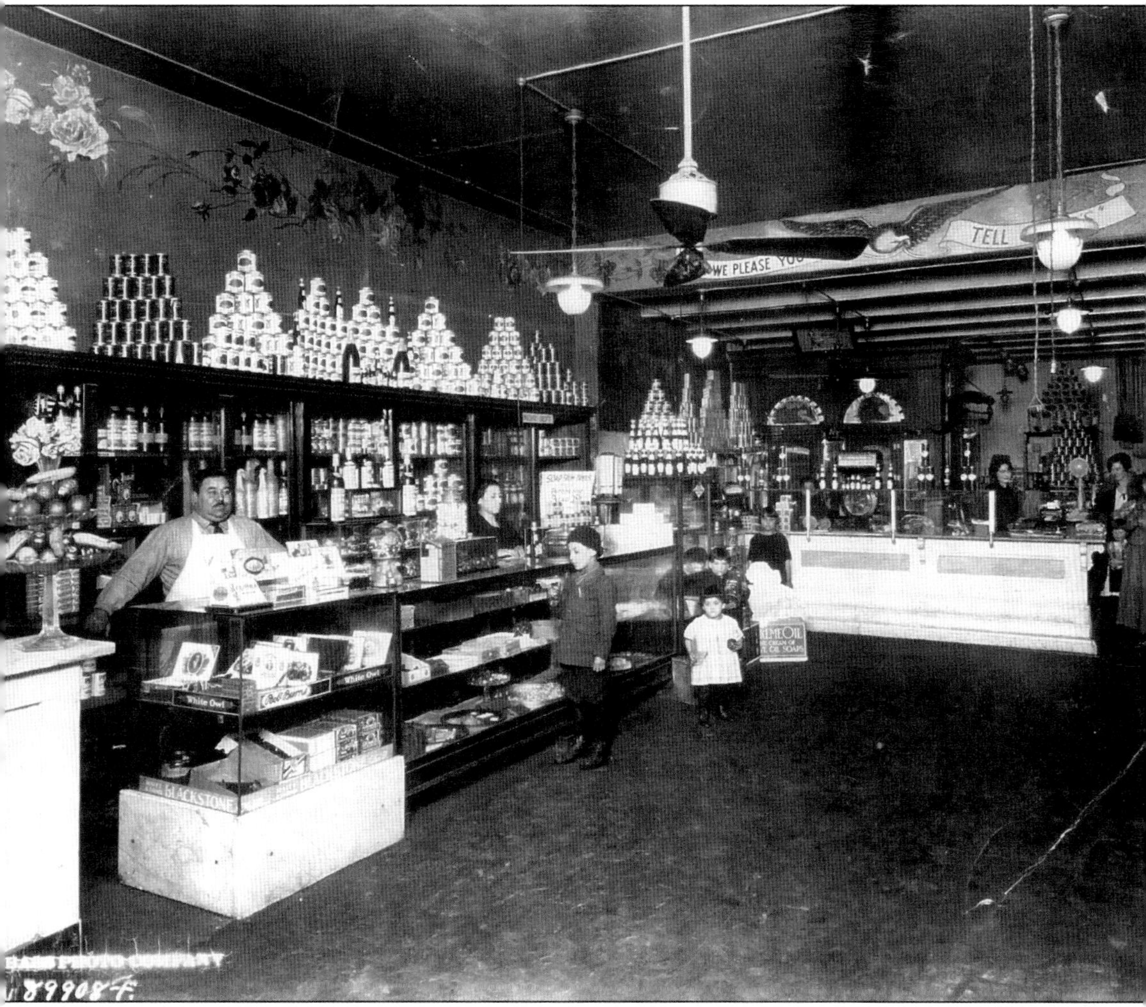

This store was located on the northeast corner of Merrill and South East Streets in the Italian neighborhood. Santoro Iozzo came from Monterosso, then in provincia di Catanzaro (Calabria), and arrived in Worcester, Massachusetts, in 1908. He recruited workers in Calabria for a bridge construction company. When these recruits concluded that he acted like an American boss named Fred, they called Iozzo Fred too. "Fred" and his wife, Rosaria Puzzello, first saw Indianapolis while he worked on the Virginia Avenue viaduct. They decided to settle here and open a grocery. Iozzo is on the left behind the counter. The lady in black at the other end of the counter is Olga Giovannoni Faenzi, born just outside Carrara (Tuscany). (Her granddaughter Carol Faenzi reports in *The Stonecutter's Aria* that Olga would be a historian's delight. She says, "It's important to keep things. I want my children to know what happened, to understand things.") (Courtesy Carol Faenzi and Joann Faenzi Wilson.)

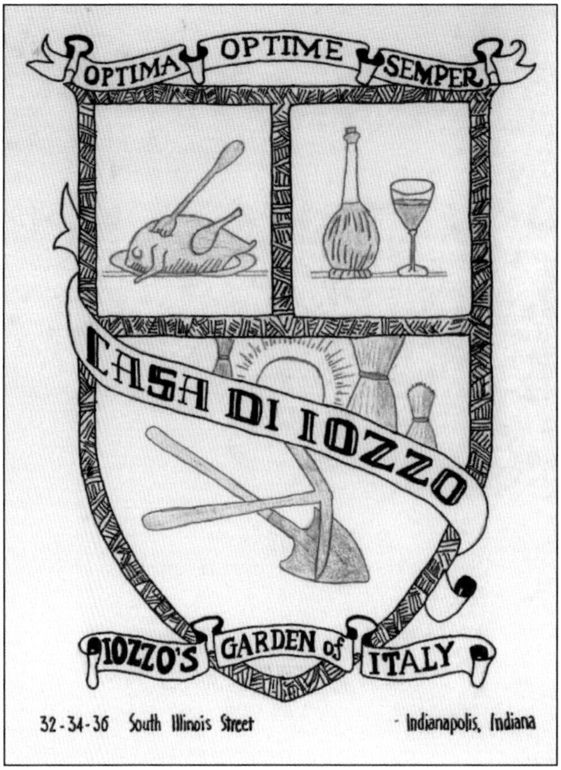

In the late 1920s, Iozzo operated two groceries on the north side. Tired of giving credit to customers and never being repaid, when the Depression hit he decided to set up the first downtown full-menu Italian restaurant. Fred, joined by his two sons, Vincent and Dominic, established Iozzo's Garden of Italy at 32–36 South Illinois Street. The Garden of Italy plate, composed of spaghetti, meatballs, and salad, cost 45¢. The Latin motto means, "The best is always better." For decorative purposes, Iozzo took some dry spaghetti and arranged it as a spray coming out of a large milk can. "So that's how spaghetti grows," commented a customer obviously ignorant of Italian food. (Courtesy Dominic Iozzo.)

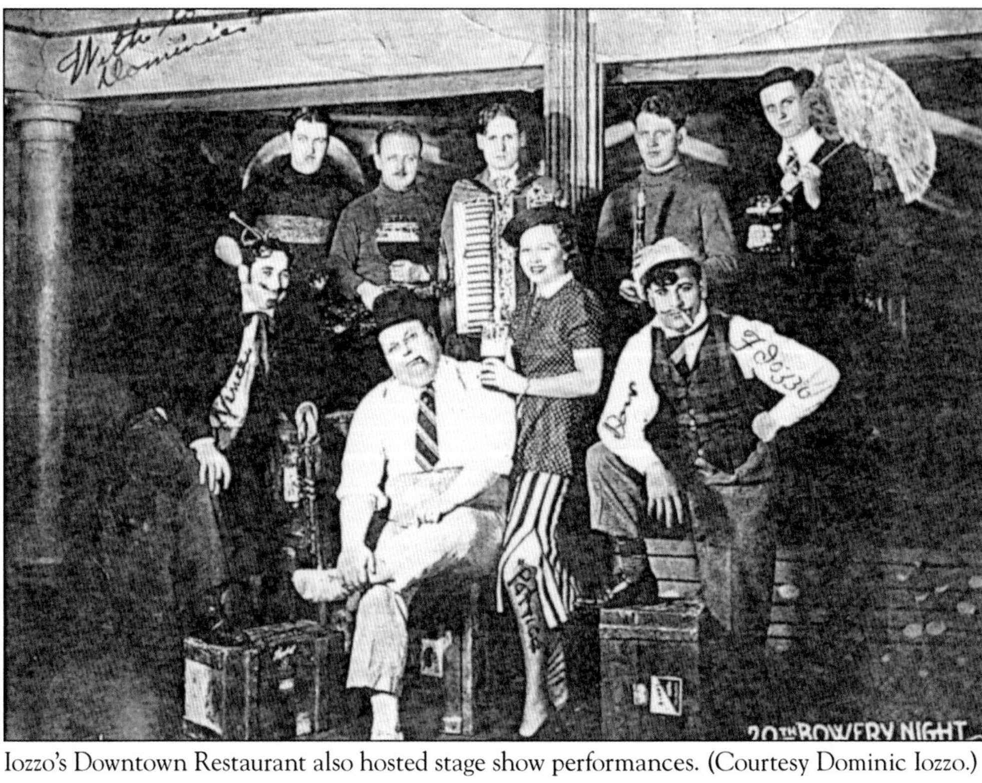

Iozzo's Downtown Restaurant also hosted stage show performances. (Courtesy Dominic Iozzo.)

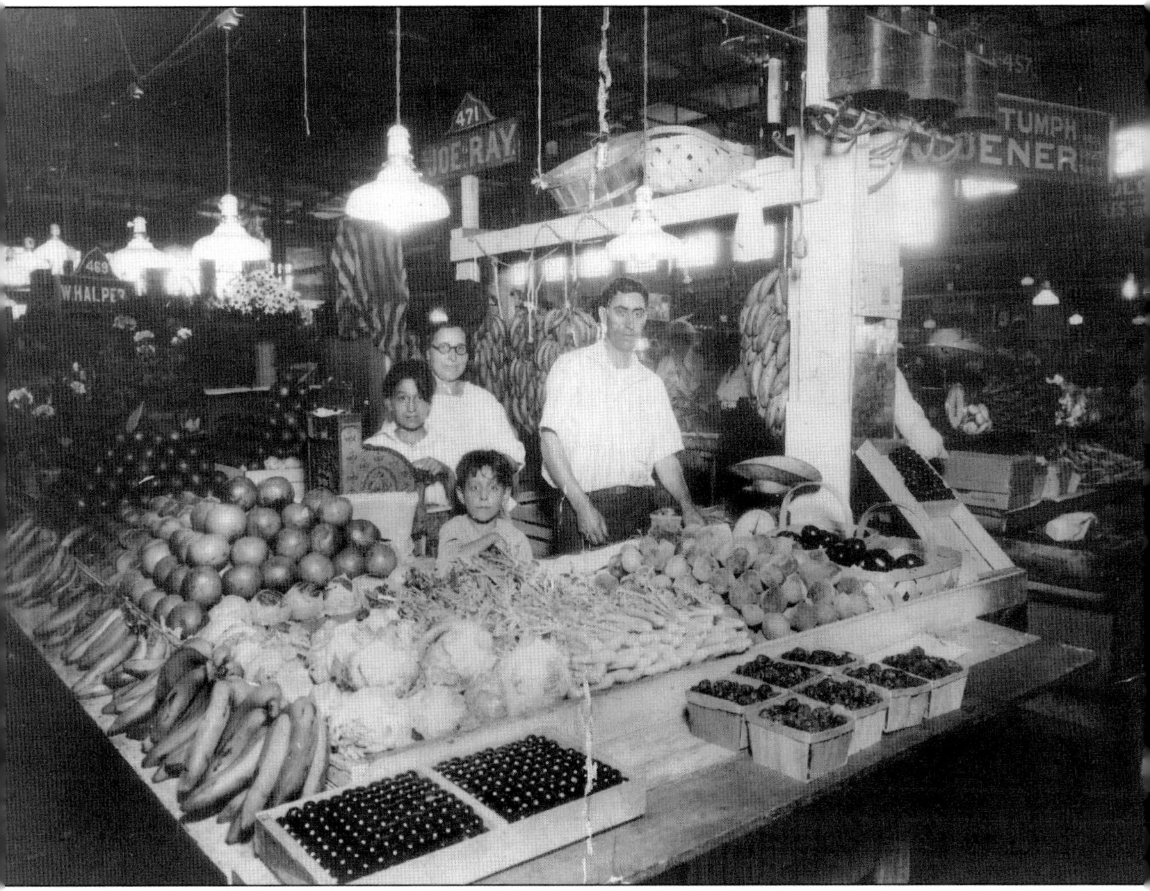

Joe and Diana Re (anglicized to "Ray" because Ellis Island officials did not like a two-letter last name) came from Sicily and entered the fruit and vegetable business. Pushcarts gave way to wagons, which yielded to market stalls. At City Market stand number 471, Diana and Joe pose with children Mike and Tony (foreground) Ray around 1925. (Courtesy Ray and Mascari, Inc.)

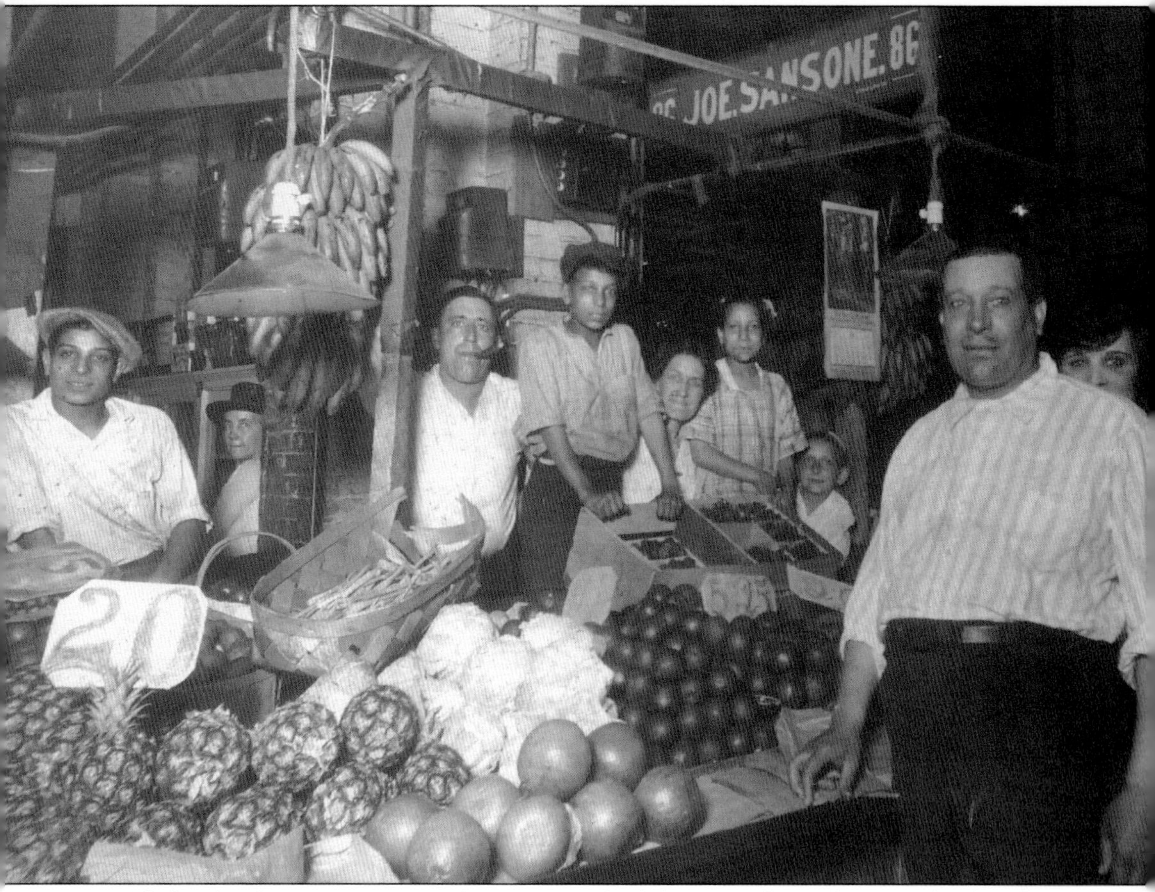

With his family, Termini native Joe Sansone (right) operated stand 86 on the first floor of Tomlinson Hall, adjoining City Market. He sold fruit like bananas, pineapples, and apples and fresh vegetables such as cabbage. When called for military service, Sansone returned to Italy and served in the navy as part of an international force working in China during the Boxer Rebellion. Upon discharge, he married a Matracia girl and traveled back to Indianapolis with his wife, mother, and father. (Courtesy Gus Stinnett.)

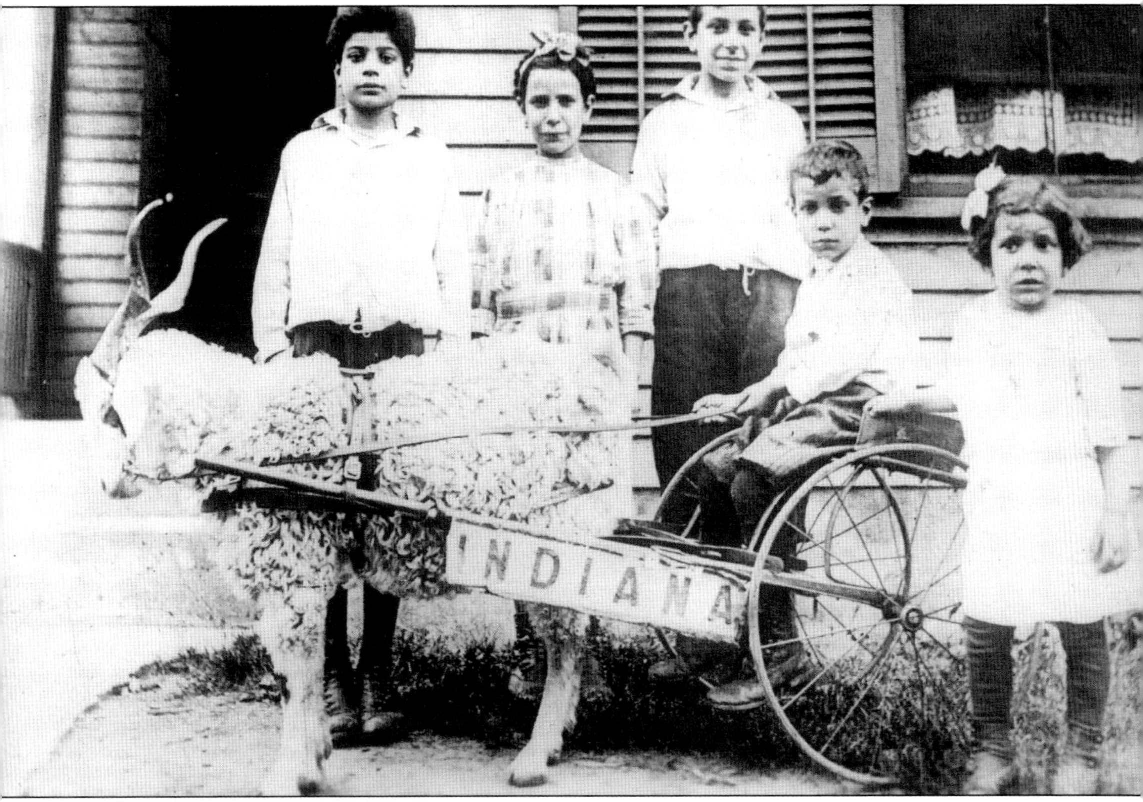

Joe Sansone's children were Americans born in Indianapolis. Pictured here, from left to right, are Vincent, Mary, Augustine (future priest), Joe, and Josephine about 1920. (Courtesy Gus Stinnett.)

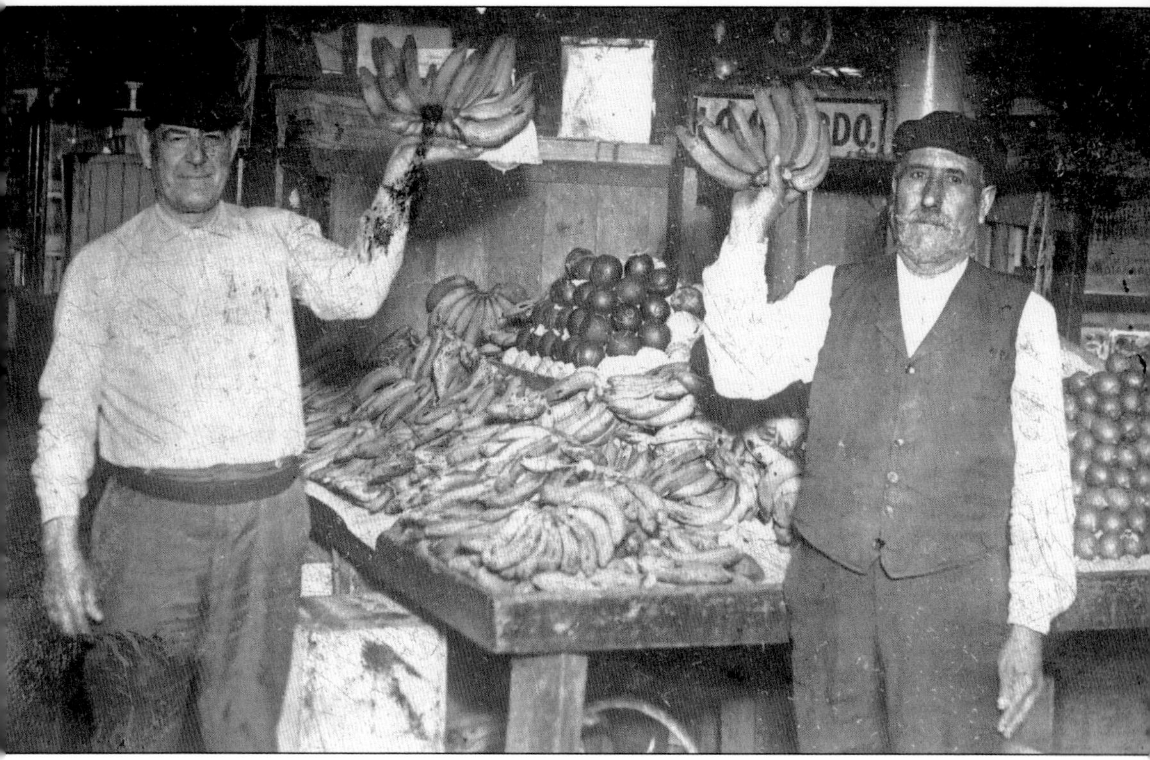

Gus Lombardo (left) advertises bananas with Salvatore Miceli around 1915. "Grandpa" Lombardo was one of several characters at City Market. Jokes and tricks attracted customers and challenged boredom. If time moved too slowly, Lombardo would feign a heart attack with proper gestures and noises, and fall to the floor. When potential customers gathered around him in concern, he would open his eyes and say, "Anyone interested in bananas today? I got these on sale!" (Courtesy Ninfa Gatto DeHilt.)

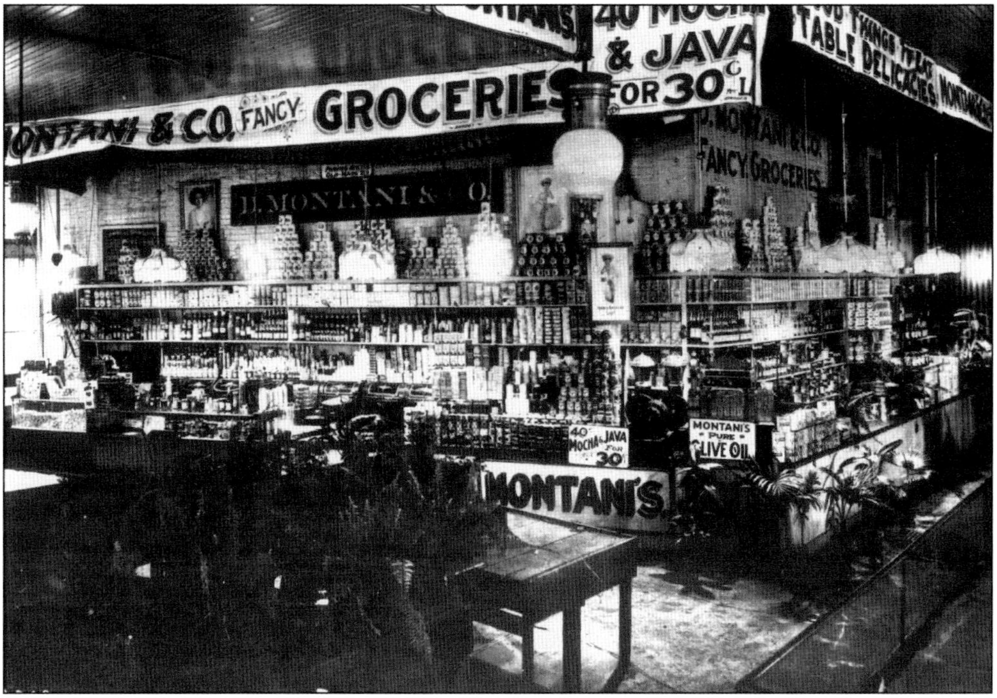

In 1881, Ferdinando Montani operated a confectionery at 127 East Washington Street. His sons and grandsons later ran a stand in City Market, as well as stores on the fashionable north side until 1978. (Courtesy John Montani.)

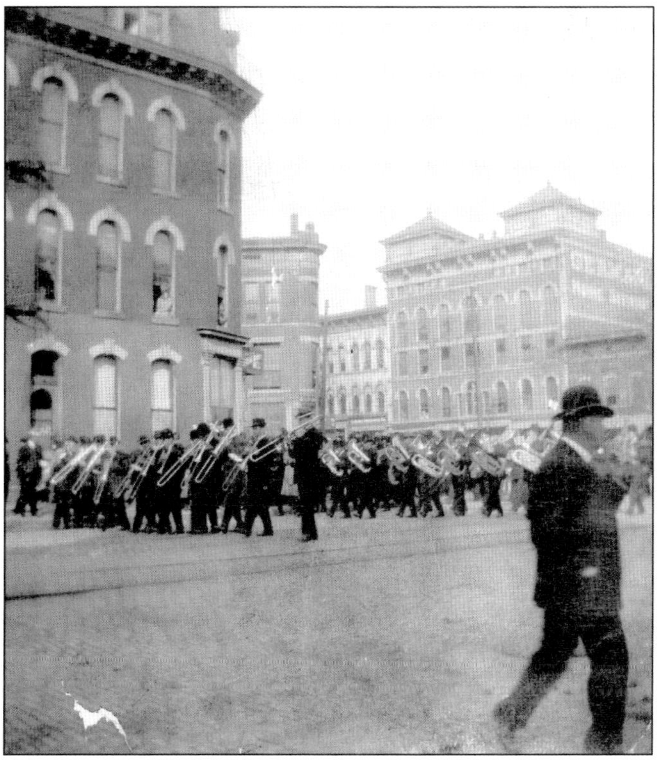

In 1907, Dominic Montani, Ferdinando Montani's eldest son, borrowed a pair of shoes from a friend. The shoes did not fit well, and he soon developed a foot sore and then a fatal infection. In respect for the well-known musician and founder of the local musicians' union, a 100-piece band accompanied his hearse to Holy Cross Cemetery. Here, band members pass the corner of Delaware and Washington Streets. Mozart (or Germania) Hall, where Italian societies met, is in the background. (Courtesy Steve Montani.)

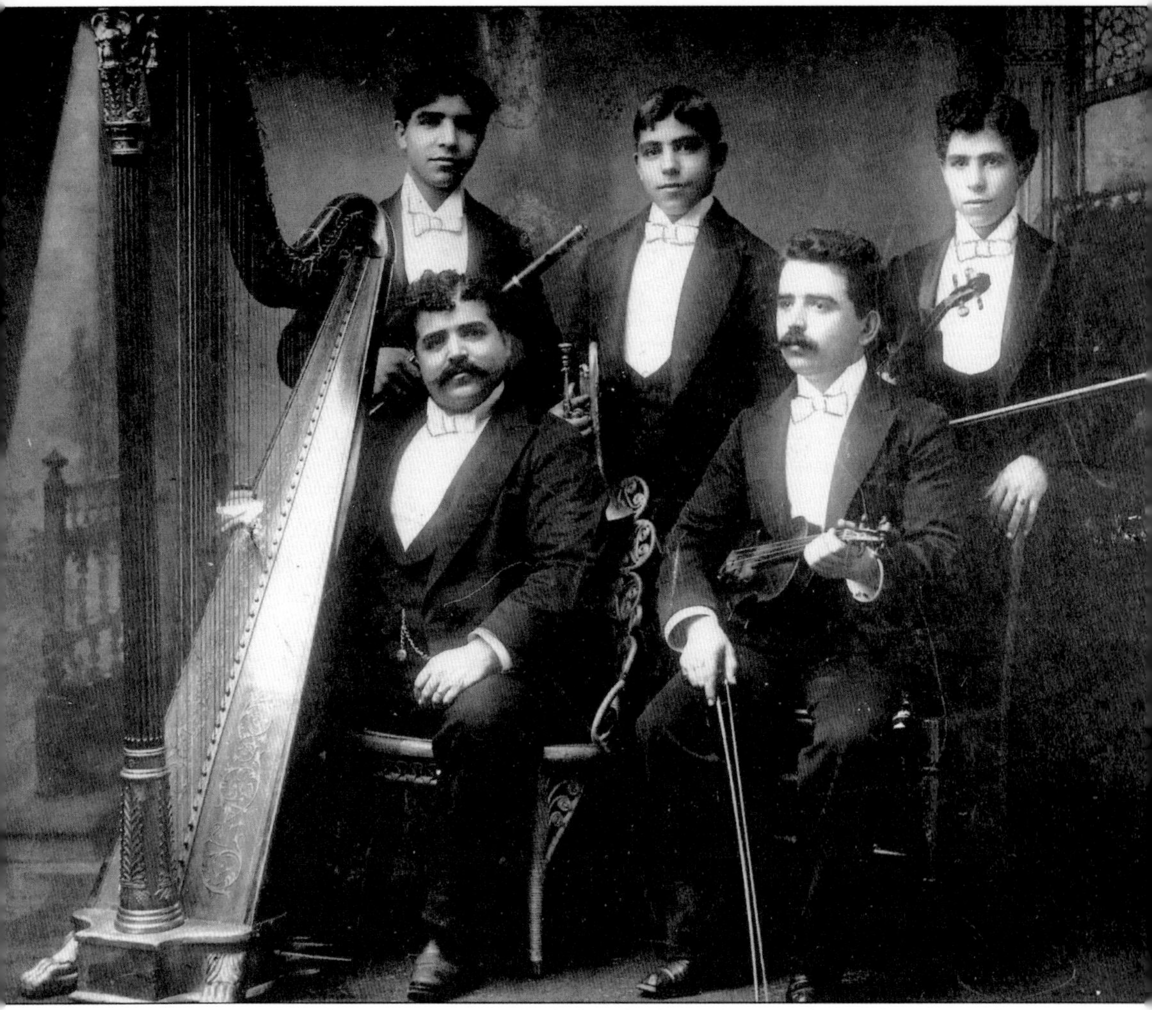

The five sons of Ferdinando Montani had already formed a popular orchestra in the 1880s, some playing together as late as the 1920s. They performed at school and church functions and at dances, private parties, and other social affairs. When waiting for a train to take them to a venue outside of Indianapolis, they would break out the instruments and play on the platform for donations from other passengers. Dominic (first row, left) was the harpist and band leader. Gaetano "Guy" (first row, right) continued to run the City Market stand and a grocery, carrying on the business started by his father. Guy played at the Claypool Hotel on Saturday nights for several years. Pasquale (second row, left), the flutist, taught at the Indianapolis College of Music, later part of Butler University. Nicola (second row, center) eventually moved to Philadelphia, composed for the St. Gregory Hymnal, and helped revive the use of Gregorian chant in the Catholic Church during the 1920s and 1930s. Anthony (second row, right), the violinist, taught music at Manual High School and in Palo Alto, California. (Courtesy Steve Montani.)

Giovanni Gioscio was born at Calvello, provincia di Potenza (Basilicata), of a long line of artists. He studied in Italy and France and worked for Bishop Giuseppe Sarto of Mantua, who was elected Pope Pius X in 1903. Gioscio entered New York in 1889 and sought work as a fresco painter. Related to the Montani family already living in Indianapolis, he settled here and married Maria Montani (sister to the orchestra members) in 1893. Always interested in church decoration, he received commissions for Catholic churches like St. Mary and old St. Joseph in Indianapolis, as well as those in Connersville and Avilla, where his work still exists.

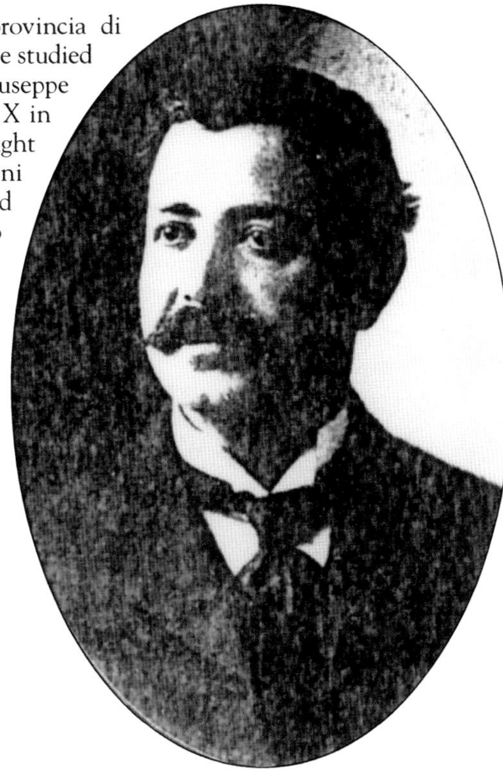

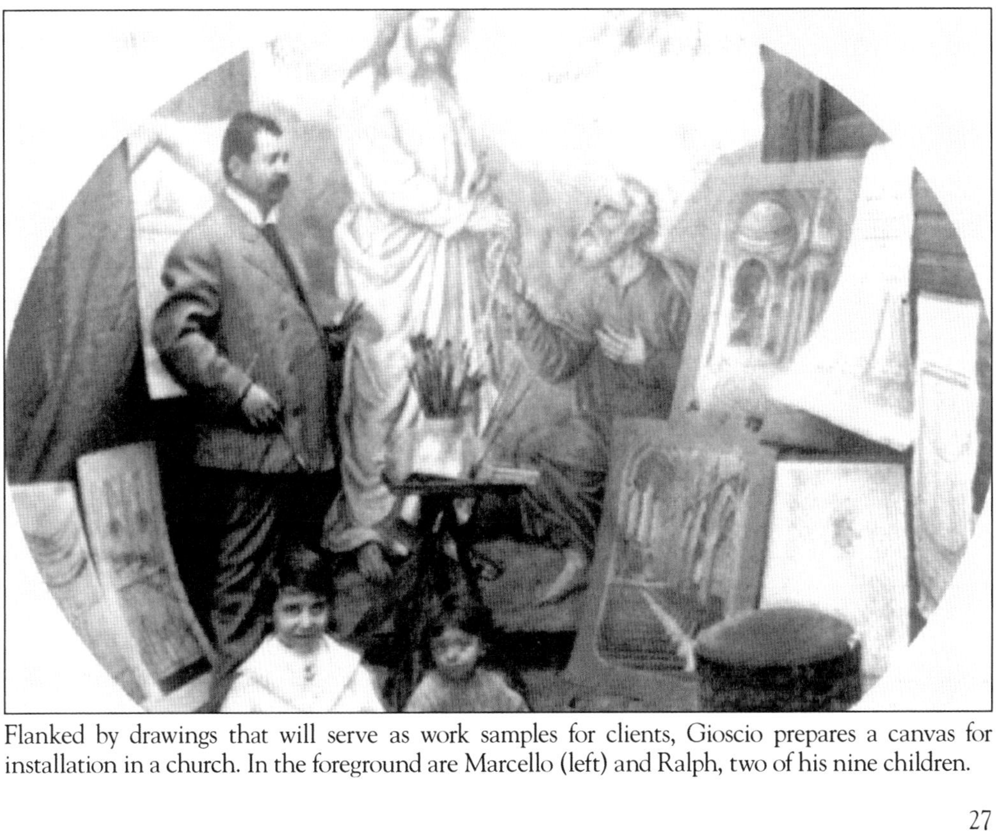

Flanked by drawings that will serve as work samples for clients, Gioscio prepares a canvas for installation in a church. In the foreground are Marcello (left) and Ralph, two of his nine children.

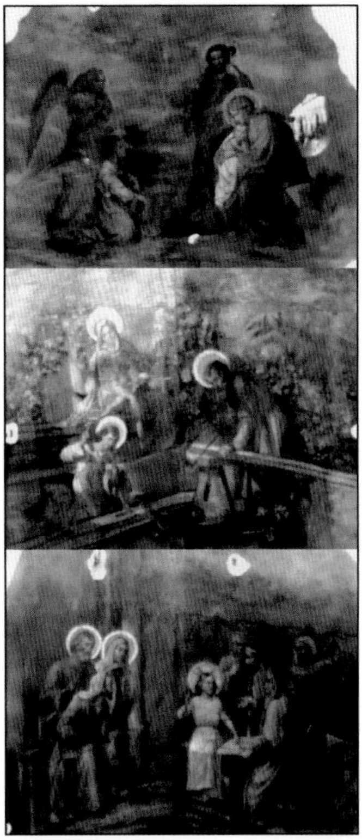

Gioscio painted *The Nativity* (upper), *The Holy Family* (center), and *Jesus in the Temple* (lower) for the ceiling of old St. Joseph's. The church was closed in 1949. Workers repainted much of the ceiling but hesitated to paint out sacred images. To use the former church as a bingo hall or as archdiocesan offices, a drop ceiling was installed. Suspension cables were mounted through the paintings. After the drop ceiling was removed and the archdiocese sold the vacant building, the damaged paintings were exposed to the light and darkened.

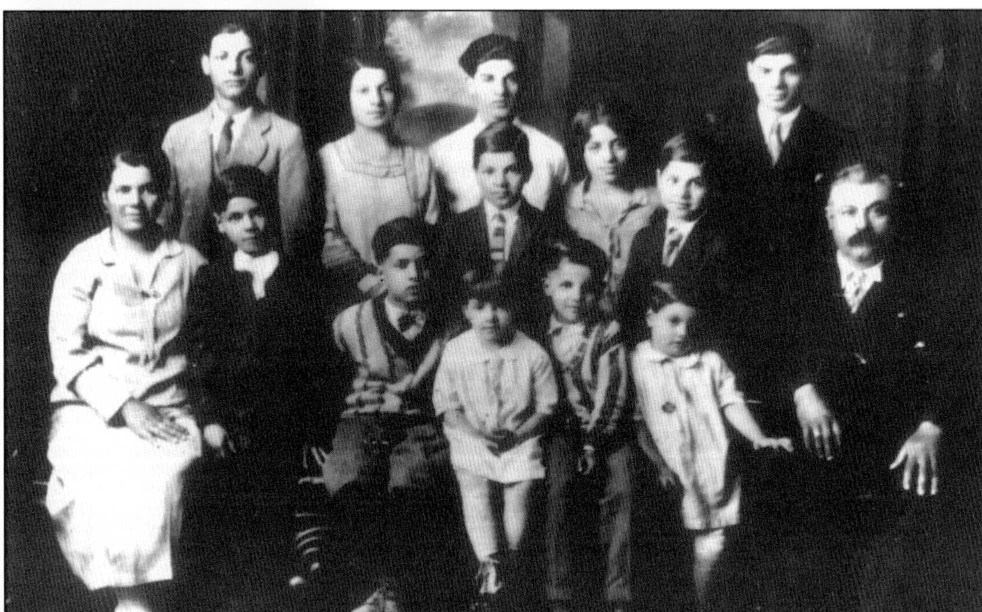

Outside observers of the Italian neighborhood always commented on the number of children running in the streets. This was understandable since families were large. In the 1920s, *The Indianapolis Star* featured the Joe and Josephine Piccione family. The couple parented 15 children, 12 of whom were still living. Joe Piccione (name pronounced "Pea-chew-nee" by locals), born in Fiumara, provincia di Reggio Calabria, was a fruit dealer in City Market. (Courtesy Charles Farah.)

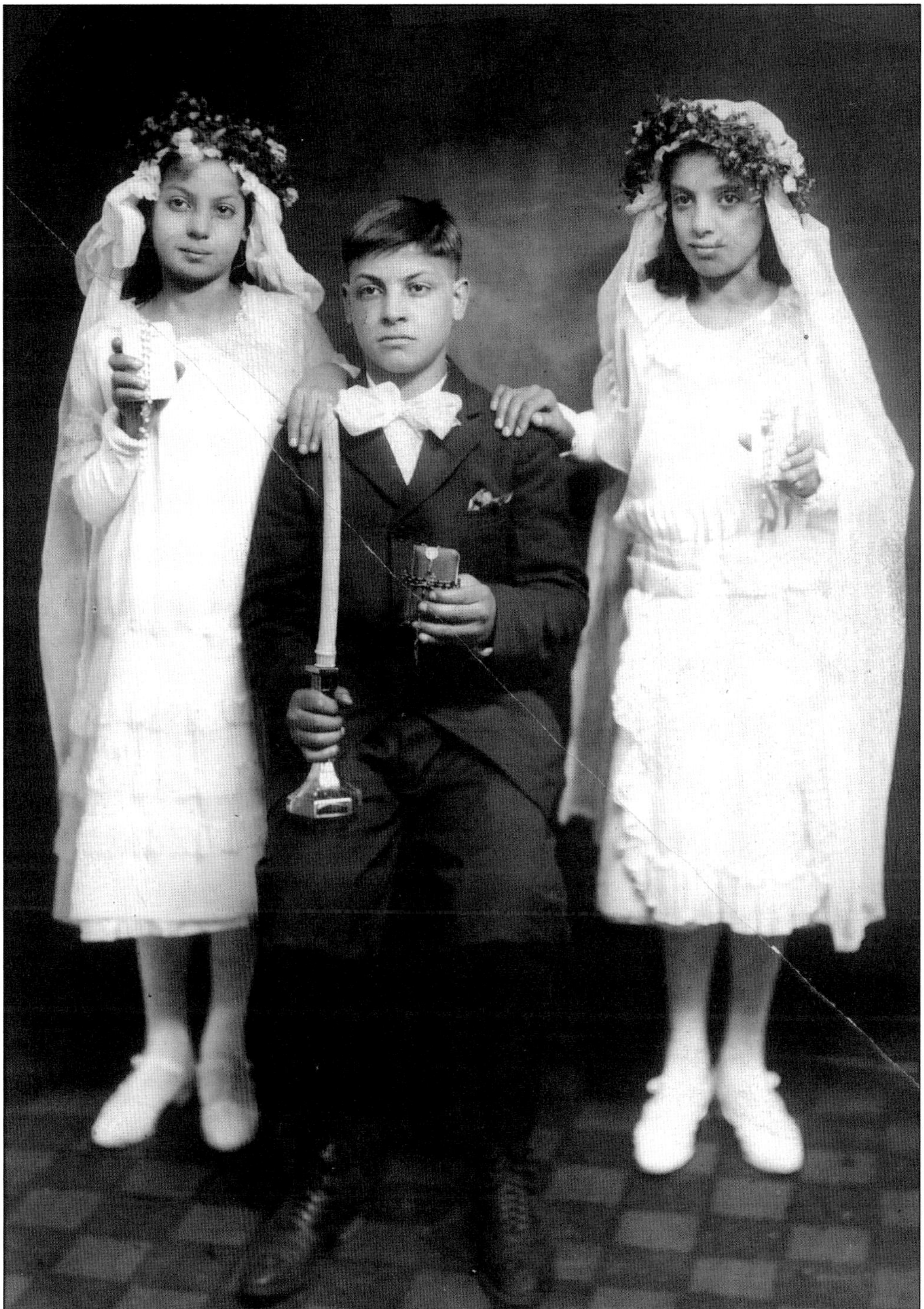

Shown here is the solemn communion of three of the Piccione children—from left, Mary, Giacomo, and Sandra—at Holy Rosary Church. They hold their special prayer books, rosaries, and a candle. (Courtesy Charles Farah.)

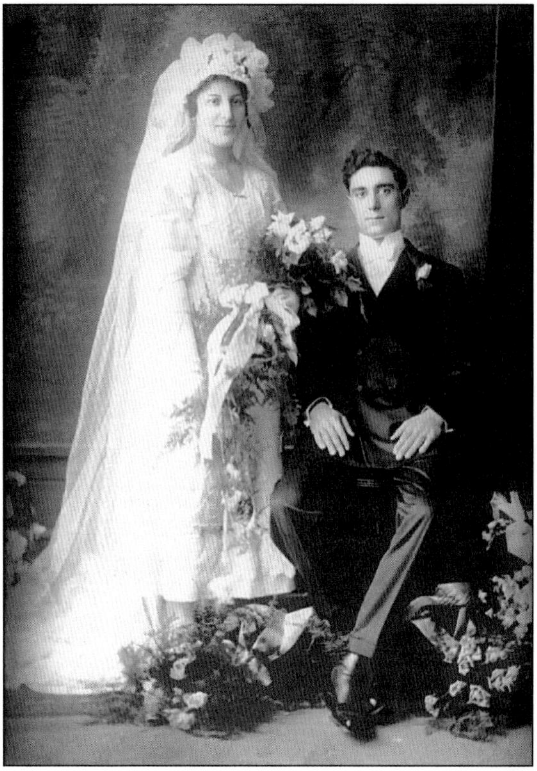

Gus Spicuzza married Rosa Mascari in 1919. He arrived from Termini Imerese at age nine in 1904. At 16, he loaded a pushcart full of bananas, and would not return home until he sold his entire supply. Later he operated a City Market stand, and like other Sicilian banana merchants, he was frugal. Gus saved 50 percent of his weekly income, so that in the interwar period he was able to invest heavily in Broad Ripple real estate. After retirement in 1955, he worked with Ray and Mascari, Murello Banana Company, and Standard Grocery chain. Gus could tell the temperature of bananas by their feel, so that only a portion of a large shipment would be ripe for sale each day. (Courtesy Rosemary Page.)

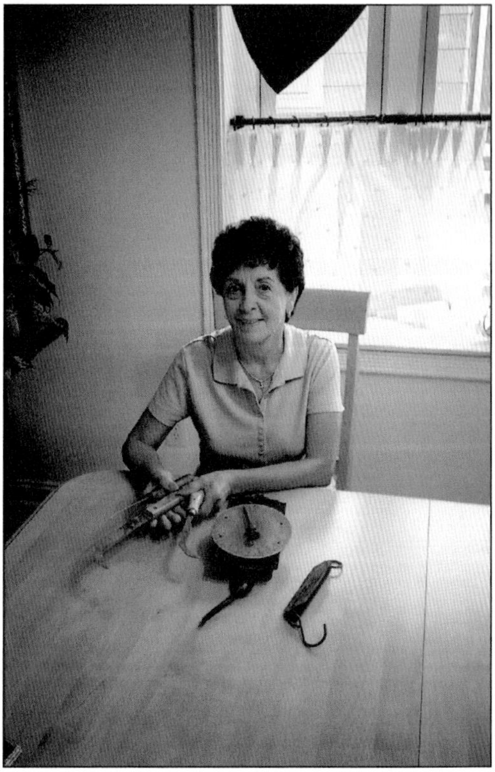

On her kitchen table, Rosemary Spicuzza Page displays banana scales and banana knives, her father's tools of the trade. As in most other houses around Holy Rosary Church, green bananas would be moved into the basement and hung in rows on strong hooks. Through placement and an artificially heated atmosphere, the bananas ripened until ready to eat.

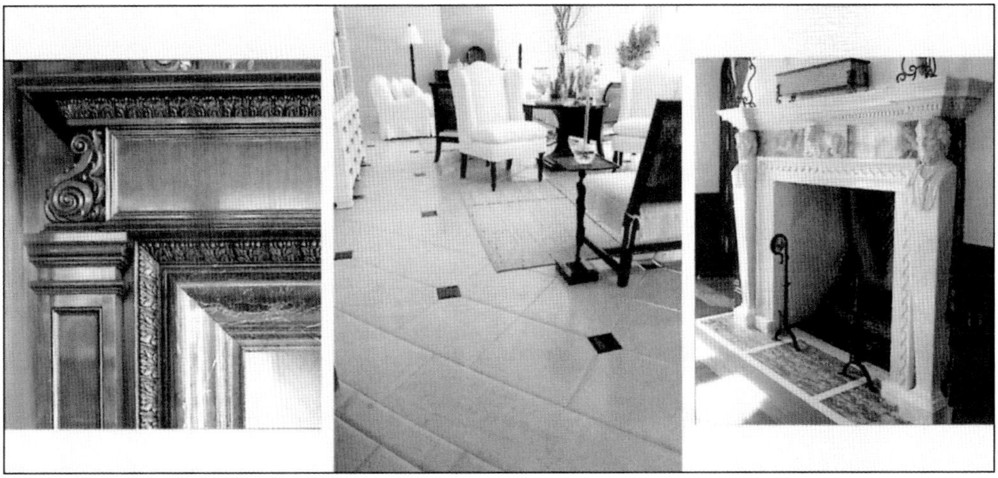

Friulani (*Furlan* in their own dialect) from northeastern Italy settled in Indianapolis as early as the 1920s, while others migrated because of a terrazzo labor shortage after World War II. Common family names were Santarossa, Toffolo, Francescon, Fargo (Fagionato), Bernardon, De Cecco, Canzian, Fontenin, Minatel, Bomben, Lovisa, Ferroli, Di Bortolo, and Finòs. The missing final vowel is usually a giveaway—this is a Furlan name. Most came from what is now the provincia di Pordenone, from towns like Fanna, San Foca, Cavasso Nuovo, and Meduno. Many Furlan specialized in terrazzo flooring and mosaic tiling. Among their worksites were city, county, and state buildings; the airport; the cathedral; Washington and Lafayette Square shopping malls; and the Notre Dame library. Today artistic moldings, artfully designed tile flooring, and classical mantels appear in Furlan business catalogs (above).

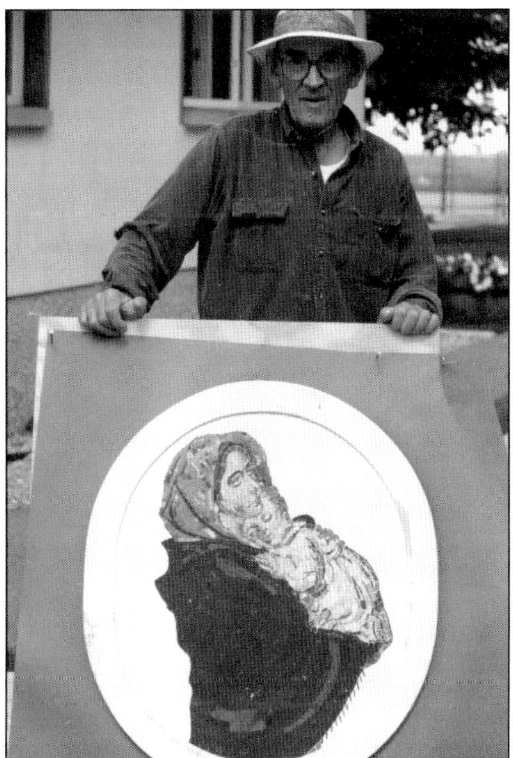

Carlo De Cecco (right) was born near Cologne in 1919, the son of a Fanna couple who found work in Germany. He joined the Alpini in the Italian army, was sent to the Russian front during World War II, was active with the partisans, and then migrated here. After retiring from the terrazzo business, he collected colored marble pieces and spent months in his garage polishing and shaping them to create this modern *Madonna and Christ Child.* (Courtesy Erna Santarossa De Cecco.)

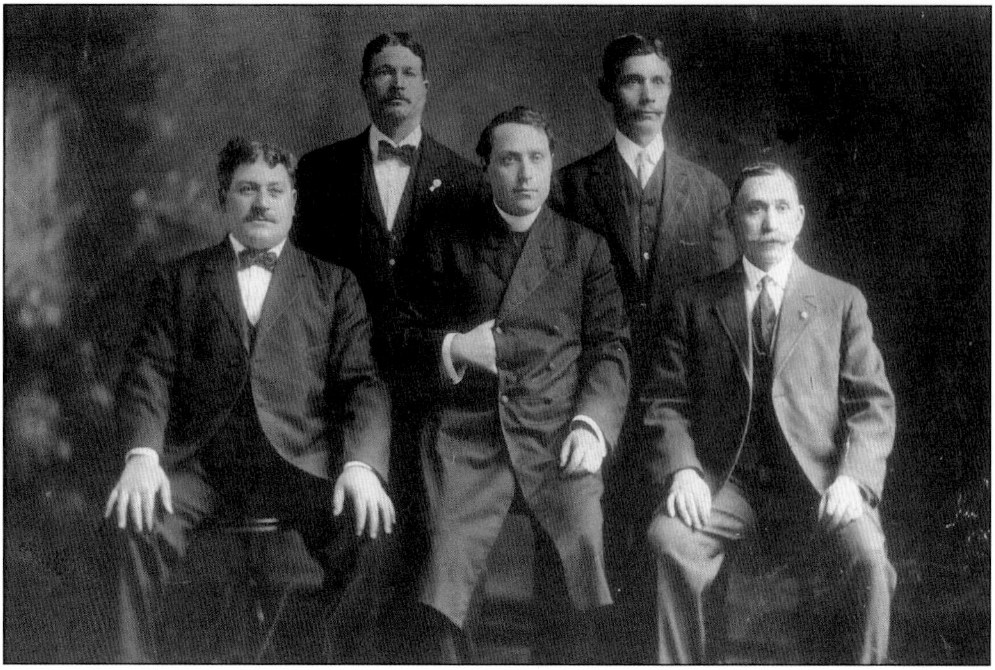

Among the stalwarts of the Italian community were the original trustees of Holy Rosary Church. Posing with Fr. Marino Priori (hand in coat) are, from left to right, Rosario Gatto, Michele Navarra, Salvatore Dagro, and Joseph Mascari. (Courtesy Angelina Navarra Kramer.)

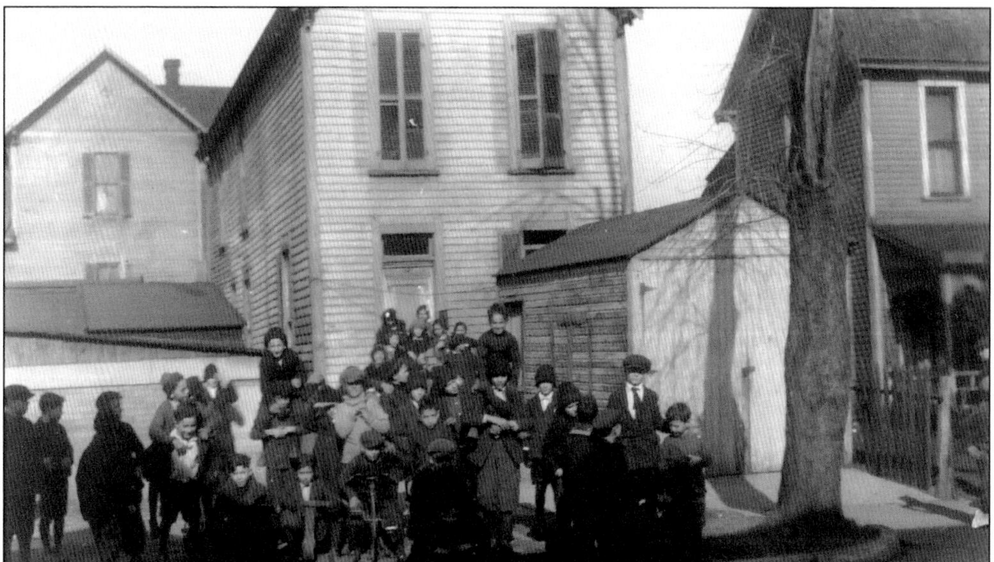

In caps and coats, neighborhood children enjoy lunch break from Holy Rosary's first schoolhouse in 1912. (Courtesy Freda Buennagel.)

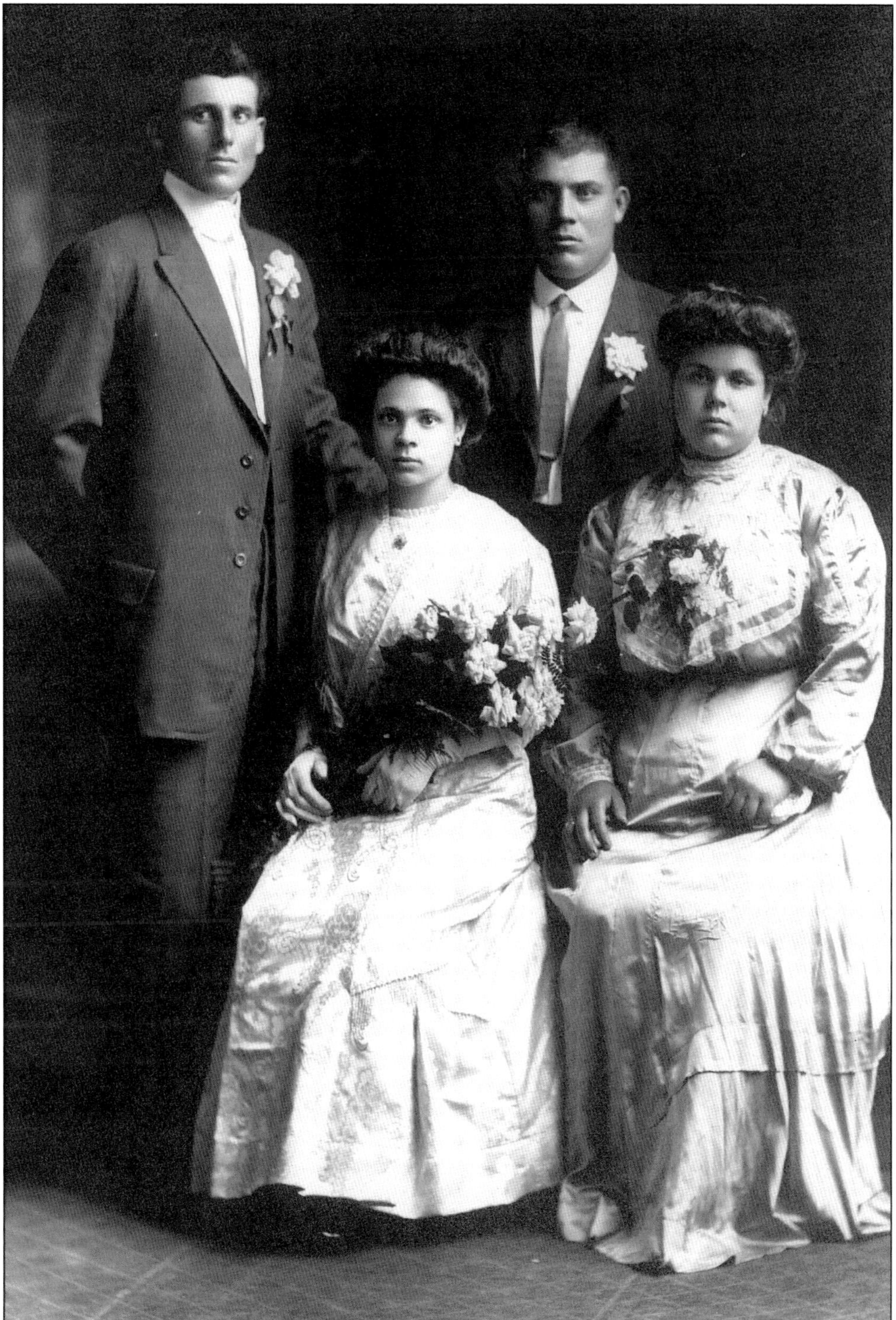

Originally from Monreale (Murreali), provincia di Palermo (Sicily), the Mirto family became Milto in America. Here, Diana sisters Anna Milto (left) and Giuseppina "Josephine" Bova pose with their husbands, Antonio Milto (left) and Salvatore "Sam" Bova. (Courtesy Joanna Milto-Bergin.)

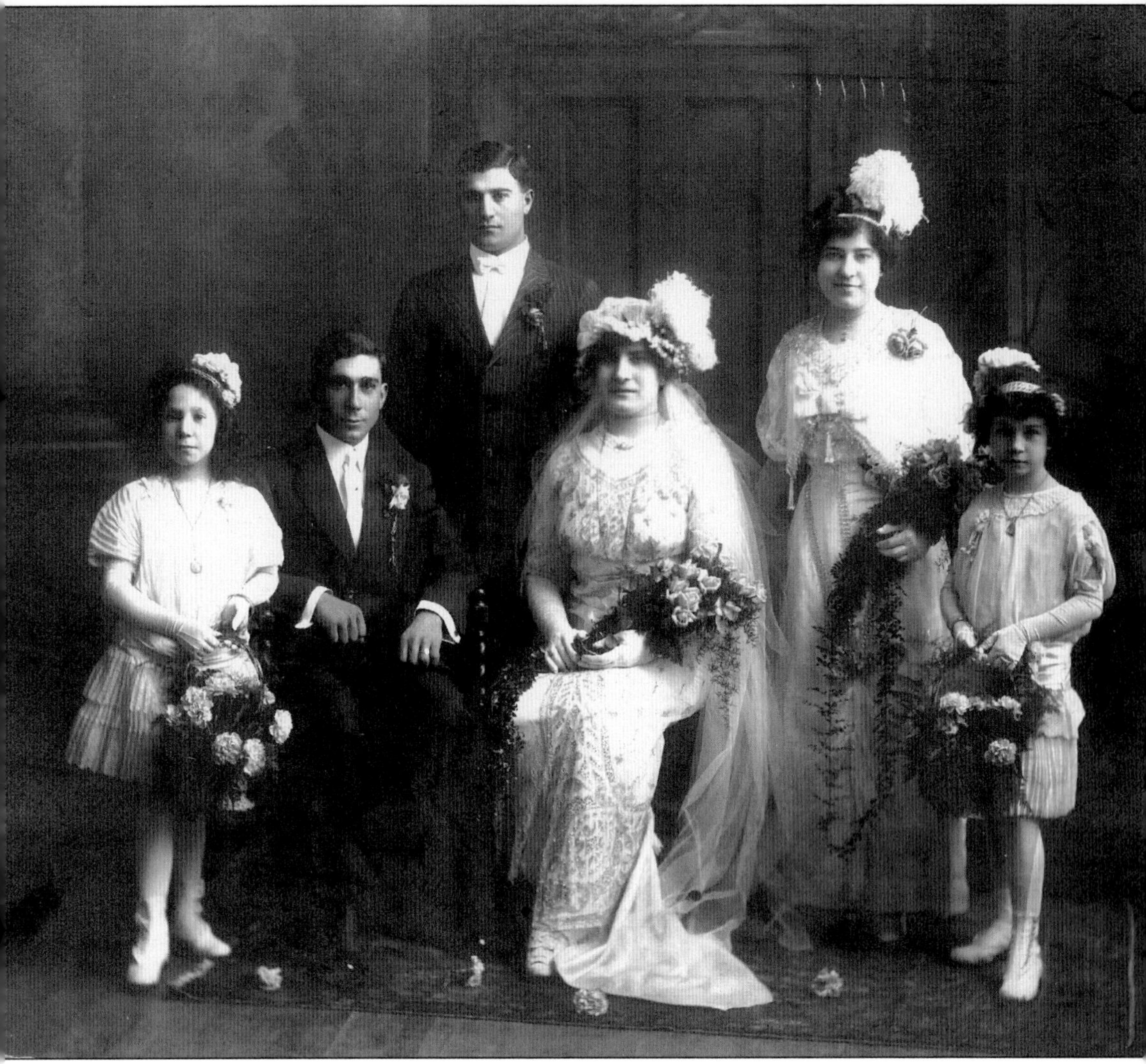

This is the formal wedding photograph of Philip H. Caito (second from left) and Josephine Miceli Caito (fourth from left).

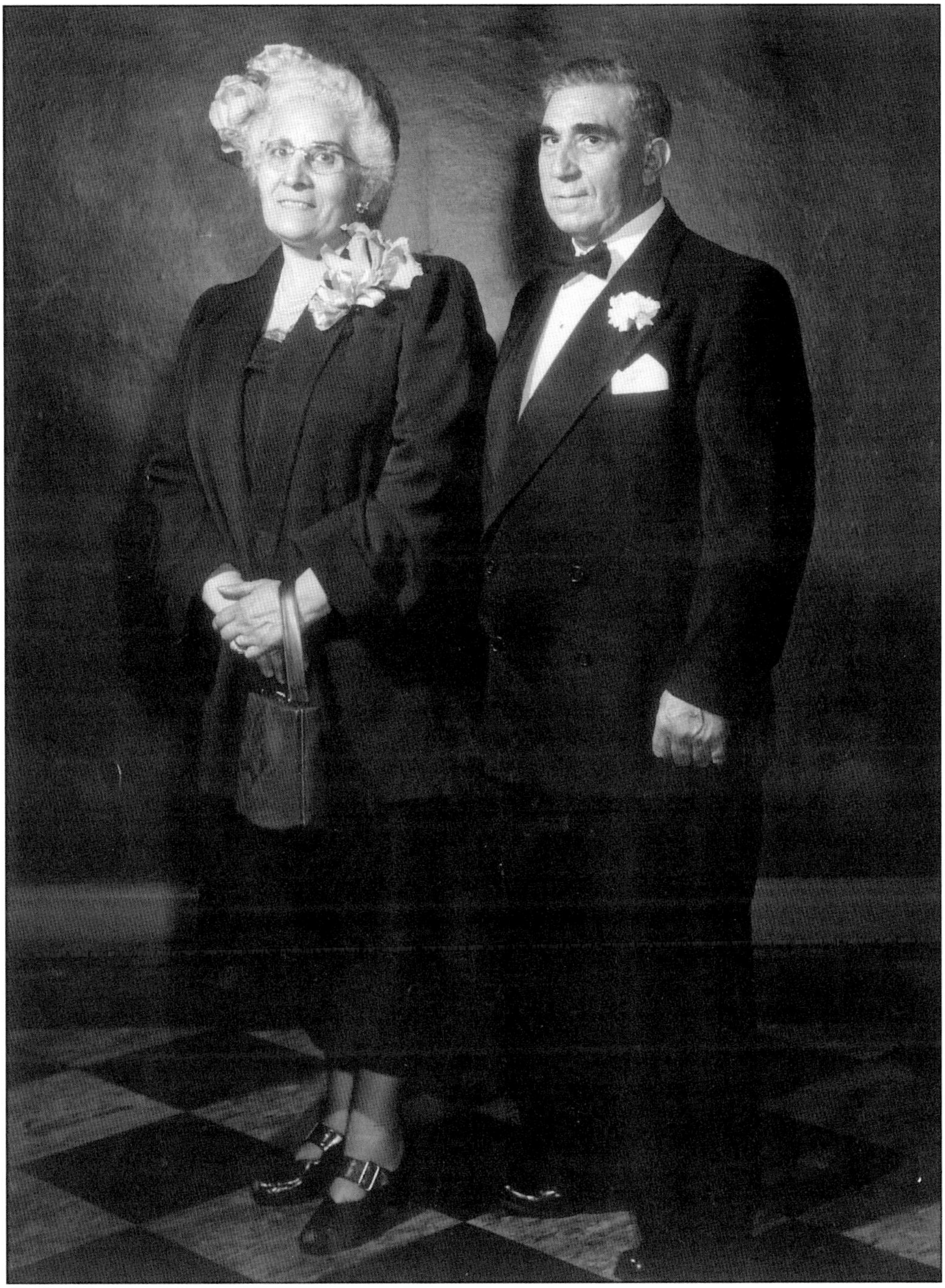

The Caitos are pictured again some 50 years later. (Courtesy Joanna Milto-Bergin.)

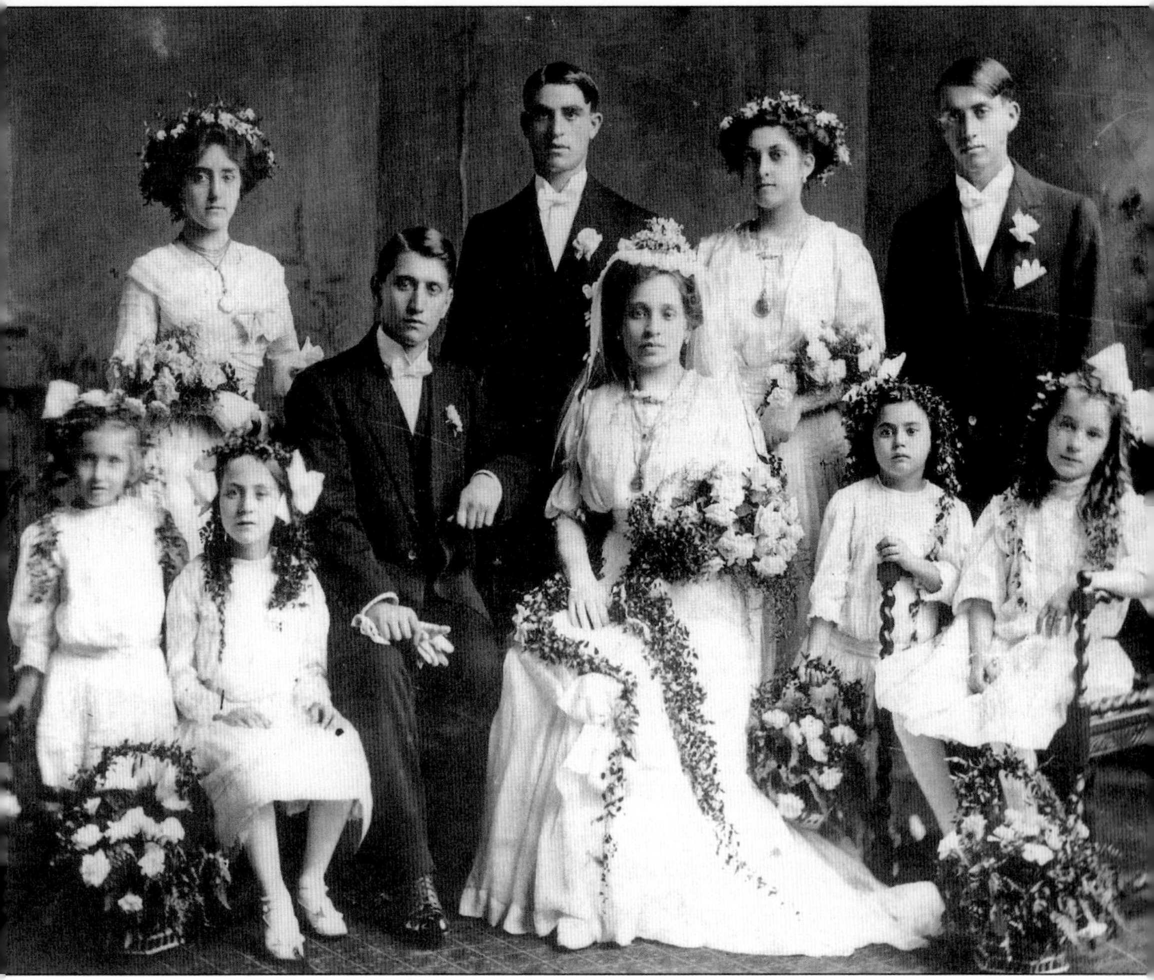

The seated couple is Charles Caldarone and Ninfa "Ann" Gatto. Upon Charles's return from the army after World War I, he saw 16-year-old Ninfa across the street. "Who is that girl?" he asked his father. The father concluded from the question that his son was interested in Ninfa, so he contacted her father to arrange marriage. Since her father had already given his word, to save face Ninfa had no choice but to marry Charlie. They married in Holy Rosary Church on September 21, 1919. From the number of attendants and elaborate decorations, it appears Ninfa's father spared no expense on his daughter's wedding. Incidentally, the marriage did not work out. (Courtesy Ninfa Gatto DeHilt.)

Two

A New People
Italian Americans

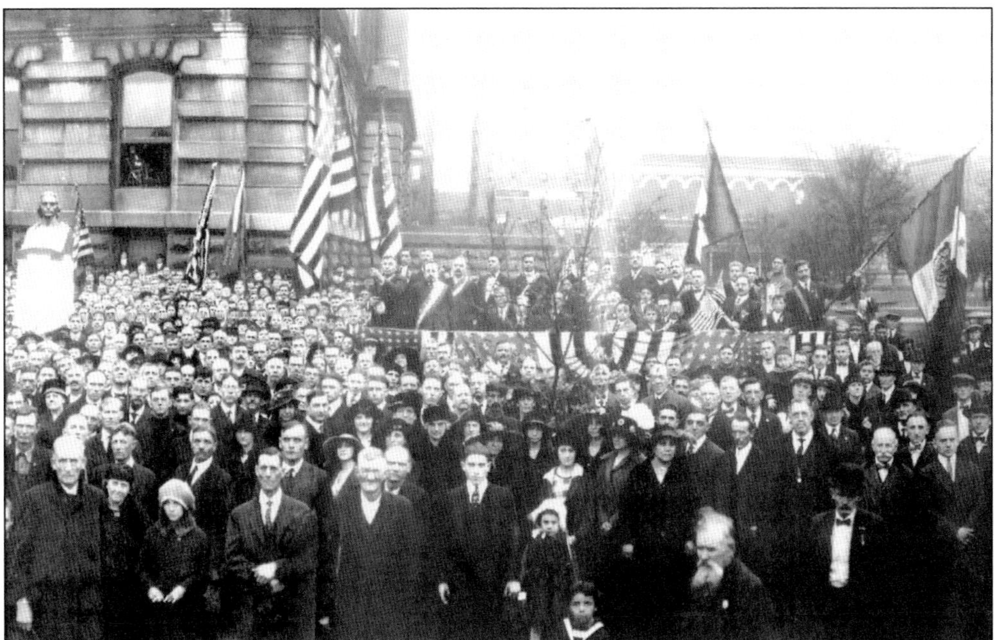

A Christopher Columbus bust with carved limestone pedestal, left, was dedicated on the grounds of the Indiana State House on October 31, 1920. Italian immigrants from Indianapolis and several other Indiana cities defrayed the cost of the monument as a salute to the discoverer and the Italian contribution to American civilization. It was the only monument erected by immigrants at the seat of Indiana government. Dr. Vincent A. Lapenta was chairman of the fund-raising committee, composed of tailors Frank DeJulio and Dominic Della Penna and commission merchant John Rosasco.

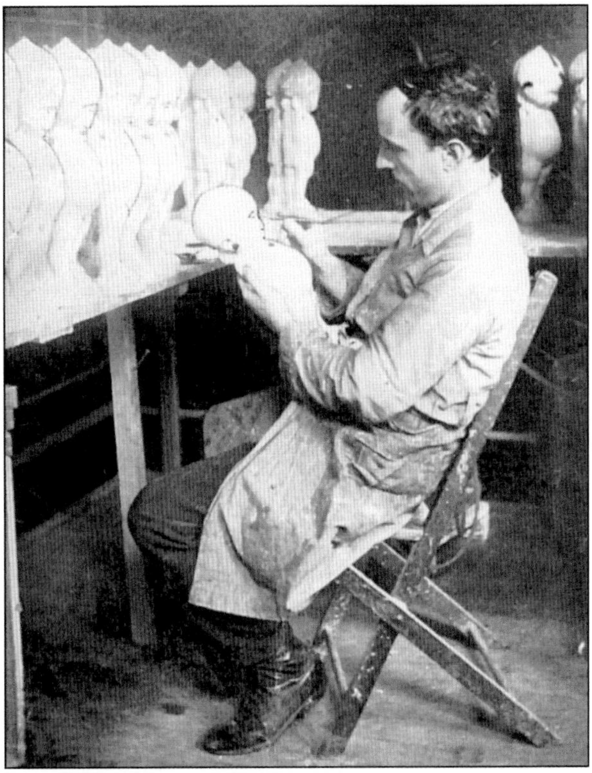

Enrico Vittori, sculptor of the Columbus bust, lived and worked in Indianapolis during the 1920s, making fireplace mantels in his shop on South Illinois Street and kewpie dolls for the Indianapolis Statuary Company. Natives of Lucca in Italy owned and operated this company. Among them were Dante Gaspari, Olindo Mariani, and Vincenzo Guerrini.

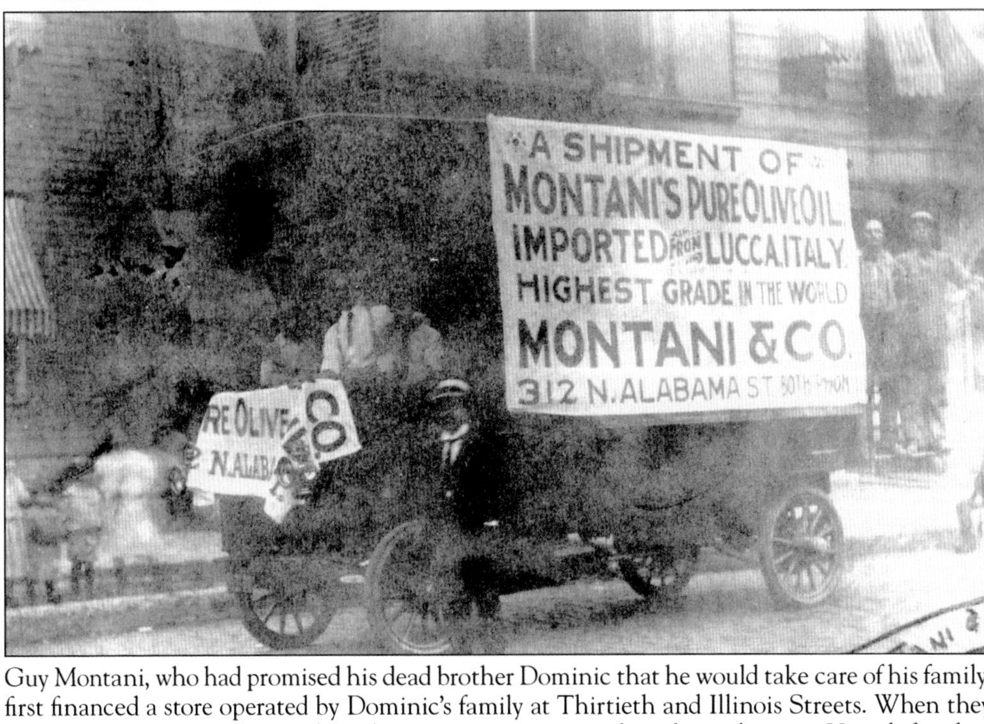

Guy Montani, who had promised his dead brother Dominic that he would take care of his family, first financed a store operated by Dominic's family at Thirtieth and Illinois Streets. When they had really great news, they took to the streets in a motorized truck to advertise. Hurrah for olive oil! This truck promotes an additional store at 312 North Alabama Street.

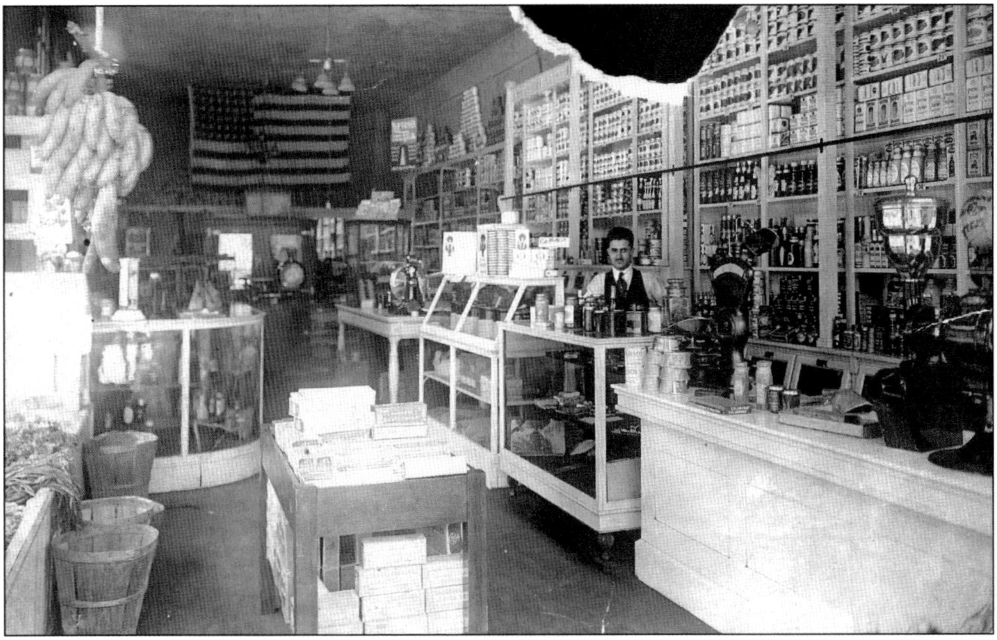

This photograph shows the Montanis' Illinois Street shop around 1918. Guy and his children would also operate stores in the Marott Hotel and at Twenty-seventh and Meridian Streets. (Courtesy Steve Montani.)

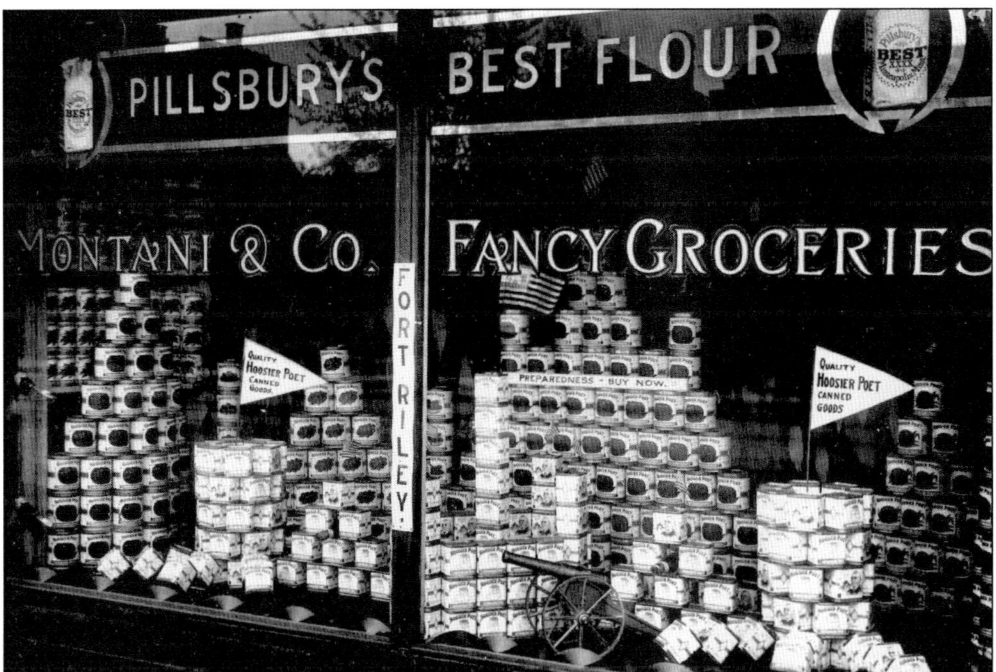

The Montanis used eye-catching window displays to advertise their products and persuade passersby to become customers. (Courtesy John Montani.)

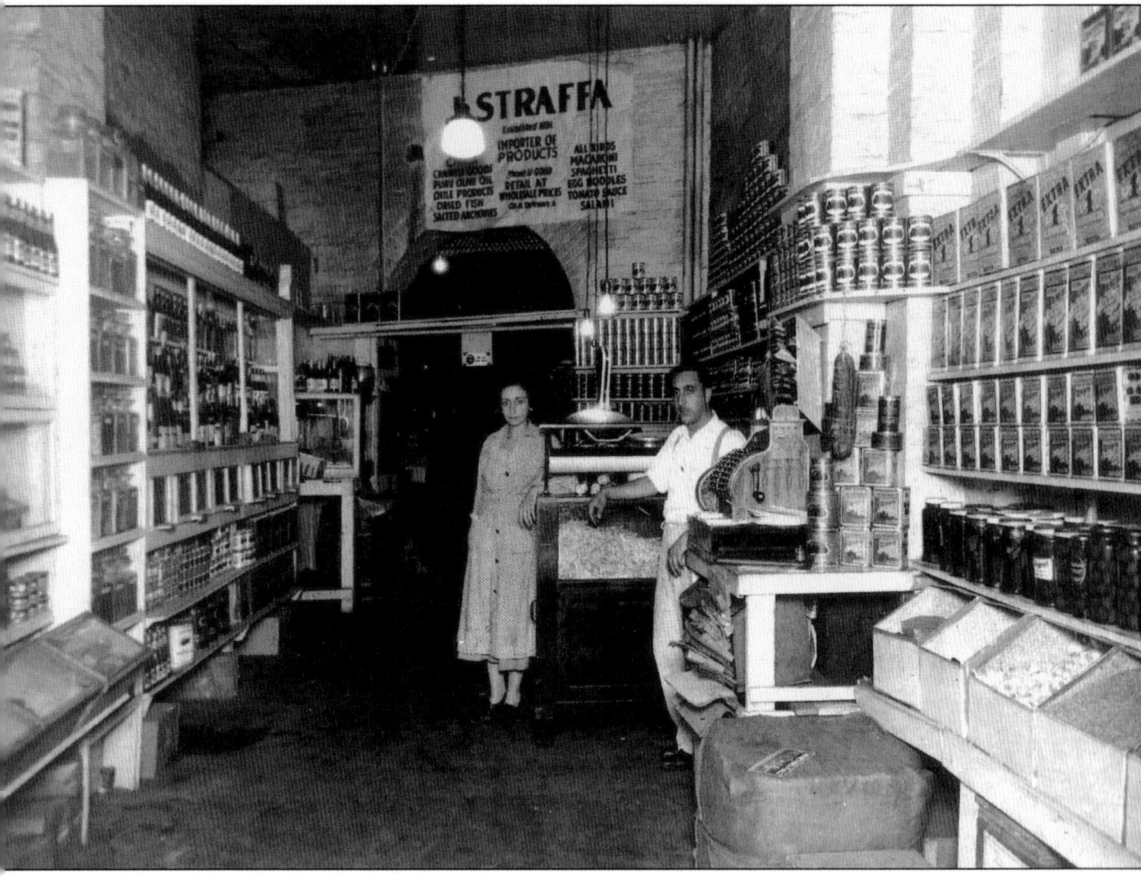

Back at City Market, Jacob and Josephine Straffa ran this store in the summer of 1932. Shoppers could buy the full stock of an Italian store—from olive oil, anchovies, and tomato sauce to pasta, olives, and salami. They carried the "fancy" grade and sold both wholesale and retail. The young clerks were daughter Rose Straffa Annarino and her husband, Anthony Annarino. Jacob Straffa was born Giacomo Straffezza and came to this country in 1888, at age 17. His wife was the former Josephine Ferracane. The Straffas donated two nave windows in Holy Rosary Church. Anthony Annarino's father came from Termini Imerese and sold produce in Cincinnati. (Courtesy Rosemary Annarino Logan.)

The family of August and Francesca d'Ascanio Scarpone lived at 149 Leota Street in 1928. August was a master of many trades. Pictured here, from left to right, are the following: (first row) Pat, August, Mary, Frances, and Bill; (second row) Ida, Chris, and Florence. (Courtesy Tom Burke.)

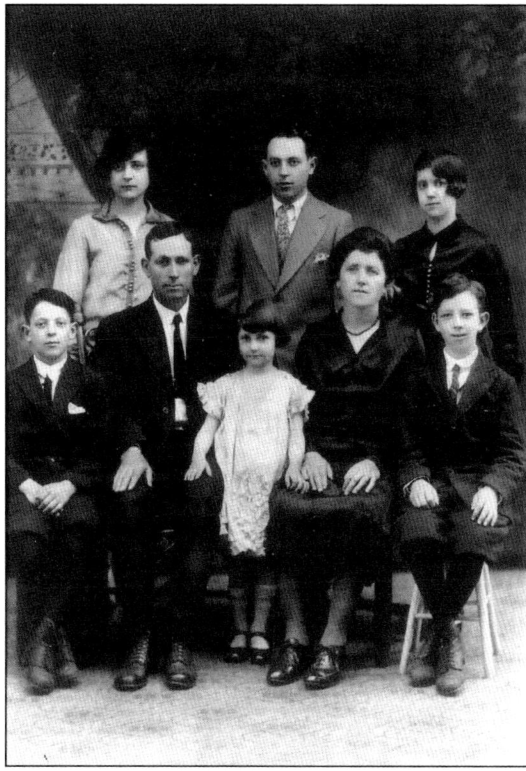

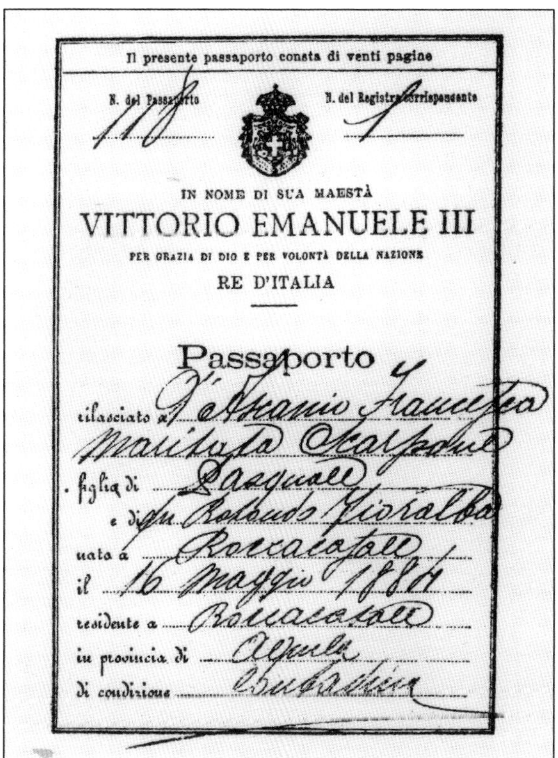

Il presente passaporto consta di venti pagine

N. del Passaporto

N. del Registro corrispondente

IN NOME DI SUA MAESTÀ

VITTORIO EMANUELE III

PER GRAZIA DI DIO E PER VOLONTÀ DELLA NAZIONE

RE D'ITALIA

Passaporto

rilasciato a D'Ascanio Francesca maritata Scarpone

figlia di Pasquale

e di

nata a

il 16 maggio

residente a

in provincia di Aquila

di condizione

This Italian passport was issued to Francesca d'Ascanio Scarpone, Crescenzo "Chris," and Ida of Roccacasale provincia di L'Aguila (Abruzzi), for all three to travel to New York in 1913. It was valid for a three-year period. Italian passports began to carry thumbnail-size photographs of their bearers only after World War I.

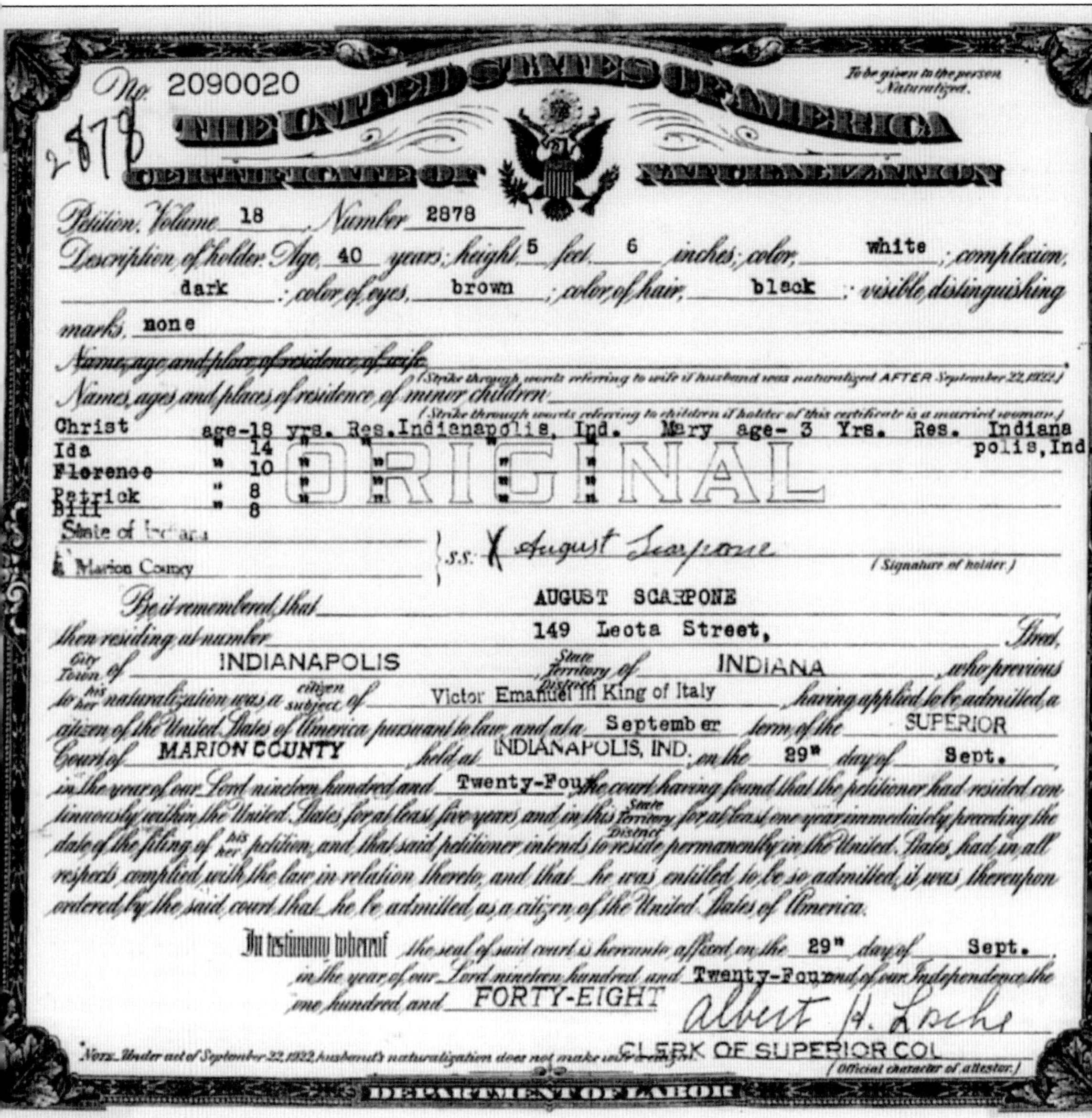
No. 2090020

2878

THE UNITED STATES OF AMERICA

CERTIFICATE OF NATURALIZATION

To be given to the person Naturalized.

Petition, Volume 18 Number 2878

Description of holder. Age, 40 years; height, 5 feet, 6 inches; color, white; complexion, dark; color of eyes, brown; color of hair, black; visible distinguishing marks, none

~~Name, age and place of residence of wife~~ (Strike through words referring to wife if husband was naturalized AFTER September 22, 1922.)

Names, ages and places of residence of minor children (Strike through words referring to children if holder of this certificate is a married woman.)

Christ age-18 yrs. Res. Indianapolis, Ind. Mary age- 3 Yrs. Res. Indianapolis, Ind
Ida " 14 " " " "
~~Florence~~ " 10 " " " "
~~Patrick~~ " 8 " " " "
~~Bill~~ " 8 " " " "

ORIGINAL

State of Indiana
Marion County } s.s. X August Scarpone (Signature of holder.)

Be it remembered, that AUGUST SCARPONE then residing at number 149 Leota Street, Street, City of INDIANAPOLIS State of INDIANA who previous to his naturalization was a subject of Victor Emanuel III King of Italy having applied to be admitted a citizen of the United States of America pursuant to law, and at a September term of the SUPERIOR Court of MARION COUNTY held at INDIANAPOLIS, IND. on the 29th day of Sept. in the year of our Lord nineteen hundred and Twenty-Four the court having found that the petitioner had resided continuously within the United States for at least five years and in this State for at least one year immediately preceding the date of the filing of his petition, and that said petitioner intends to reside permanently in the United States, had in all respects complied with the law in relation thereto, and that he was entitled to be so admitted, it was thereupon ordered by the said court that he be admitted as a citizen of the United States of America.

In testimony whereof the seal of said court is hereunto affixed on the 29th day of Sept. in the year of our Lord nineteen hundred and Twenty-Four and of our Independence the one hundred and FORTY-EIGHT

Albert H. Losche

CLERK OF SUPERIOR COURT (Official character of attestor.)

Note: Under act of September 22, 1922, husband's naturalization does not make wife a citizen.

DEPARTMENT OF LABOR

The naturalization certificate of August Scarpone showed that his minor children became citizens, but that his wife was excluded from citizenship if he naturalized after 1922. This peculiarity in the law was a step toward excluding some immigrants from automatic citizenship before enactment of the quota system in 1924.

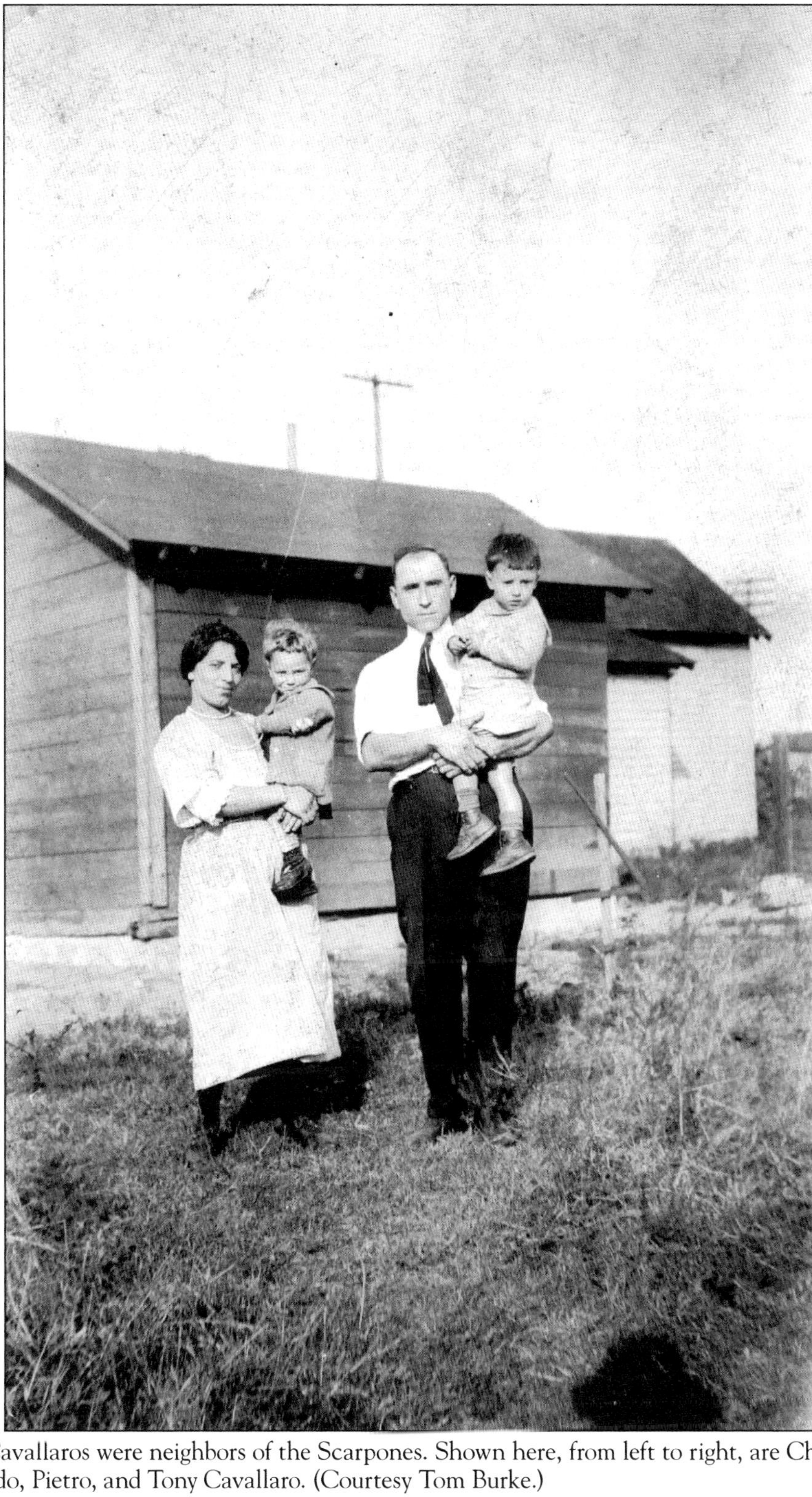

The Cavallaros were neighbors of the Scarpones. Shown here, from left to right, are Christina, Orlando, Pietro, and Tony Cavallaro. (Courtesy Tom Burke.)

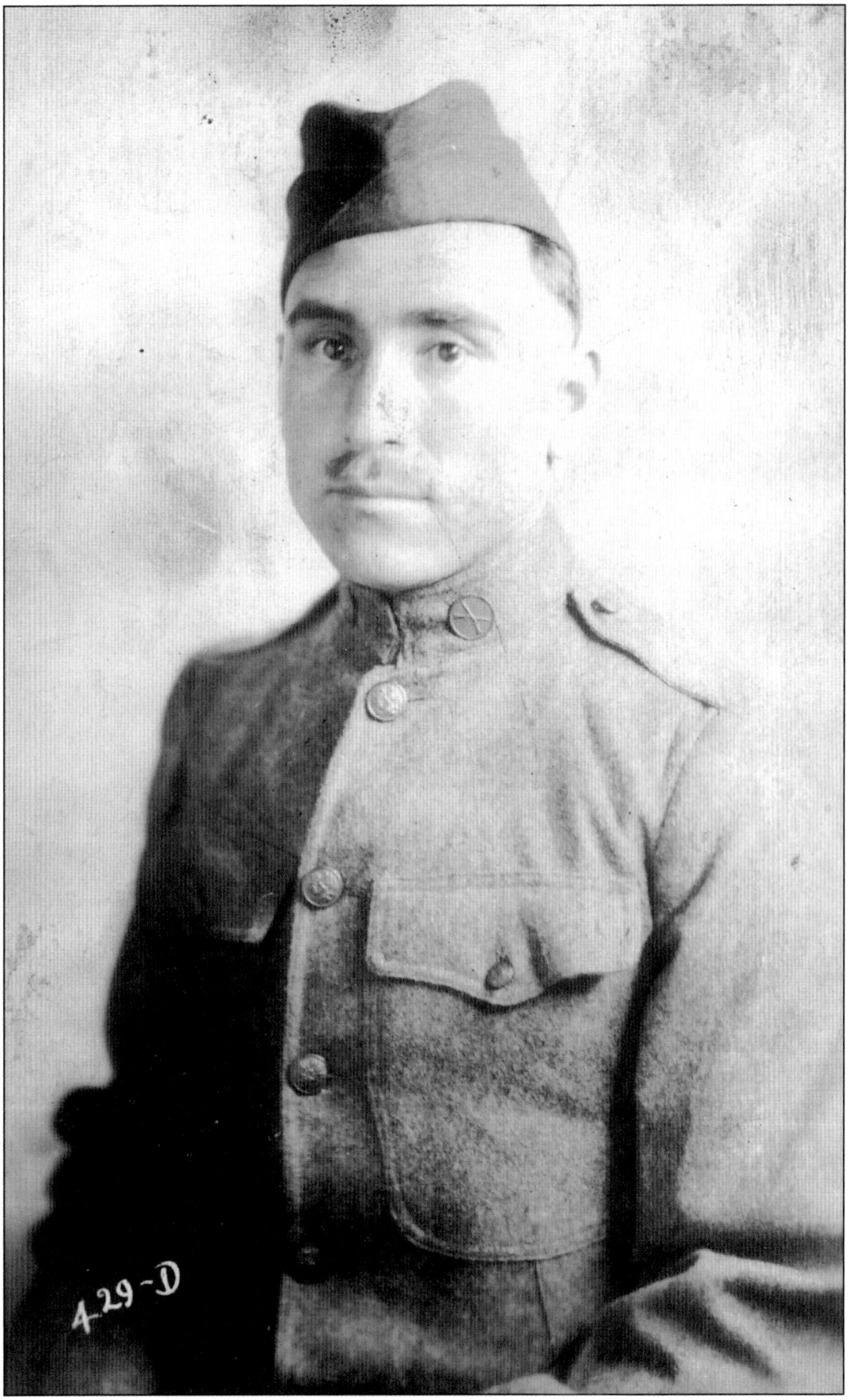

Pietro Cavallaro, born in Roccacasale, wears his military uniform during World War I. Italian Americans were members of the United States military, attesting to their patriotism. Yet only a few years later, the Ku Klux Klan would consider "foreigners" a threat to the American way. (Courtesy Tom Burke.)

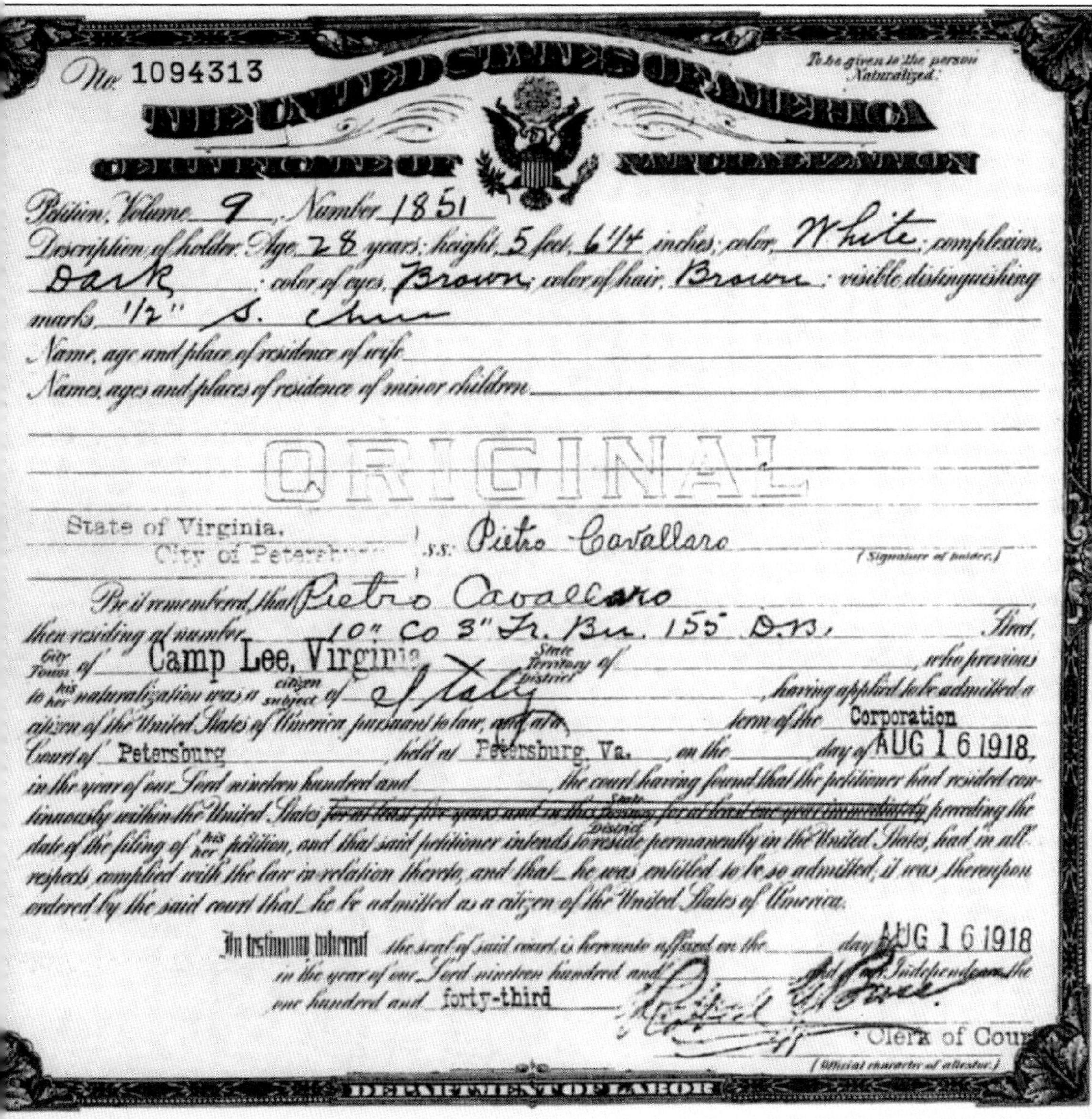

No. 1094313

To be given to the person Naturalized.

THE UNITED STATES OF AMERICA

CERTIFICATE OF NATURALIZATION

Petition, Volume 9, Number 1851

Description of holder: Age 28 years; height 5 feet, 6 1/4 inches; color White; complexion Dark; color of eyes Brown; color of hair Brown; visible distinguishing marks 1/2" S. Chin

Name, age and place of residence of wife

Names, ages and places of residence of minor children

ORIGINAL

State of Virginia, City of Petersburg } ss: Pietro Cavallaro (Signature of holder.)

Be it remembered, that Pietro Cavallaro then residing at number 10" Co 3" Tr. Bn. 155 D.B. Street, City of Camp Lee, Virginia, who previous to his naturalization was a subject of Italy, having applied to be admitted a citizen of the United States of America pursuant to law, at a term of the Corporation Court of Petersburg held at Petersburg, Va., on the day of AUG 16 1918, in the year of our Lord nineteen hundred and , the court having found that the petitioner had resided continuously within the United States ~~for at least five years and in the ... for at least one year immediately~~ preceding the date of the filing of his petition, and that said petitioner intends to reside permanently in the United States, had in all respects complied with the law in relation thereto, and that he was entitled to be so admitted, it was thereupon ordered by the said court that he be admitted as a citizen of the United States of America.

In testimony whereof the seal of said court is hereunto affixed on the day AUG 16 1918 in the year of our Lord nineteen hundred and and of our Independence the one hundred and forty-third

Clerk of Court (Official character of attestor.)

DEPARTMENT OF LABOR

Because he was an immigrant who served in the army, Cavallaro automatically obtained American citizenship at the military base from which he was discharged. (Courtesy Tom Burke.)

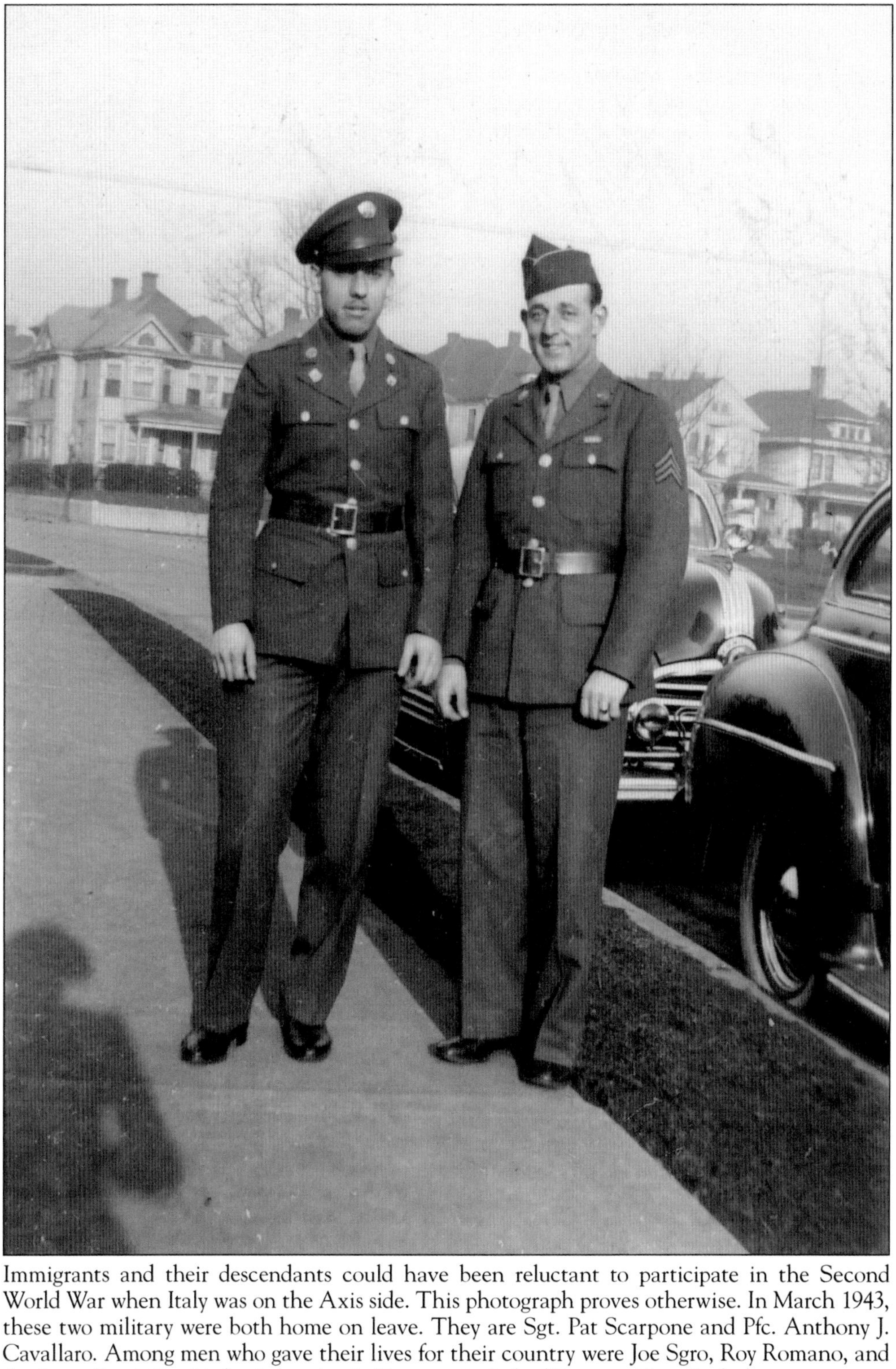

Immigrants and their descendants could have been reluctant to participate in the Second World War when Italy was on the Axis side. This photograph proves otherwise. In March 1943, these two military were both home on leave. They are Sgt. Pat Scarpone and Pfc. Anthony J. Cavallaro. Among men who gave their lives for their country were Joe Sgro, Roy Romano, and Anthony Sergi. Sergi is buried at Anzio-Nettuno in Italy. (Courtesy Tom Burke.)

Joseph Peter and Margaret Genco Morone stand proudly before the grape arbor in their yard at 1101 Newman Street, just north of Arsenal Technical High School. Born Giuseppe Pietro Morrone in Santa Ninfa, southwest of Palermo, Joseph emigrated in 1907 to find work on the Great Northern Railroad in Minnesota. He returned home to marry and took the transatlantic trip again in 1923. On the way back to Minnesota, the couple stopped in Indianapolis to visit relatives who persuaded them to settle where the weather was warmer. Joe found a job as section foreman with the Big Four Railroad. "It wasn't unusual because of accident or other emergency for him to be called away from dinner, even Christmas dinner, to take care of a railroad problem," remembered his son Nino. (Courtesy Antone "Nino" Morone.)

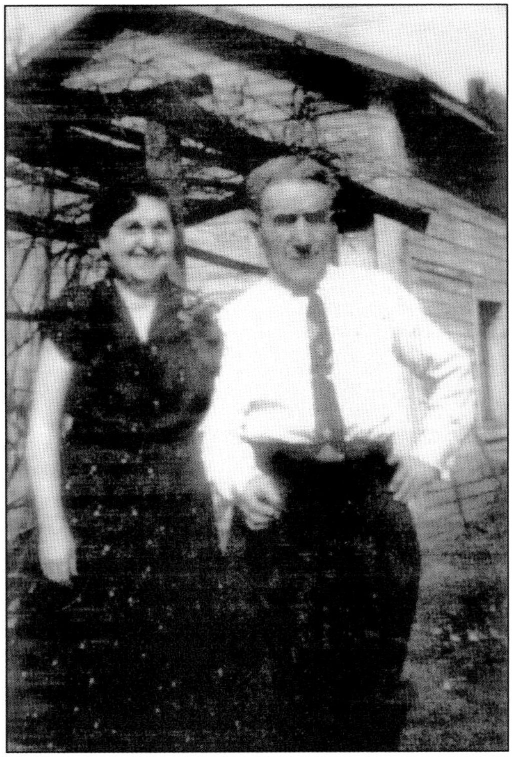

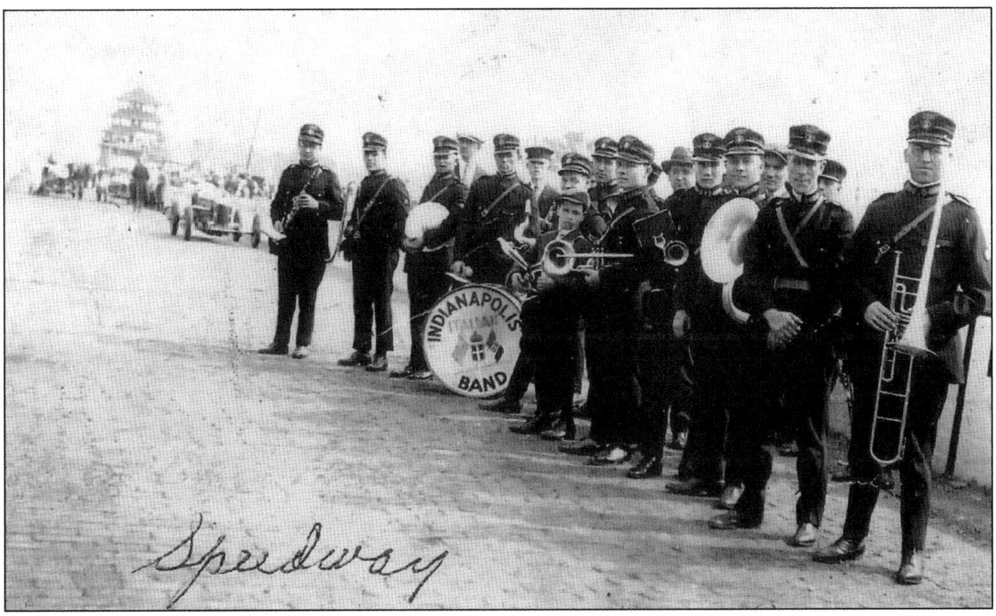

In 1923, grocer Fred Iozzo incorporated the Italian Musical Association, whose purpose was to maintain a military concert band. He bought instruments and uniforms and hired a professor from New York to train members. The Indianapolis Italian Band appeared at turn one on the brick pavement before the old Pagoda at the Indianapolis Motor Speedway around 1927. Identified here are two Liggera brothers (far left and far right), Marian Taddei, Augusto Scarpone (with drum), Pietro Cavallaro, Guirrine "Guidin" Colarocca, and Sabine Carbone. (Courtesy Tom Burke.)

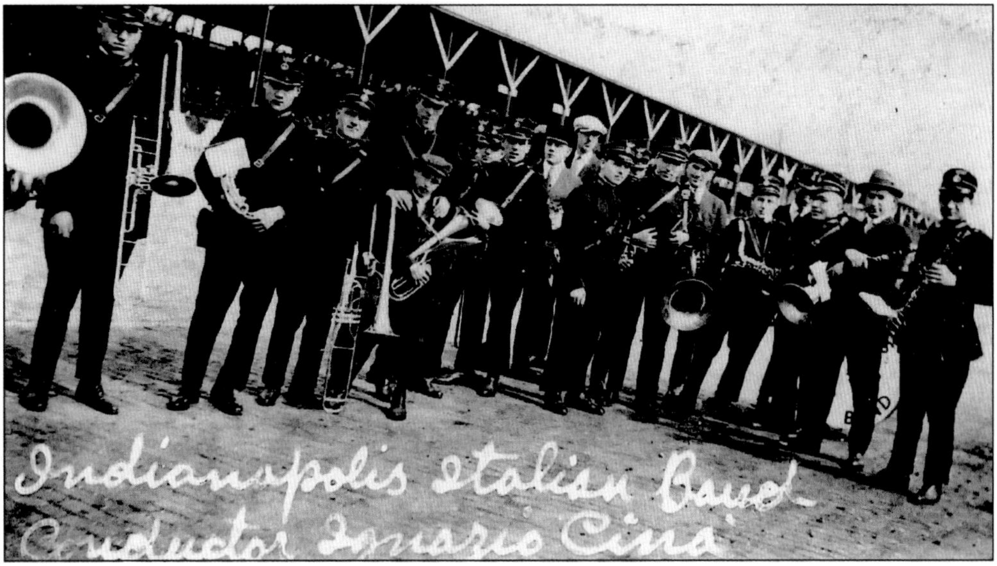

Indianapolis Italian Band members, some of whom hailed from Roccacasale, provincia di L'Aquila (Abruzzi), and lived around Georgia and Bates, east of College Avenue, are seen with their backs to the stands in the first turn at the Indianapolis Motor Speedway. Alas, the upkeep of the band became too expensive for founder Fred Iozzo. Because it lacked community financial support, the group was disbanded. Iozzo's son remembered that uniforms of various sizes hung in the family closet for years. (Courtesy Tom Burke.)

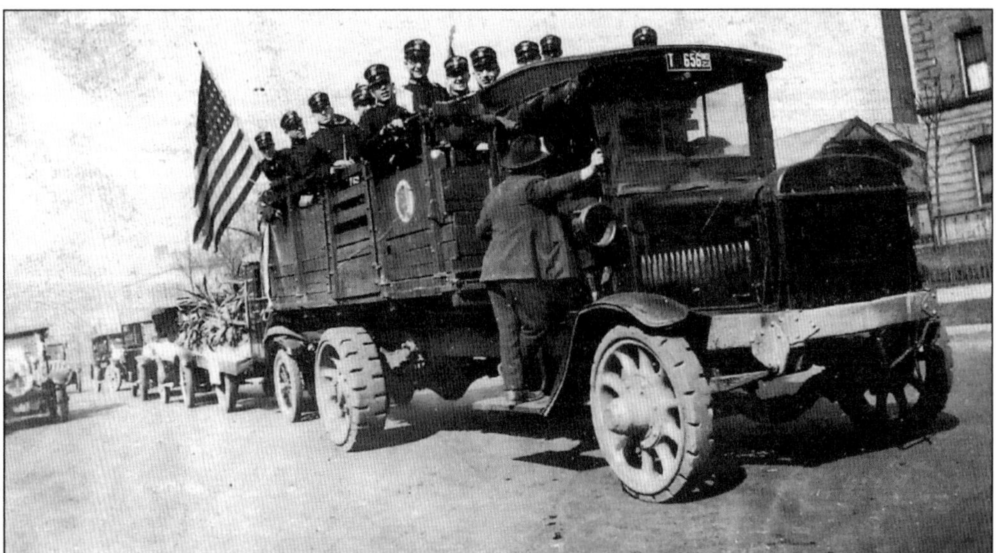

Italian bandsmen wave the American flag on a truck in 1923. (Courtesy Tom Burke.)

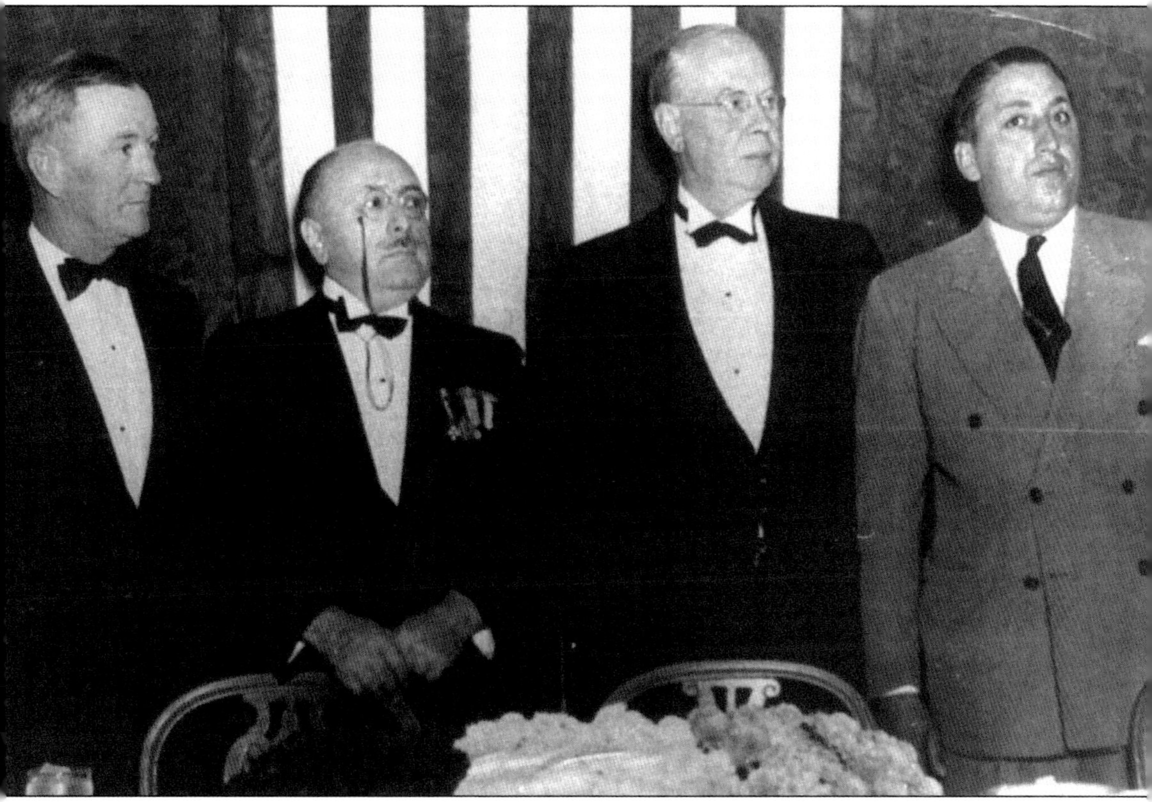

The number of Italians in Indianapolis may be small in comparison to Germans or Irish, but important personalities recognized their contribution to city life and attended Italian community events. These people are seated at the head table in the downtown Claypool Hotel for the annual Columbus Day dinner on October 12, 1939. Pictured from left to right are Judge H. Nathan Swaim, Indiana Supreme Court; surgeon-scientist Vincent A. Lapenta, honorary Italian consul for Indiana; Reginald H. Sullivan, mayor of Indianapolis; and Salvatore "Tudie" Miceli, Sicilian banana king, president of the Francesco Crispi Society for several years, and dinner chairman.

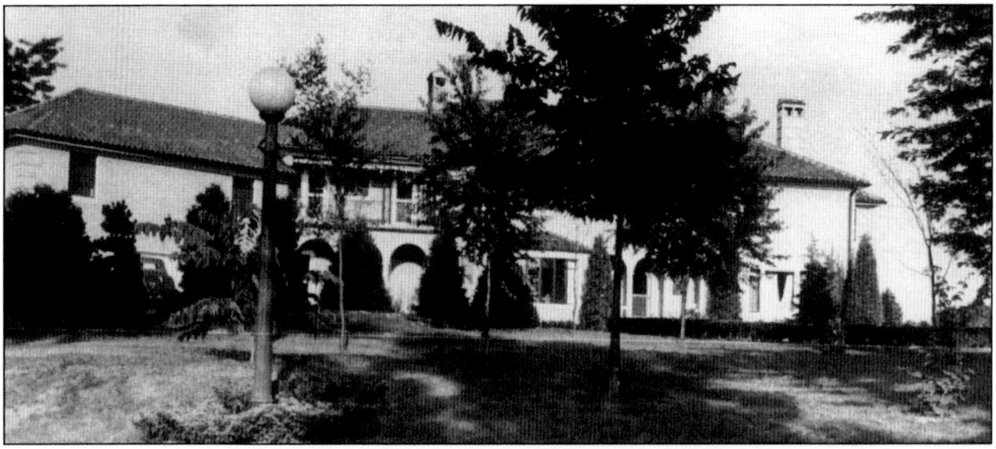

This home, located north of White River in the 6400 block of North Meridian Street, belonged to abdominal surgeon Vincent A. Lapenta. Son of an Italian army officer and nephew of the bishop of Ischia (his birthplace), Lapenta received hismedical degree at the University of Naples in 1906 and studied at Harvard Medical School in 1909. He moved to Indianapolis in 1911, after meeting Italians at the 500 race who expressed need for a doctor who spoke their language. Lapenta developed a serum used during the war to staunch hemorrhage, and in 1930, the king of Italy made him a knight officer of the Royal Crown of Italy. Appointed honorary consular agent for Italy in Indiana in 1921, he lectured on Fascist foreign policy in the 1930s. Publicly, Lapenta usually wore a monocle and a tuxedo and sash with medals, cutting *una bella figura*. When Italy declared war on the United States in 1941, he was interned as an enemy alien for 16 months along with 27 others. He died in 1946, saluted by peers as a victim of war.

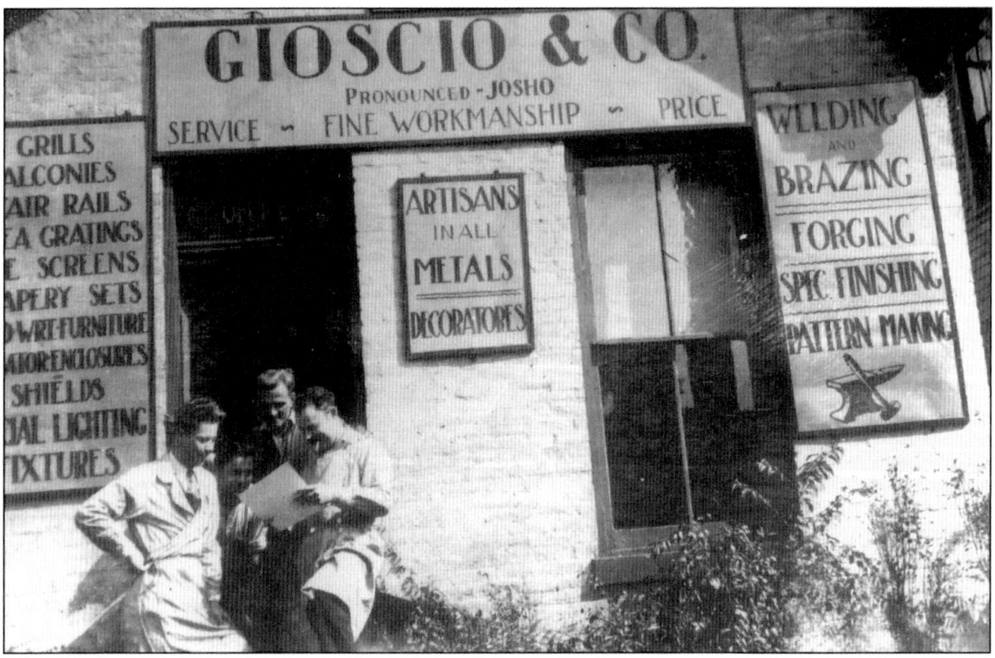

Gioscio and Company, at 129 North Noble Street (now College Avenue), specialized in artistic wrought-iron designs. Dominic (second from left) and Fred Gioscio (right), sons of painter and decorator Giovanni Gioscio (pronounced "Josho"), study a design with their employees. Fred designed fireplace irons, porch rails, and church candelabra and candle stands. (Courtesy John Gioscio.)

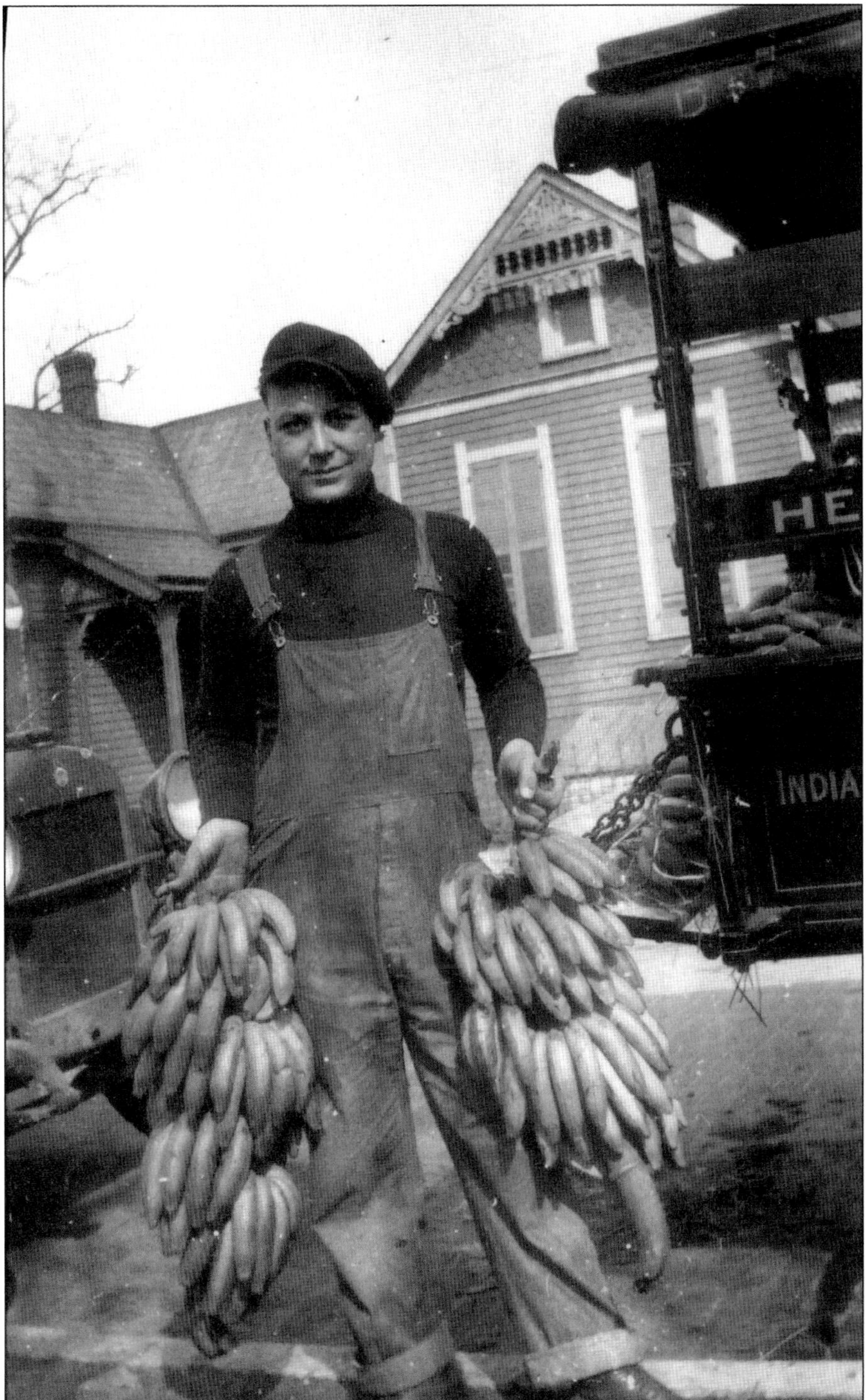

Their parents were ordinary Sicilian immigrants, but Tony and Joe Murello were very successful in the produce business from the 1920s to 1940s. Here Joe reminds us that banana is king. (Courtesy Margaret LaGrotto.)

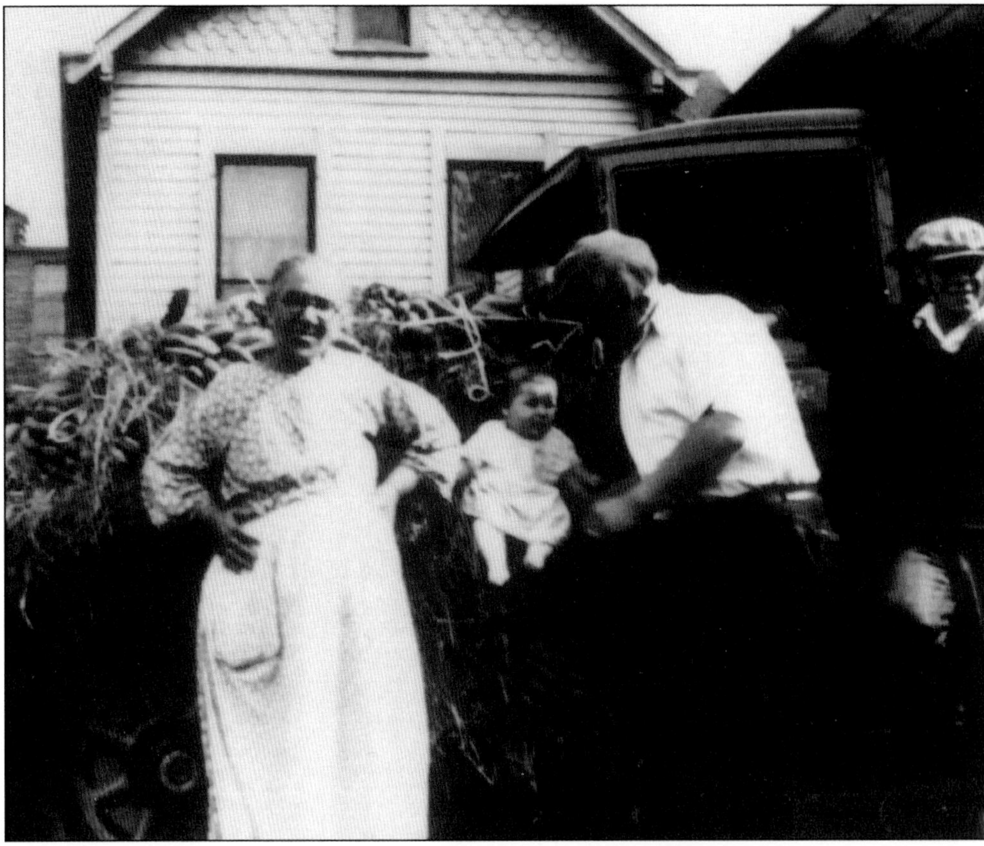

From left to right, Margaret Catalano Murello stands before the Merrill Street family home with granddaughter Margaret, son Joe, and neighbor Salvatore Caruso. (Courtesy Margaret LaGrotto.)

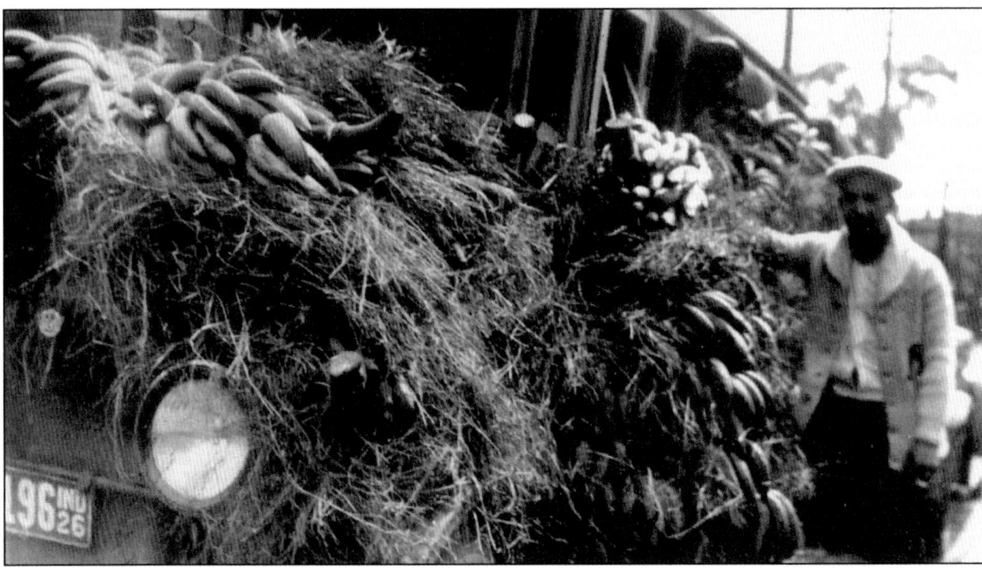

Tony Murello places straw on the truck fender to transport bananas without bruising in 1926. (Courtesy Margaret LaGrotto.)

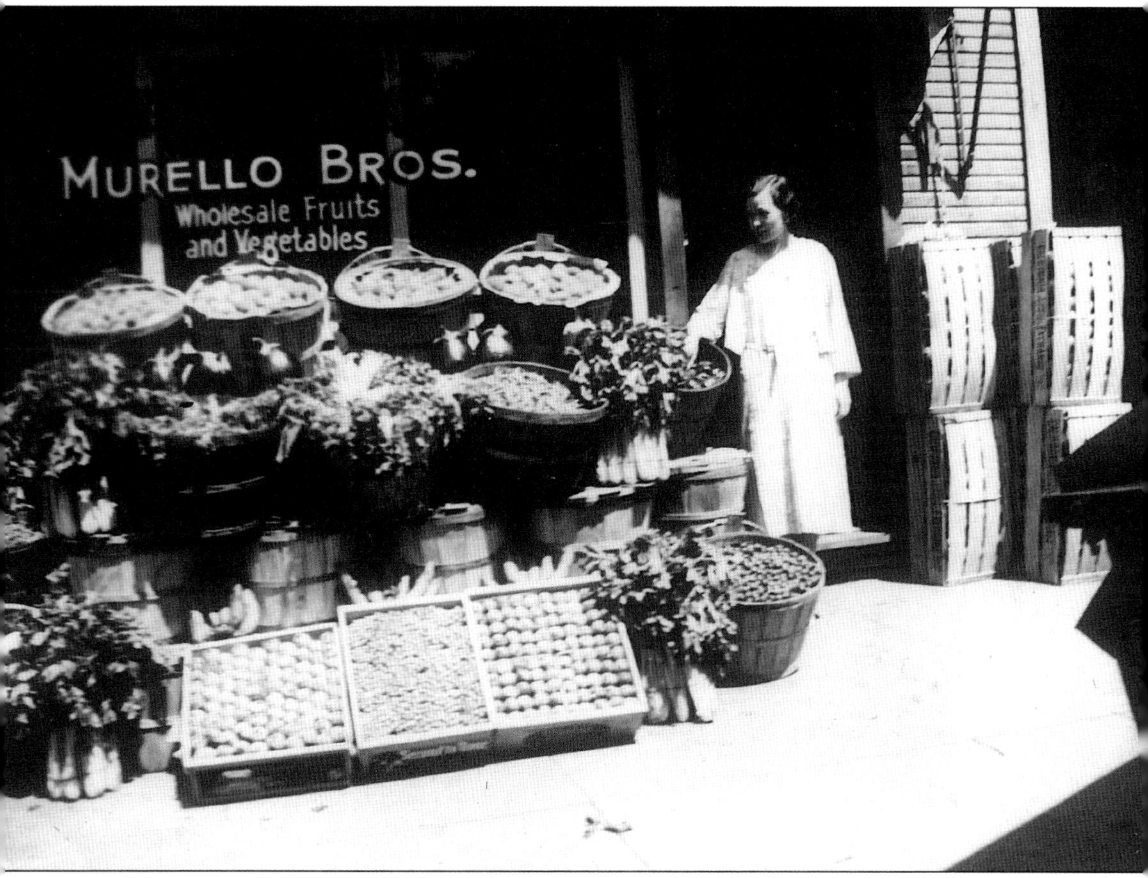

Joe Murello's wife, Helen, checks the first-rate display prominent in front of the Murello Brothers business. (Courtesy Margaret LaGrotto.)

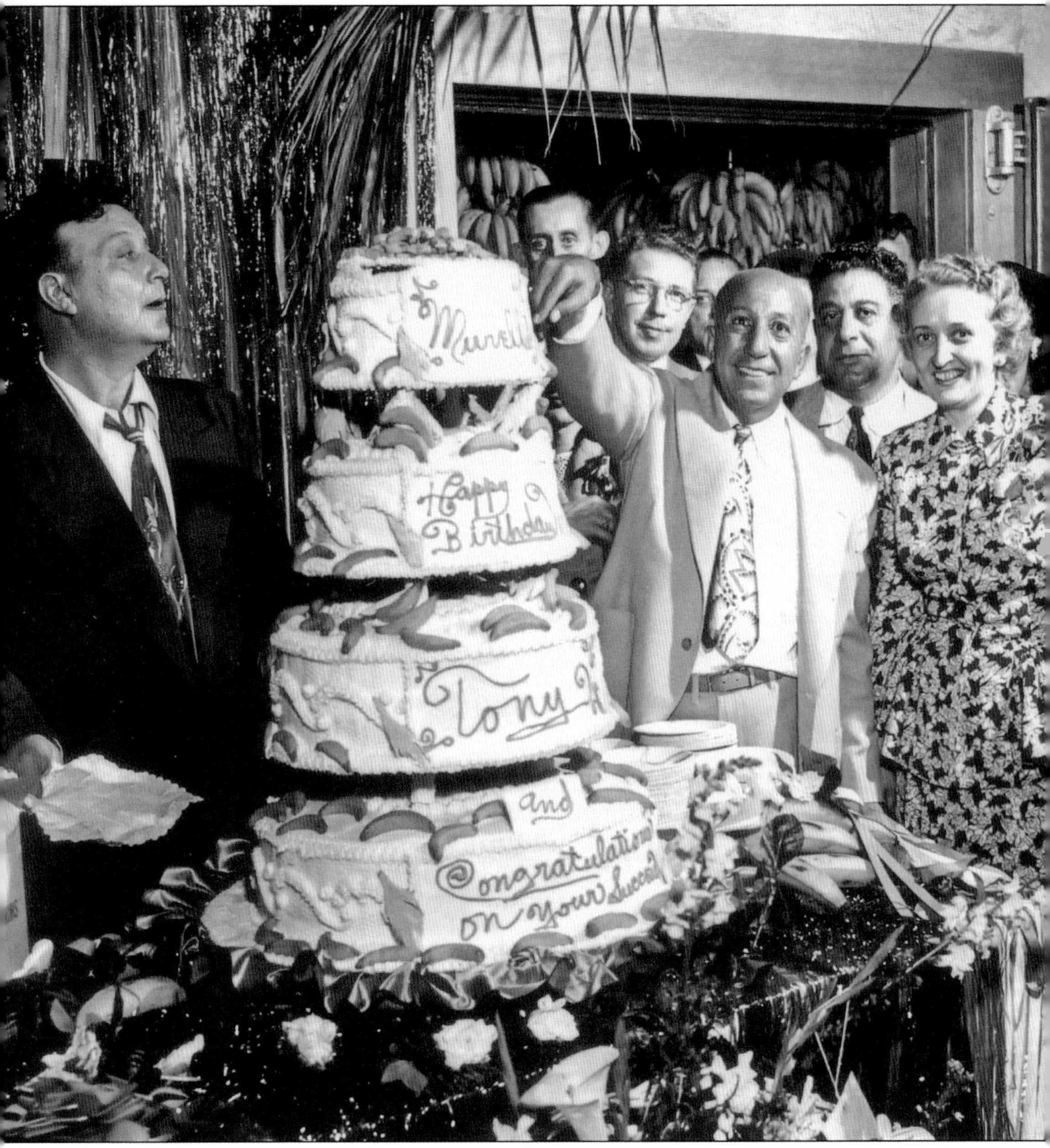

Interviewees always mention Tony Murello's many moneymaking activities, his popularity with women, and his marriages. In the winter, when he had to live in Miami Shores, Florida, for health reasons, he reportedly began sending rum along with bananas back to Indianapolis. During World War II, his Miami base facilitated hiring ships to transport bananas from Caribbean islands. His firm was the only one to sell bananas in town. After the war, Murello built a warehouse with banana warmers on South East Street at a reputed cost of $85,000. Here, he takes center stage in front of a banana vault during his birthday party around 1948, to which he invited the neighborhood. His brother Joe is on the left of the cake, while his wife, Christine, is on the right. Tony's only bad luck was a fire that destroyed his warehouse in 1952. (Courtesy Helen Murello.)

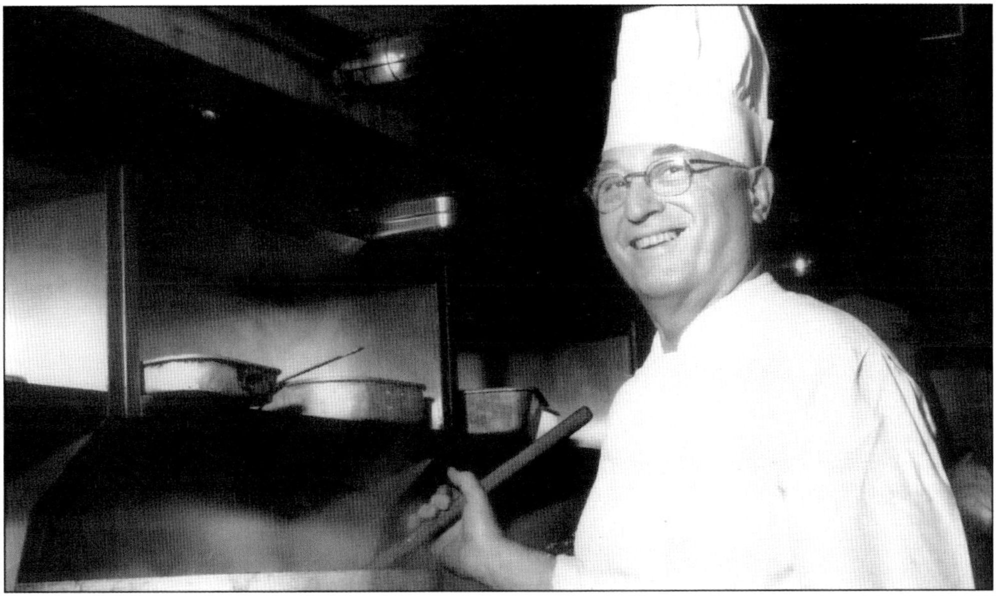

Ottavio "Otto" Faenzi was 16 years old in 1913, when he departed Sorano, provincia di Grosseto (Tuscany). He arrived in New York one year before the assassination of the Archduke Franz Ferdinand. The smile on Otto's face reflects the enjoyment he felt preparing meals for members and guests of Indianapolis's exclusive Columbia Club for 35 years. He retired in 1962 and died in 1996 at age 92. Otto is one of the characters in *The Stonecutter's Aria*, written by his granddaughter Carol Faenzi in 2005. (Courtesy Joann Faenzi Wilson.)

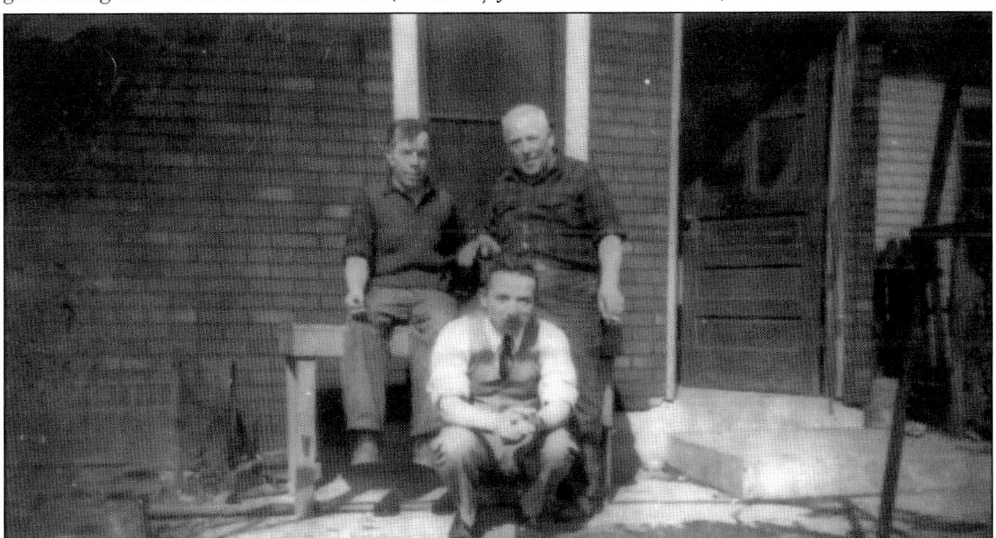

In Carisolo, provincia di Trento (Trentino-Alto Adige), knife sharpeners returned from abroad with money, so many ambitious men took up the trade, sold small inherited landholdings to purchase a transoceanic ticket, and departed for Canada, the United States, Australia, and Brazil. Early on, the Carisolo contingent resided mostly on Georgia Street near Shelby Street. After work, this area became the social hub in their new world, far removed from the cool, fresh Alpine air to which they were accustomed. Pictured in front of a house on Georgia Street are Vito Povinelli (left) and Gabriele Maestri, with Gabriele's son Rudy in front.

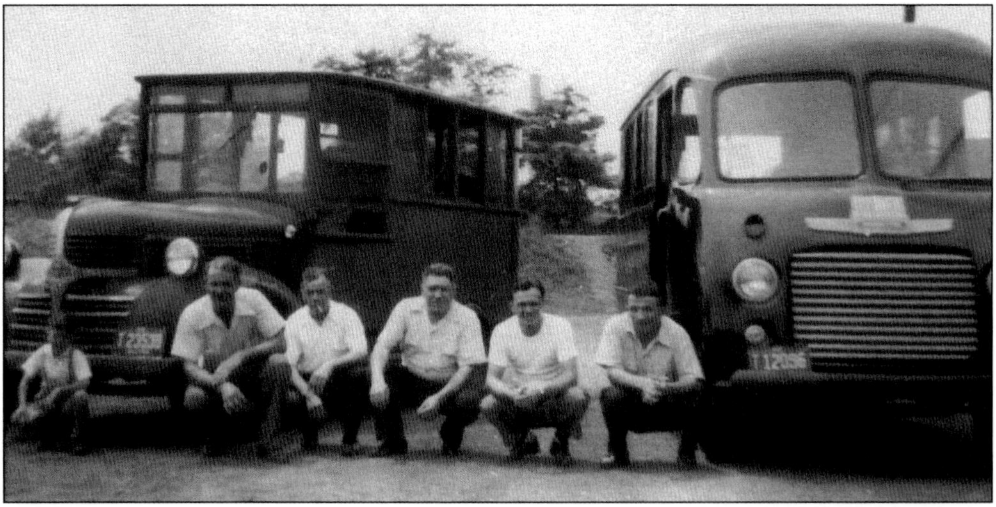

Engaged in the knife-sharpening profession were, from left to right, Narcisso Povinelli, George Povinelli, Vito Povinelli, Gabriele Maestri, Pete Povinelli, and Rudy Maestri. As an Austrian soldier, Vito Povinelli was captured on the Russian front during World War I and evacuated through Vladivostok. He came to Indianapolis in 1921, followed some 10 years later by his sons Anselmo "Sam" and Pietro "Pete." When cousin Rodolfo "Rudy" Maestri joined the Povinellis after World War II, trucks bearing their names had a virtual monopoly on knife sharpening throughout central Indiana. They supplied or rented cutlery to hundreds of restaurants, groceries, and other customers. They then returned to sharpen those blades or replace the rental set so customers always felt on the cutting edge.

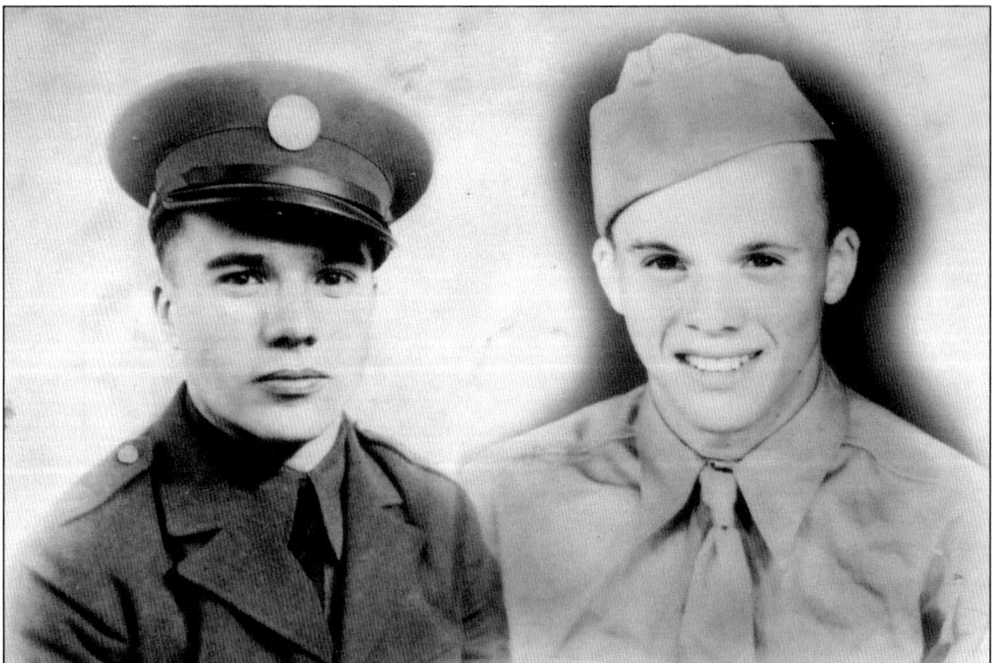

Sam Povinelli (left) and his brother Pete both served in combat during World War II. At first, Italian-born soldiers were sent to the Pacific theater to avoid fighting other Italians, but later they were considered an asset in the European theater. (Courtesy Ray Povinelli.)

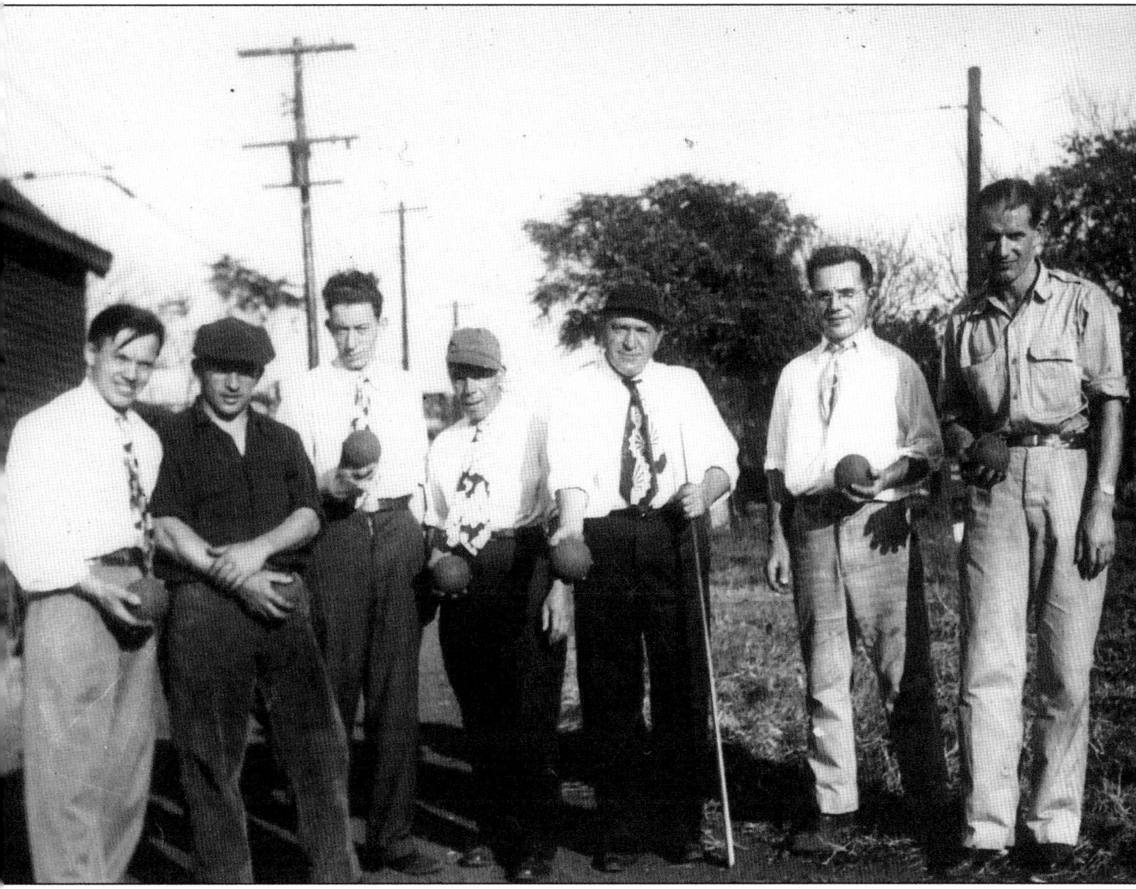

Povinelli and Maestri family members, natives of the Trentino, played bocce in the alley behind their residence on Georgia Street in 1938. (Courtesy Ray Povinelli.)

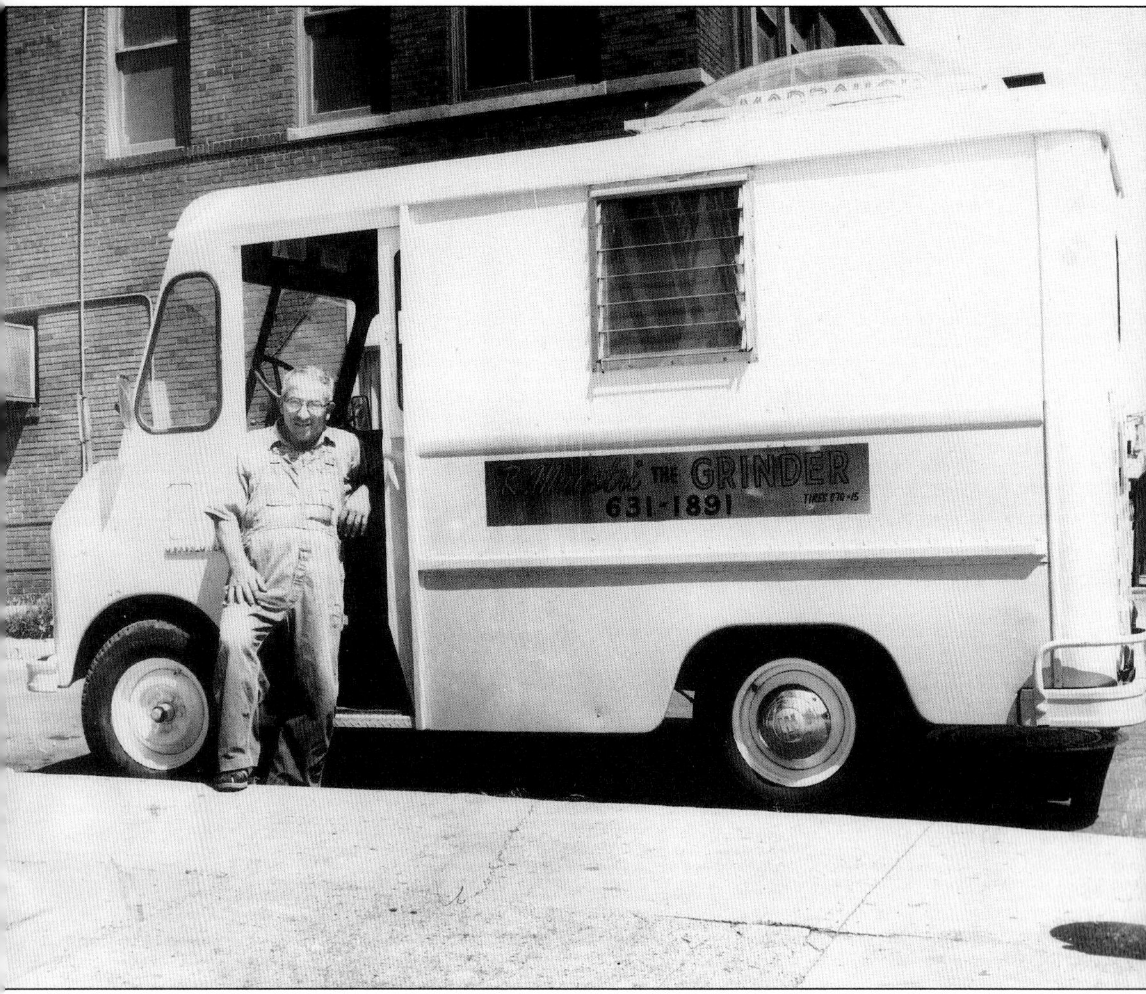

Rudy Maestri stands with his new truck around 1960. The size and condition of the truck reflect the success of the sharpening business. (Courtesy Aldo Mina.)

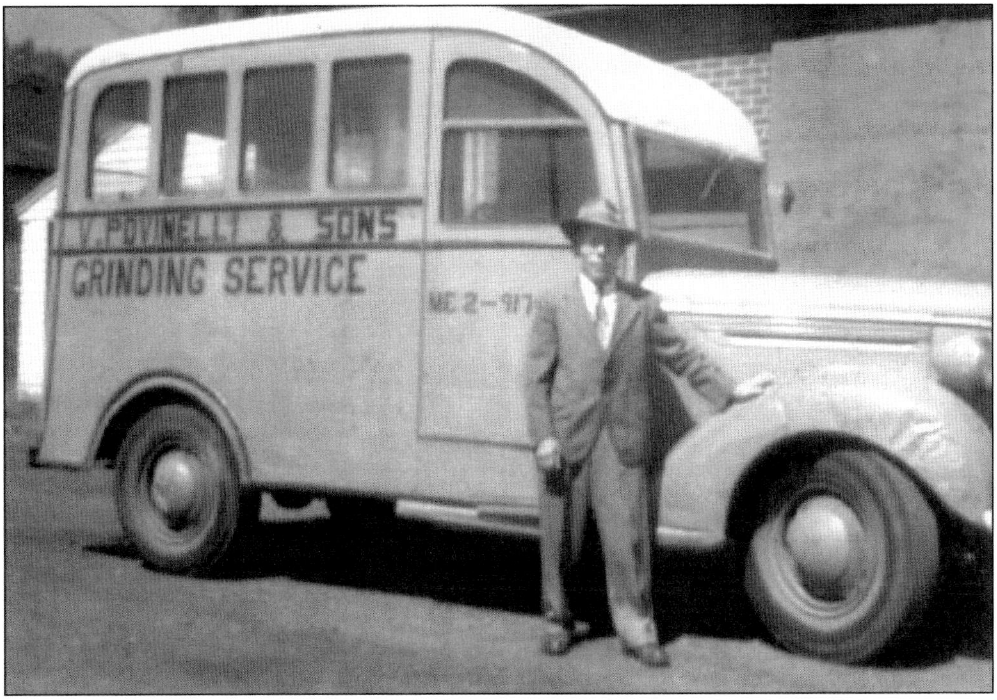

Vito Povinelli poses with his last truck before retirement. (Courtesy Ray Povinelli.)

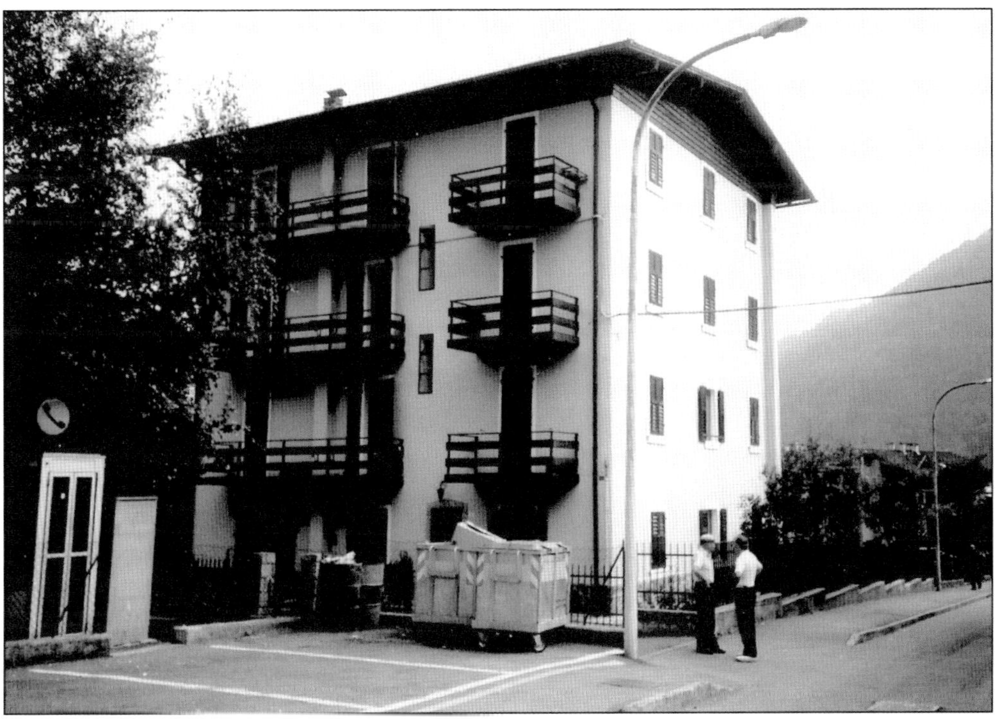
To build this four-story house, Vito Povinelli sent the money he made grinding knives in Indianapolis back to Carisolo.

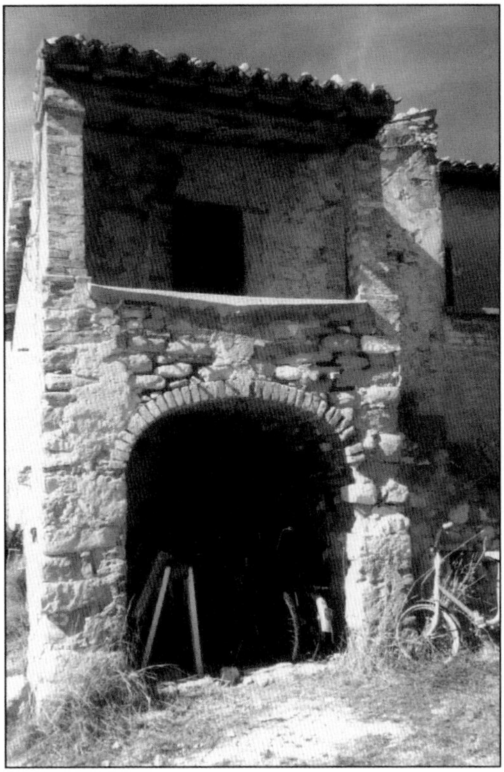

In this house on Via Madonna del Croce in Castiglione a Casauria, provincia di Pescara (Abruzzo), Antonio Vespa (Vespo) was born. In 1898, he married Paolina di Donato Vespa, born in nearby Tocca di Casauria. They emigrated in 1906 with two sons. Antonio peddled vegetables, worked for the Big Four Railroad, and ran a City Market stand. By 1915, Paolina had five more sons, and they moved to 624 East Georgia Street. Then he began his grinding business, sharpening knives and mower blades. When Paolina died in 1919, Antonio wrote to a family in Sulmona and asked for their daughter Antonette Christillini in marriage. She journeyed to Indianapolis, married him sight unseen, gave birth to one girl, and remained married until her death in 1952.

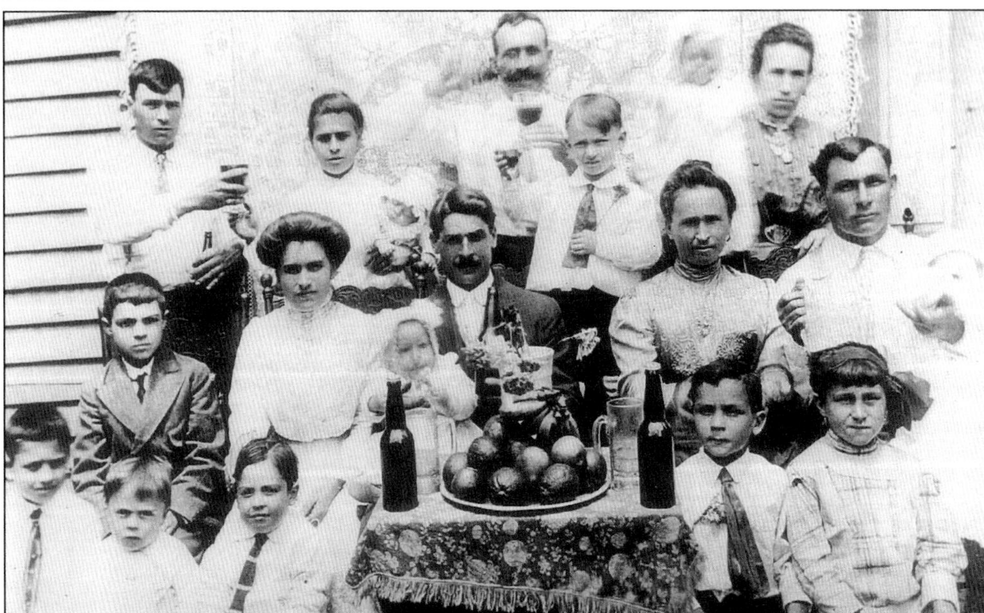

Four families, undoubtedly neighbors, joined for a formal photograph about 1912. Identified here are Jerry, Danny, Eddie, and Frank Vespo (lower left) and Antonio and wife Paolina Vespo with baby Jimmy (upper left). Pasquale Uberta, his wife, and their two children are on the lower right. (Courtesy of Mary Jo Chandler)

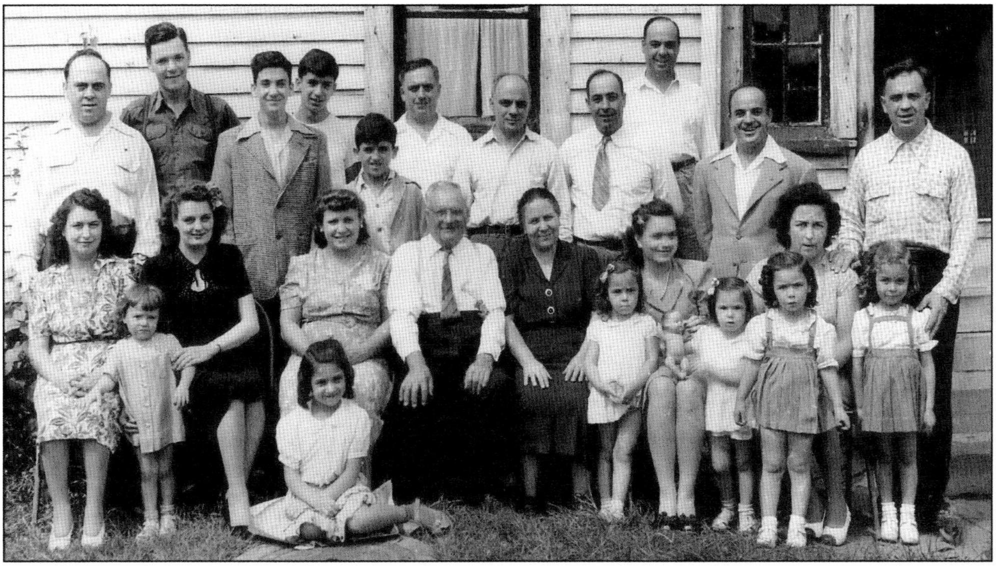

In 1946, the Vespo family held a reunion at Antonio and Antonette's house, at 1108 Fletcher Avenue. In attendance were the following, from left to right: (first row) Anna Raia, Karen, Rose Vespo Booth, Carmelia Suozzi, Antonio, Antonette, Toni, Anita, Cherie, Patsy Vespo Hesson, Maria de Jesus Gonzales, and Rosie Vespo Thompson; (second row) Eddie, John Booth, Anthony, Paul, Danny Jr., Danny Sr., Jerry, Jimmy, Freddie, William "Woody," and Frank. TAll the men in the second row except John Booth, Paul, and Danny Jr. are the sons of Antonio. Seated over the sewer cover is Mary Jo Vespo Chandler. (Courtesy Mary Jo Chandler.)

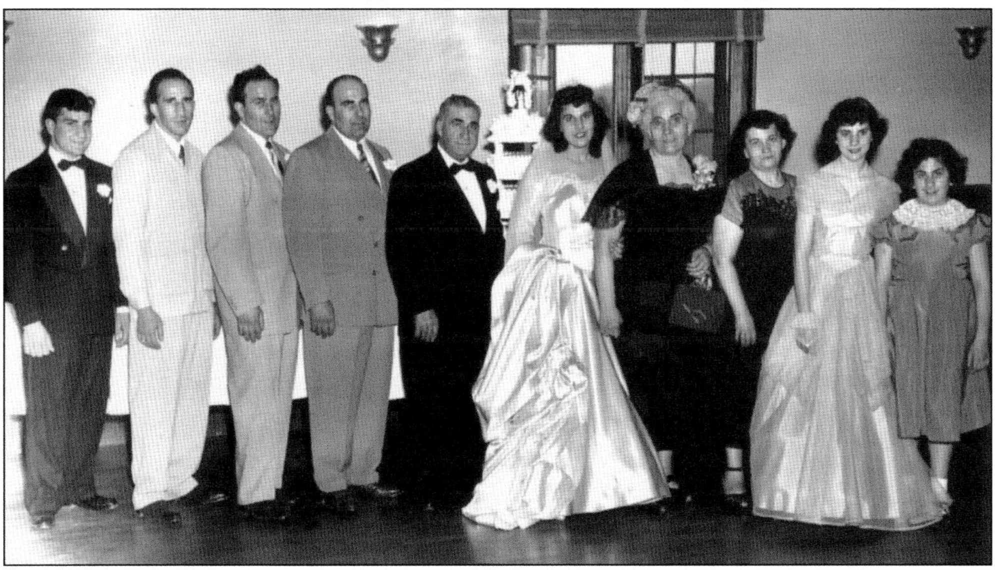

A polite rule to follow within the Italian community is never to criticize someone harshly in the presence of others, because the others are probably related. Family loyalty discourages public criticism (criticism within the family is a different story). The wedding photographs above and on page 62 illustrate the extensiveness of relation in two first families. Members of this wedding party all bear the Caito name except as listed. Pictured from left to right are Salvatore, Mike, Gus, Philip Jr., Philip H., Angeline Caito Milto, Josephine Miceli Caito, Magdalene, Anna Rose, and Mary Jane. (Courtesy Joanna Milto-Bergin.)

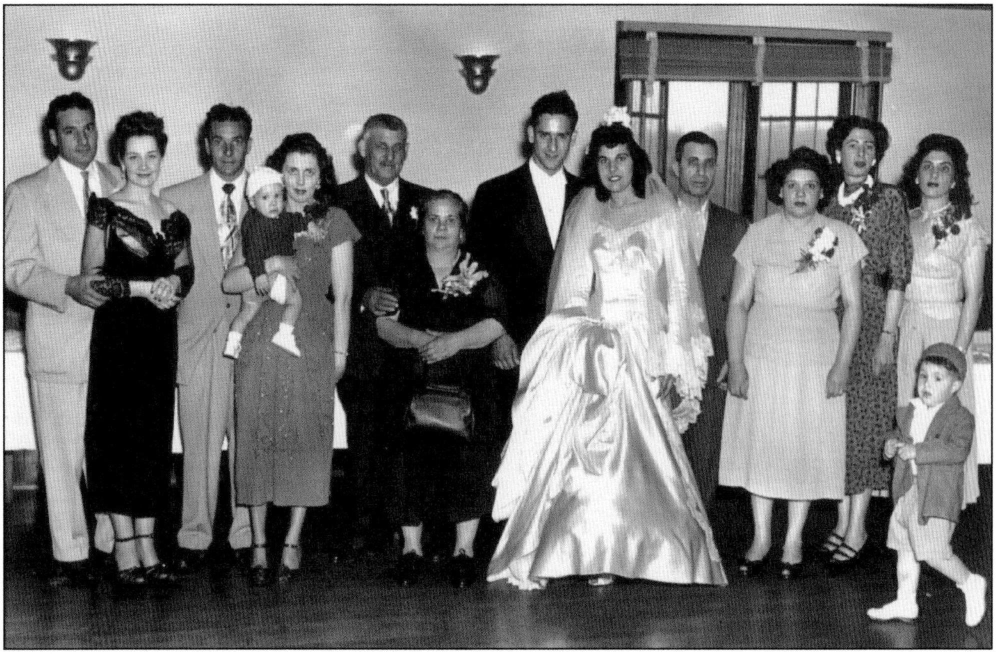

All pictured here bear the Milto name except as noted. Shown here, from left to right, are Gus; Dorothy; Sam; Vivian with baby Anthony; Antonio; Anna Diana Milto; Philip; Angeline Caito Milto; Joseph Pons and his wife, Josephine Milto Pons; Frances; and Sarah. The little boy is unidentified. (Courtesy Joanna Milto-Bergin.)

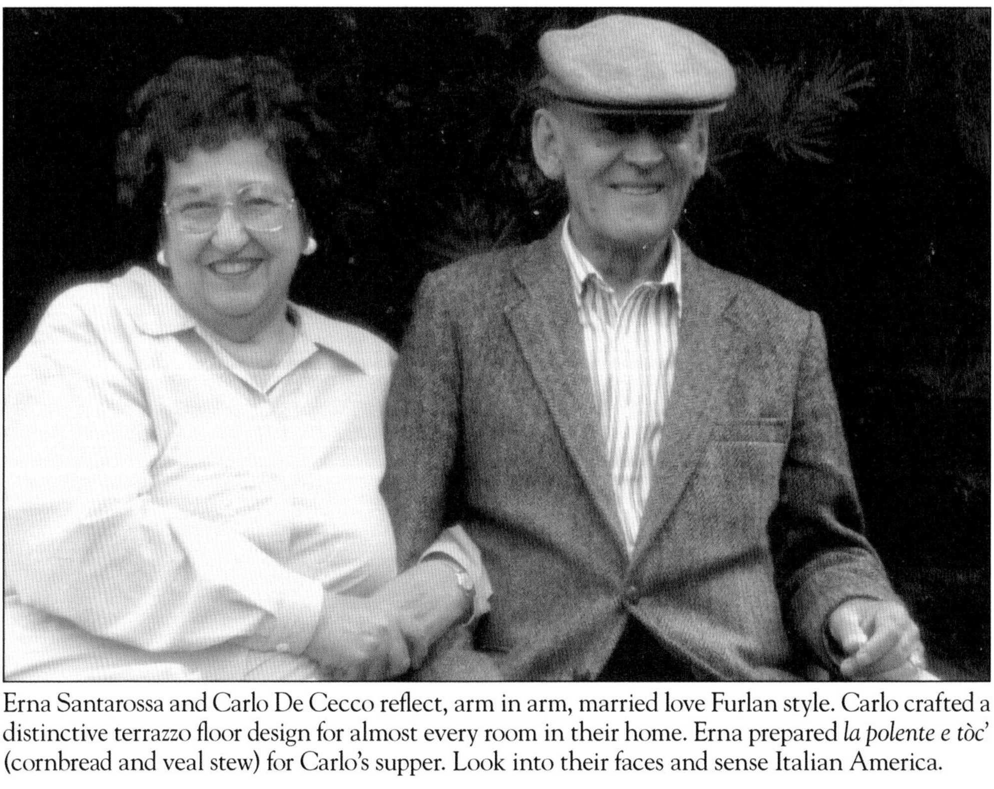

Erna Santarossa and Carlo De Cecco reflect, arm in arm, married love Furlan style. Carlo crafted a distinctive terrazzo floor design for almost every room in their home. Erna prepared *la polente e tòc'* (cornbread and veal stew) for Carlo's supper. Look into their faces and sense Italian America.

Three

REVIVAL
ITALIAN-BORN IN THE COMMUNITY

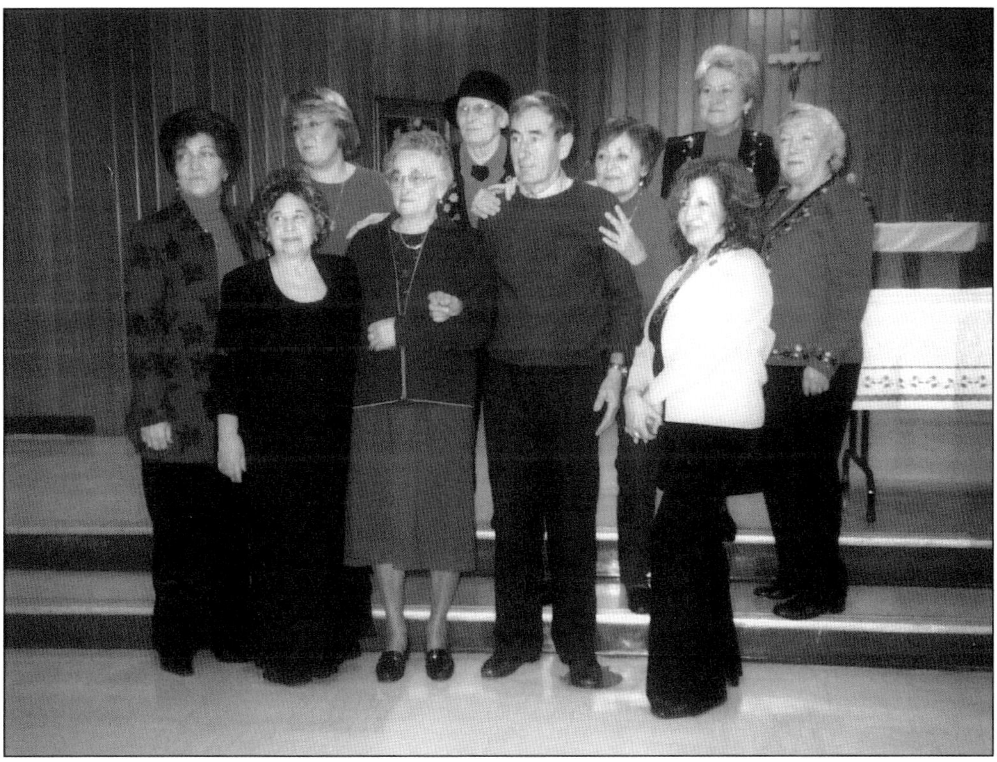

Italian immigrants who arrived in the United States in 1955 celebrated the 50th anniversary of their journey by attending the 2005 Christmas party sponsored by the Italian Heritage Society. Seen here, from left to right, are the following: (first row) Germana Mella, Rina LaMonaca, Elisabetta Ferroli, Mario Ferroli, and Antonietta Pizzi; (second row) Teresina D'Angelo, Silvana Ferri, Anna Maria Graffitti, Rina Wright, and Anita Simeone.

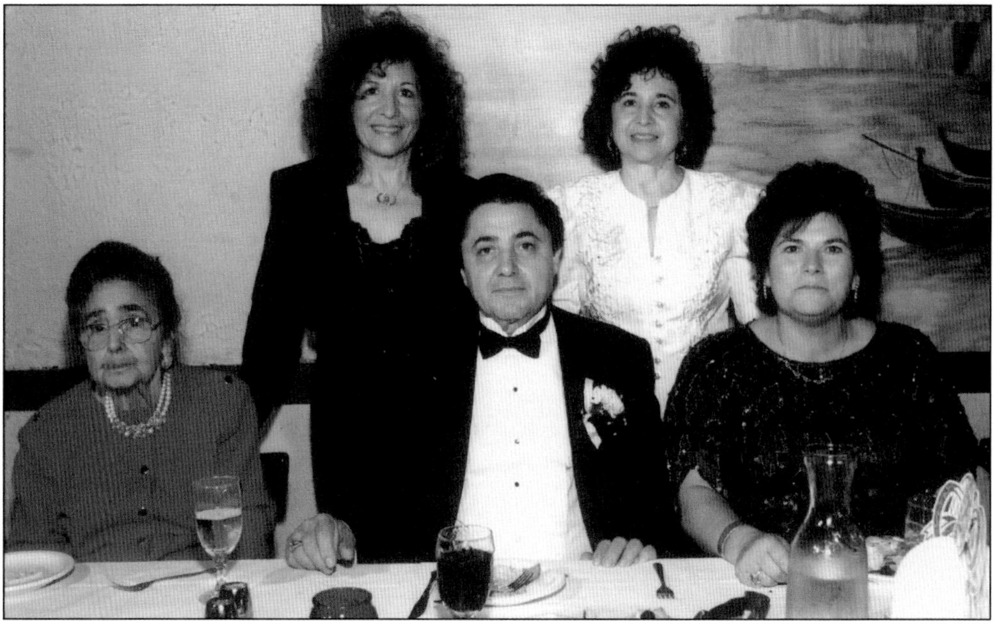

Guerino and Carmela Martinelli Cento came from Roccaforte del Greco, provincia di Reggio Calabria, in 1955 and opened Napoli Villa restaurant five years later. The restaurant, relocated in Beech Grove, was the scene of the 25th wedding anniversary party of their son Paul Cento and his wife Lisa in 1992. At table with *antipasto e vino* are, from left, Carmela, Paul, and Lisa. Behind them are Paul's sisters Antonietta Pizzi and Caterina LaMonaca. Paul operated a downtown shoe repair shop; Antonietta and her husband Frederico Pizzi, also from Roccaforte, operate Napoli Villa. Other Centos and Pizzis run restaurants in Broad Ripple and Zionsville. (Courtesy Paul and Lisa Cento.)

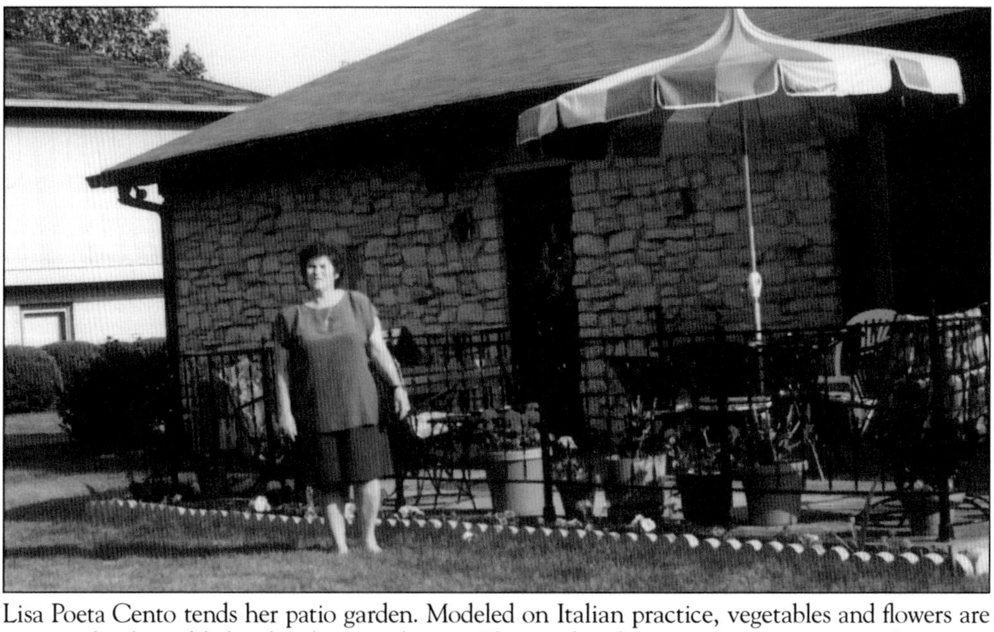

Lisa Poeta Cento tends her patio garden. Modeled on Italian practice, vegetables and flowers are commonly planted behind Italian residences. This garden, however, incorporates an American flair with a charcoal grill sitting alongside statuary and fountain. (Courtesy Paul and Lisa Cento.)

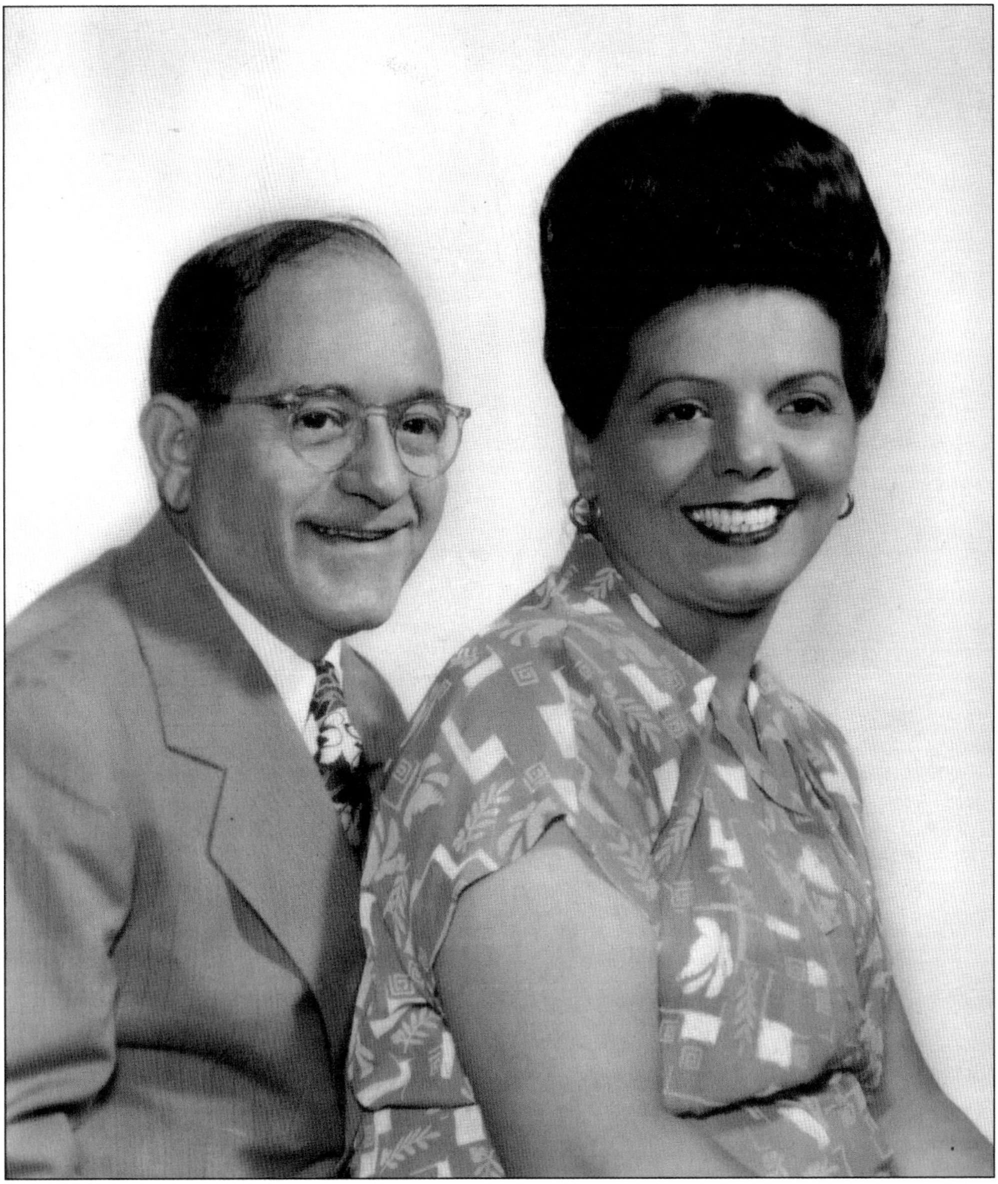

When Joe Modaffari reached Ellis Island in 1913, he reported his hometown as Condofuri, provincia di Reggio Calabria. He and his brother Paul worked briefly for U.S. Rubber, enlisted in the army during World War I, and then opened a fruit and vegetable stand in City Market. Paul dreamed of operating a restaurant and finally did in 1934. The one-room Milano Inn was located at 230 South College Avenue, across the street from U.S. Rubber and expanded several times. This early downtown restaurant was advertised as "gourmet-patronized." Paul hired an artist to decorate a frieze around the restaurant showing the U.S. Army occupying Rome. By 1960, the Modaffaris employed 15. After Joe and Paul died, Paul's widow, Mary Iacoppino Modaffari, managed the restaurant until her own death. Passed briefly to Pat Sgro, the restaurant was then operated by the Leo LaGrotte family. This photograph shows Paul and Mary Modaffari. (Courtesy Phil De Fabis.)

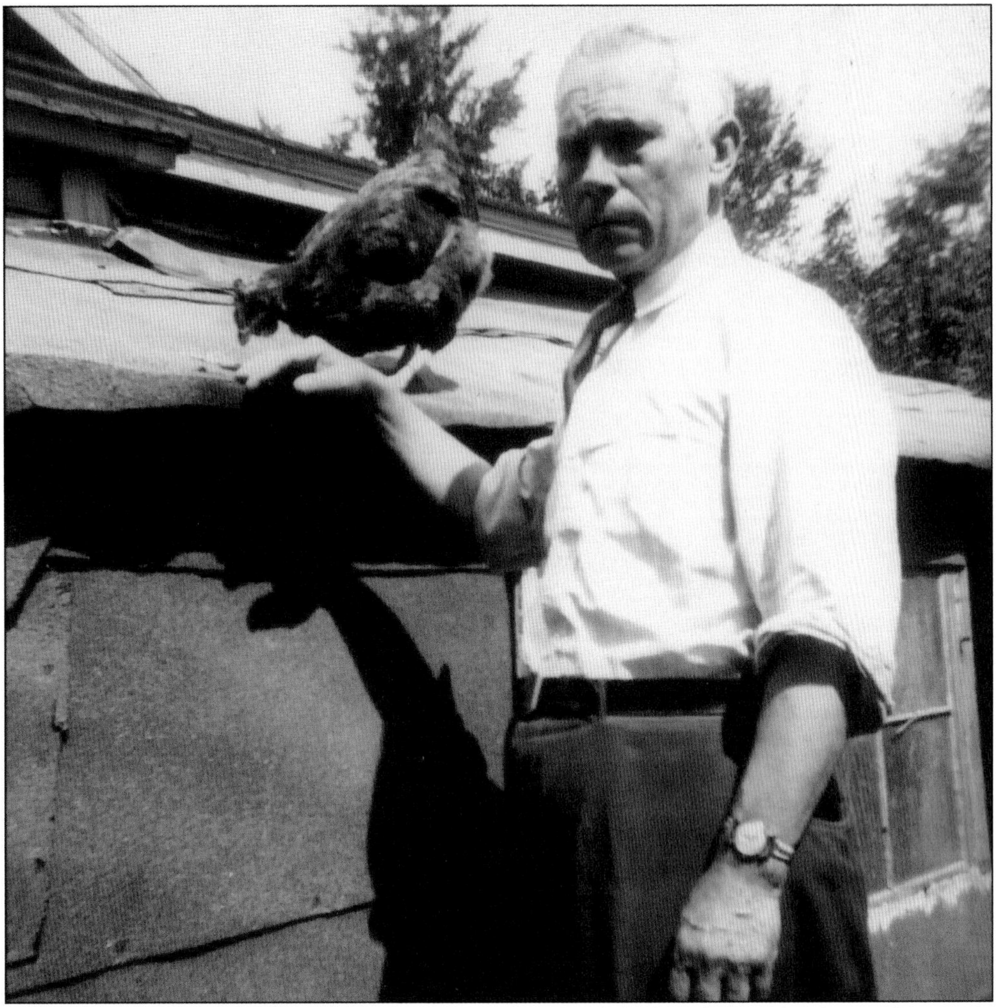

Salvatore Minà considers eggs for Sunday breakfast or fried chicken for Sunday dinner. (Courtesy Aldo Mina.)

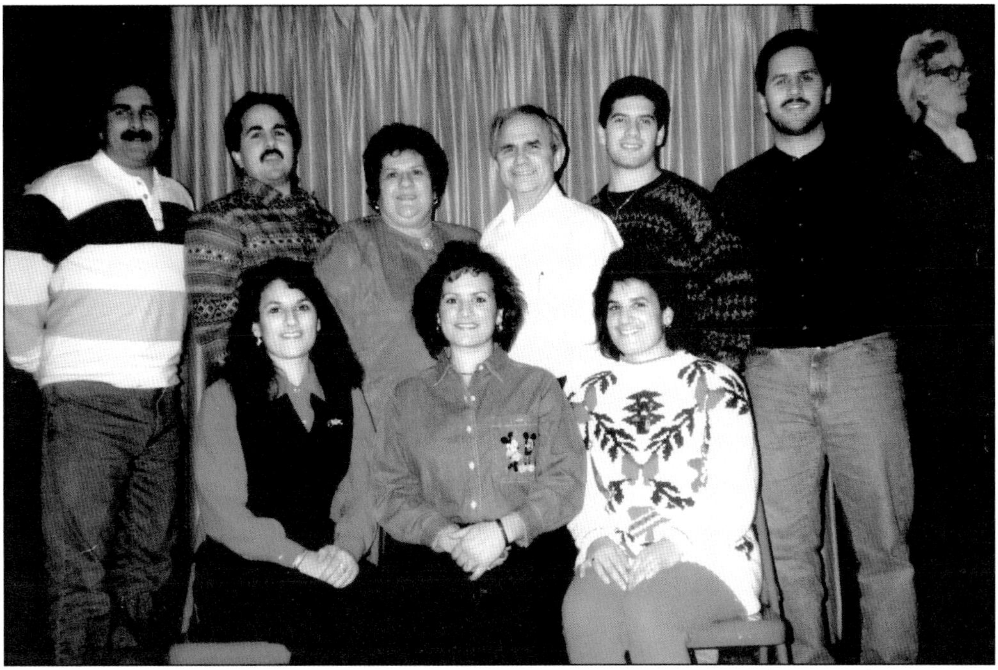

A young married man from San Pietro di Caridà, provincia di Reggio Calabria, Salvatore Minà arrived in Indianapolis in 1921. Since his wife disliked America (her brothers were killed in mine violence), she and the children remained at home. The Depression and World War II prevented permanent reunion. Finally, son Aldo, at age 16, came to live with his father and learned to be a tailor. His last employer before retirement was the fashionable Jacobsen's in Keystone-at-the-Crossing. Aldo married Ada Maestri of the knife-sharpening family and they parented seven children. Shown here, from left to right, are the following: (first row) Angie, Mary Ann, and Enza; (second row) Aldo Jr, Dominic, Ada, Aldo, Gino, and Anthony. (Courtesy Aldo Mina.)

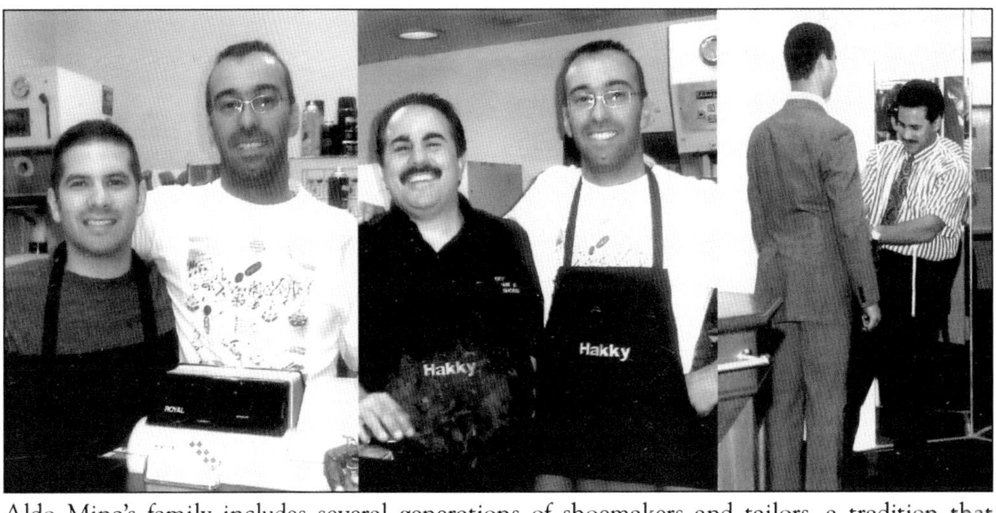

Aldo Mina's family includes several generations of shoemakers and tailors, a tradition that continues today. In these photographs, Mina sons are at work. Gino (far left) and Dominic (center, left) visit with their cousin from Italy in their shoe repair shops. Anthony the tailor (far right) checks out a fit. (Courtesy Aldo Mina.)

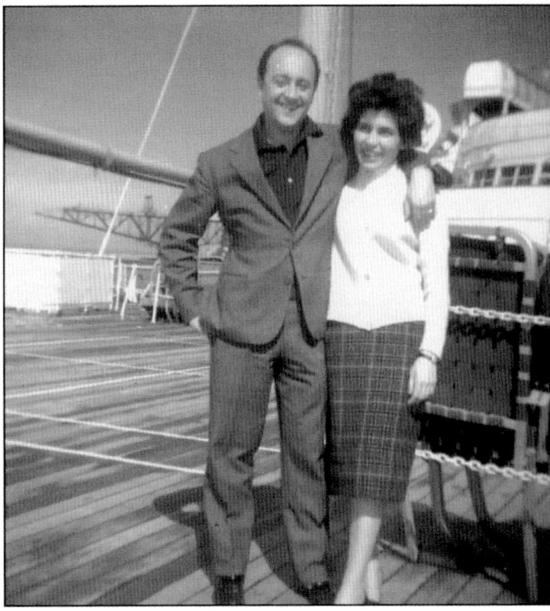

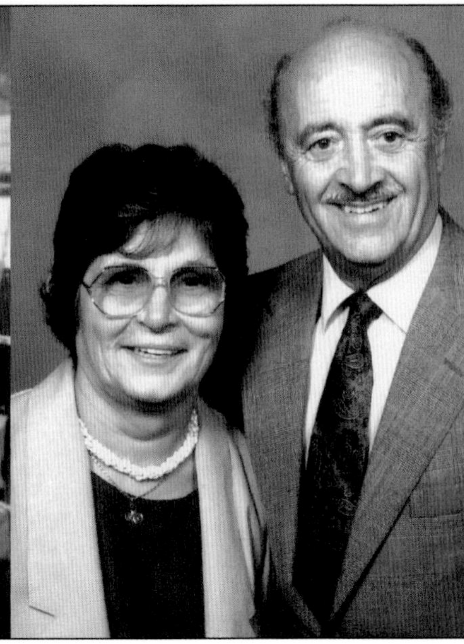

Pietro Ferri's grandfather departed Broccostella, provincia di Frosinone (Lazio) for Rome; there Pietro and his parents were born. Silvana Lentini Ferri, Pietro's wife, is related to the noble Lucangeli family. After World War II, Pietro and Silvana sailed aboard the Constitution to America (left). Block's department store hired Pietro, who was experienced in selling retail clothing to the rich and famous in Rome. He worked for just about every Block's and Lazarus in town before retirement (right). Pietro participated in the Italian-American Club, founded the Columbus Commission '92, and headed the Italian Heritage Society. The Ferris have two children: architect Tom who designed the Italian Heritage Society pin, and bank computer specialist Laura. (Courtesy Pietro Ferri.)

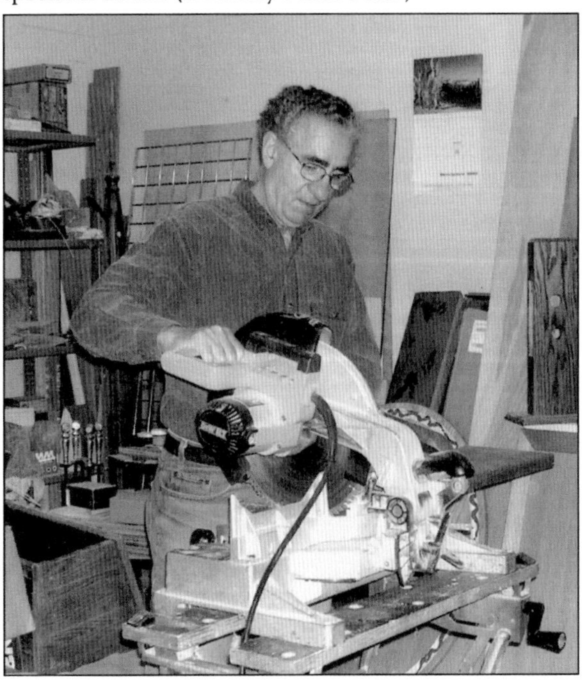

Angelo Piga, born in Padria, provincia di Sassari (Sardinia), joined the customs police and rose to the rank of first lieutenant. He immigrated to Indianapolis in 1969 to marry the woman he loved, Caterina Odorico. A master carpenter, Angelo has worked on the restoration of the Hamilton County Courthouse and the finishing of the Indiana State Museum. He and his wife received the Italian Heritage President's Award for their contributions to the preservation of Italian heritage in 2005. (Courtesy Caterina Piga.)

Maria Odorico was born in Sistiana, provincia di Trieste, and emigrated with her husband and daughter Caterina in 1963 to be with her four sisters and parents. Maria is an excellent seamstress, the sewing machine her constant companion. Caterina, also born in Sistiana, keeps the Italian community informed by editing *L'Italia*, the Italian Heritage newsletter. (Courtesy Caterina Piga.)

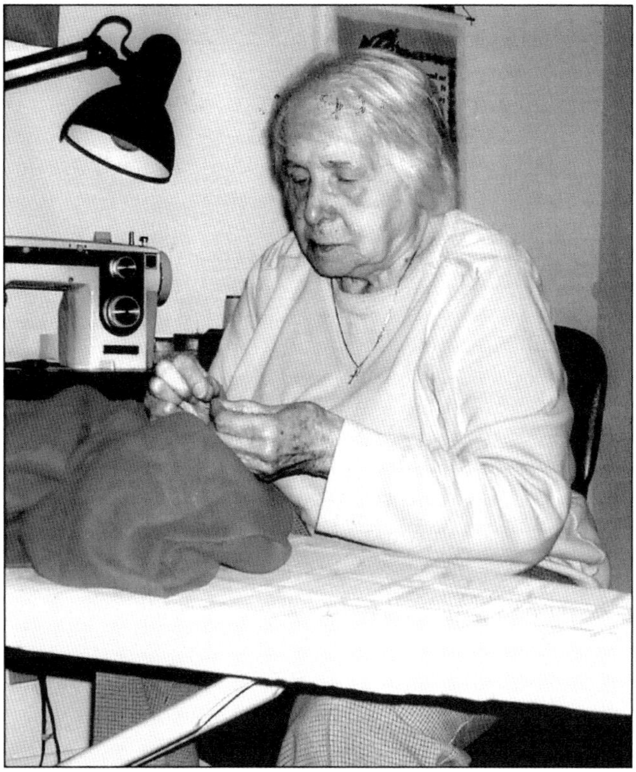

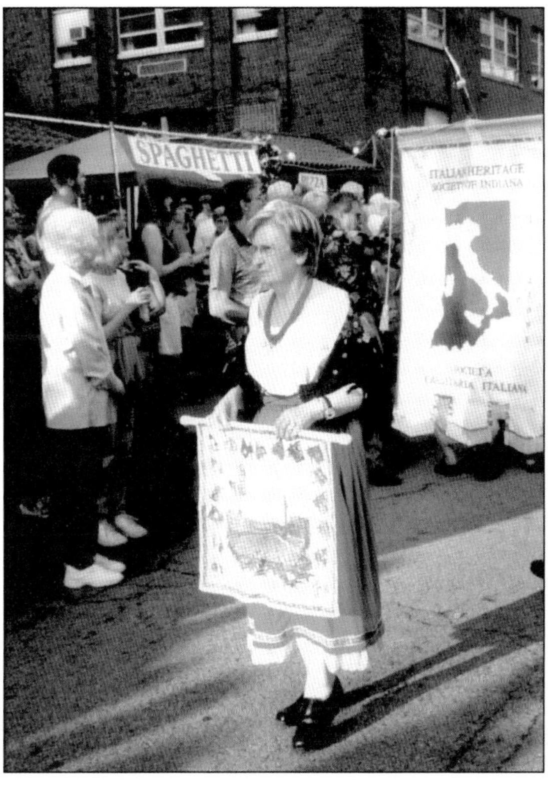

Born in Nave, provincia di Brescia (Lombardy), Evelina "Evi" Greotti McPherson lived in Germany and various places in Italy before accompanying her American husband, Allen, to Indianapolis after his military discharge in 1986. She has taught Italian classes and been active in the Italian Heritage Society. Here, she participates in the religious procession during the Italian Street Festival.

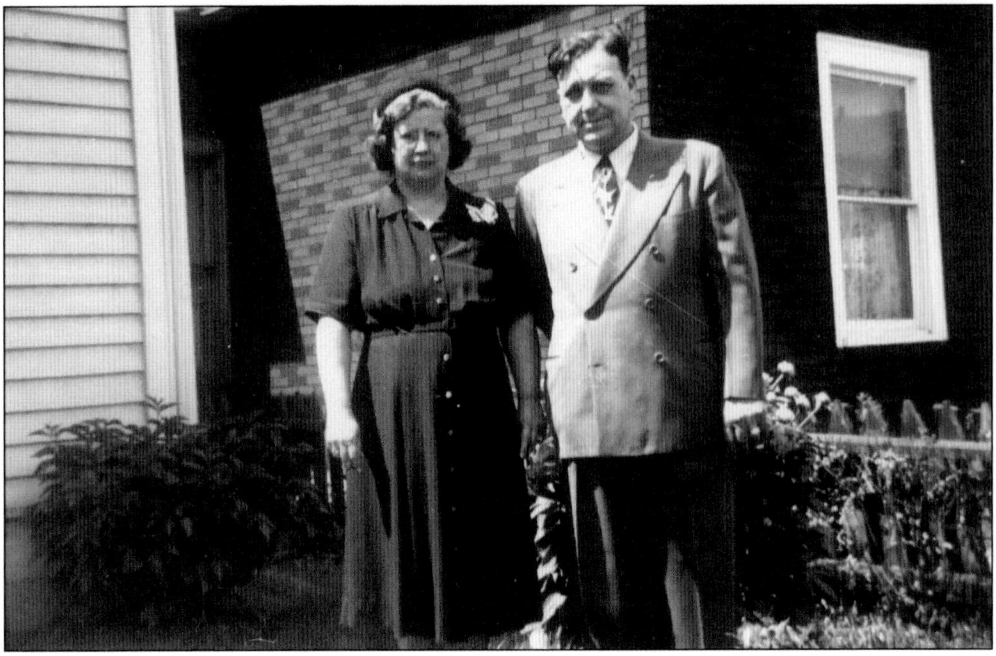

Helen Murello, shown with her husband Joe, was one of three women who were particularly knowledgeable about the social and personal aspects of the Italian community. Helen had such extensive contacts and insights that many did not know she was of Irish rather than of Italian background. (Courtesy Margaret LaGrotto.)

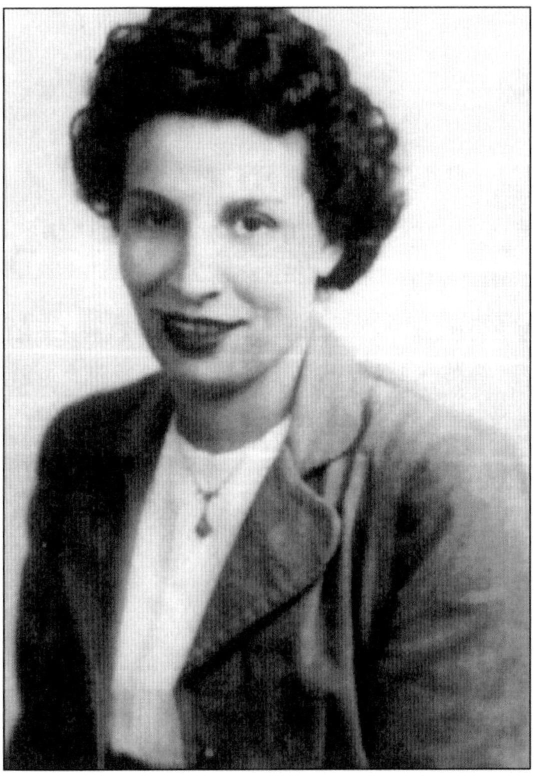

Mary Sansone Mascari, seen here, and Josephine "Josie" Mascari Sigreto were also great historical sources. Mary married Salvatore "Harpo" Mascari, step-grandson of grocer John Bova Conti. She always lived in the house where she was born on Stevens Street, in the shadow of Holy Rosary Church, until her death in 2005 at age 86. She could report the saintliness and sinfulness of the priests at Holy Rosary, and remember who dated whom in the 1940s. She recalled womanizers, luckless produce businessmen, disobedient children, and docile wives. Josie was to Merrill Street what Mary was to Stevens Street. A niece of Frank Mascari, the first Sicilian in town, Josie could relate family traditions by taking a stack of wedding photographs in hand and identifying not only the brides and grooms but also the members of their wedding parties. At the same time she would offer personal comments on each of them.

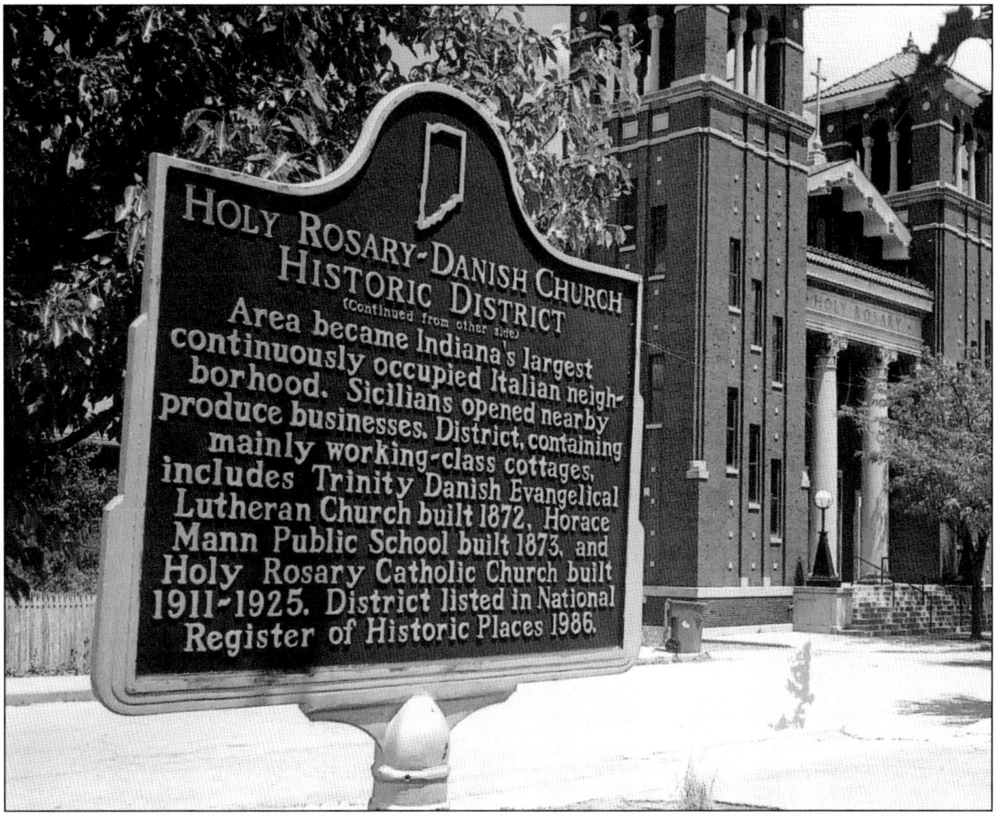

In June 2000, the state of Indiana honored the early Italians of the city when it erected a historical marker at the corner of South East and Stevens Streets. It saluted the Holy Rosary–Danish Church Historical District, listed on the National Register of Historic Places in 1986. The district is named for the two major institutions in the Virginia-East Triangle—Holy Rosary Italian Catholic Church and the First Trinity Danish Evangelical Lutheran Church, located at McCarty and Noble Streets from 1872 to 1956. National Register nomination was unprecedented for an ethnic, working-class neighborhood.

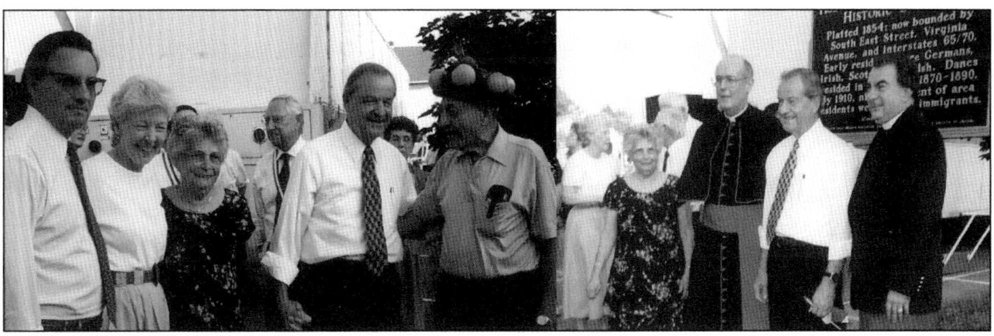

Italian old-timers Mary Sansone Mascari and "Uncle" Pete Corsaro assisted the governor in unveiling the marker. Seen at left are, from left to right, councilman Frank Short; Judy O'Bannon, wife of the governor; Mary; Gov. Frank O'Bannon; and Pete. Pictured at right are, from left to right, Judy O'Bannon, conversing with Jerry Roland and the author; Mary Mascari; Holy Rosary pastor Msgr. Joseph Schaedel; Governor O'Bannon, holding an Italian flag just given to him by a child; and Lutheran pastor Jeff Iacobazzi of First Trinity (also of Italian ancestry).

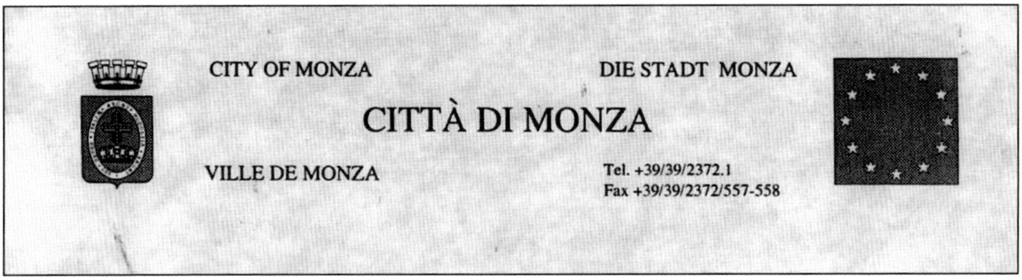
CITY OF MONZA

DIE STADT MONZA

CITTÀ DI MONZA

VILLE DE MONZA

Tel. +39/39/2372.1
Fax +39/39/2372/557-558

Leaving the homeland was so traumatic for some immigrants that they refused to speak Italian in the family circle, especially in front of their children. "We are in America now," they would say, "and to go to school and find good jobs you need to know English." The establishment of sister city relationships indicates that the attitude toward Italy and Italian has changed. Now Italian Americans seek cultural exchange with the Old Country through visiting diplomats, politicians, students, teachers, musical groups, and businessmen. The city of Monza outside Milan signed a sister city agreement with Indianapolis in 1994; both are sites of well-known auto races.

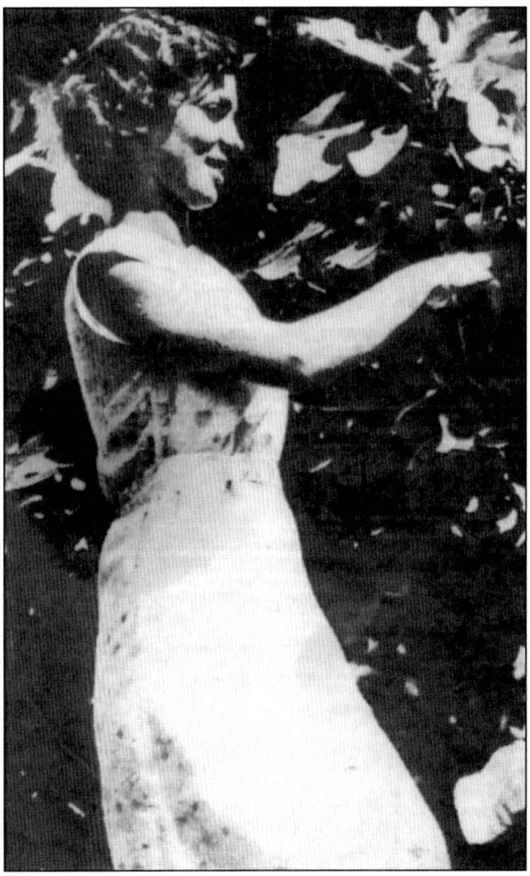

Figs do not naturally grow in central Indiana because of cold winters, but if the limbs are tied close to the trunk and a sheltering structure built around each tree, they flourish. Santina Bondi of 713 Greer Street picks fruit from the two trees her father, Nicholas Bondi, was given seven or eight years earlier. "The figs are fine," Santina says, "but taking care of the trees is a lot of trouble." Bees and other pests, smelling the sweetness, become real challenges at harvest time. (Courtesy Matthew Iaria.)

Four

BUSINESS AND SPORTS

COMMUNITY ECONOMICS AND ATHLETICS

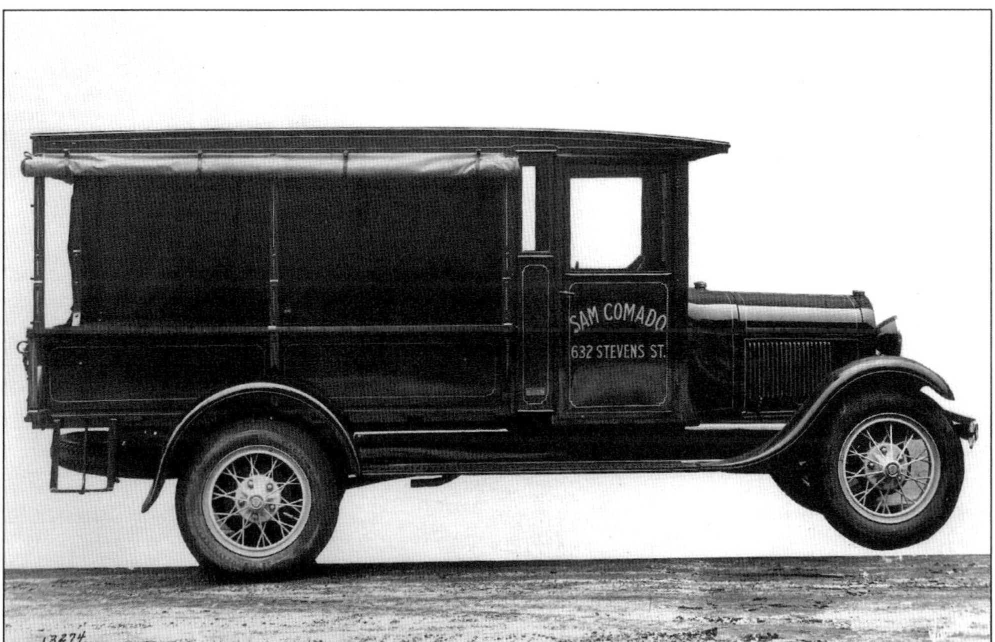

City Market stands were slowly giving way to corner groceries. Selling retail meant that extending credit was expected, and credit could easily become a real financial burden for the merchant, especially with the advent of the Great Depression. Profits from selling wholesale were more stable because of the clients' cash flow. Thus, the use of trucks became the way to larger profits. Shown here is one of three models built by the Guedelhoefer truck builders on Kentucky Avenue around 1940. Guedelhoefer demonstrated its business connection to the Italian community by donating a stained-glass window to the new Holy Rosary Church. (Courtesy Loretta Guedelhoefer and the Indiana Historical Society.)

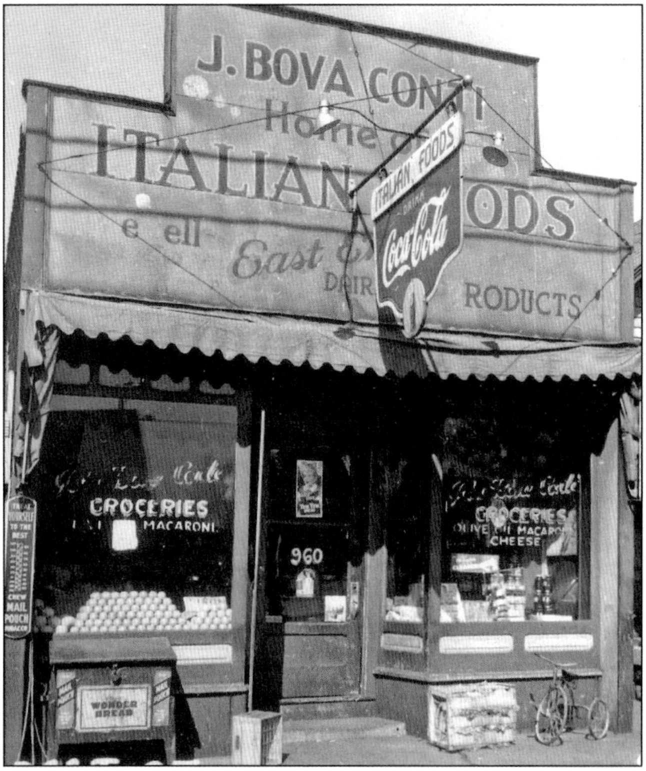

The Bova Conti grocery, 960 South East Street, was more than a neighborhood landmark; it was the most popular grocery store in the Italian neighborhood. John Bova Conti's business account book for 1924 to 1927 shows that he imported heavily from Italy and supplied stores from Columbus and Terre Haute to Kokomo and Richmond. After visiting relatives in Indianapolis, customers from smaller towns would stop at Bova Conti's to buy 20 pounds of dry pasta for the month. Among his attractive prices were one gallon Berio olive oil, \$3; one bottle, Florio Marsala, \$2.25; five pounds, Sicilian caciocavallo, \$3.75; and one case, Brioschi, 75¢. (Courtesy Mary Mascari and Indiana Historical Society.)

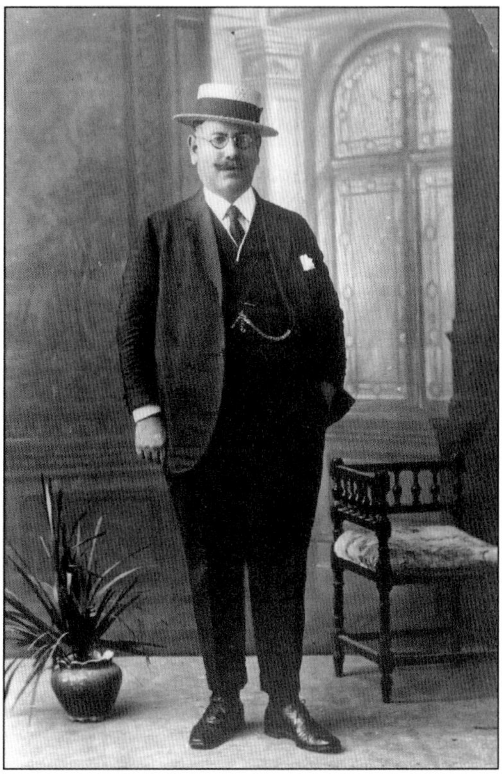

John Bova Conti (1877–1937) and his brothers ran a family business that made liqueurs and cordials. Seeking adventure, he left Palermo for Indianapolis. There, he found the widow Mascari and her son Tommaso having difficulty running a grocery; he moved in to run the business and married the widow. John was a well-educated, well-liked speaker of fluent Sicilian, Italian, and English. (Courtesy Mary Mascari and the Indiana Historical Society.)

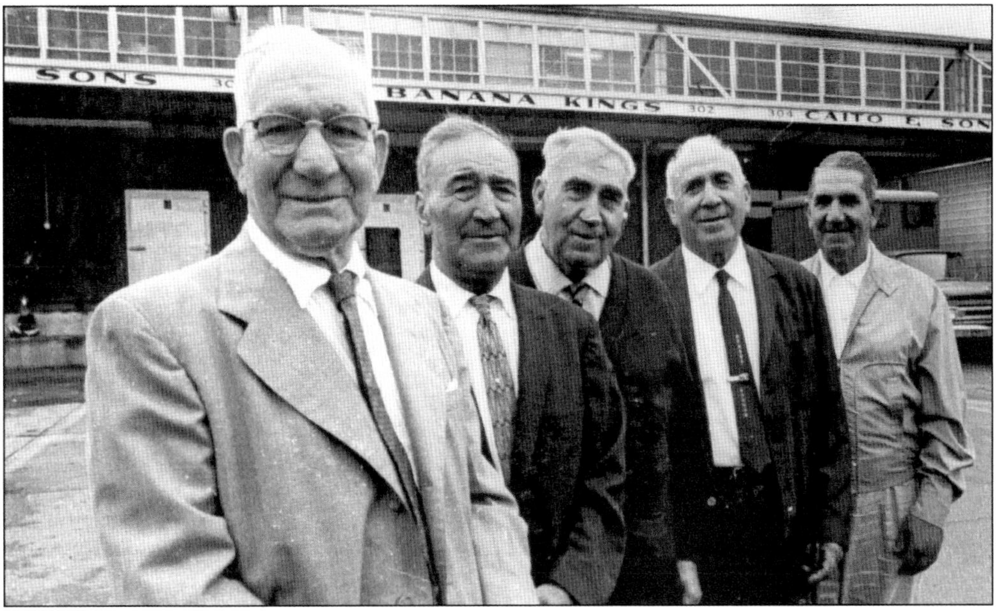

In a rare photograph, standing outside the Indianapolis Produce Terminal, are the five sons of Michelina and Philip Caito—from left to right, Gus, Joseph, Phil, Tony, and Mike. The terminal, a truck and railroad facility for the wholesale distribution and marketing of fruits and vegetables, was a major cooperative effort in a highly competitive business. In 1947, several Italian investors purchased the bankrupt Brightwood Airport at 4101 Massachusetts Avenue. Designed by the U.S. Department of Agriculture, the terminal opened on this site in 1954. Its first officers were Gus A. Comella, board chairman; Philip J. Caito, president; Philip Caito, Jr., vice-president; Cosmas A. Mascari, secretary; and Salvatore Mazza, treasurer. Today the site, occupied by Indianapolis Fruit Company, is adjacent to Interstate 70.

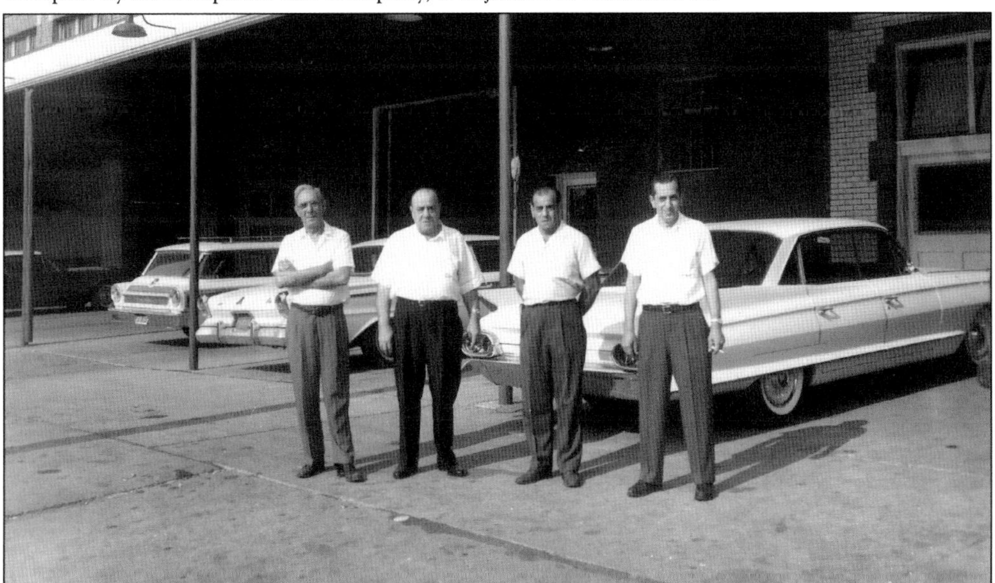

Standing in front of Ray and Mascari, Inc., in the old neighborhood are, from left to right, Gus Spicuzza, Gus Mascari, Frank Mascari, and Mike Ray.

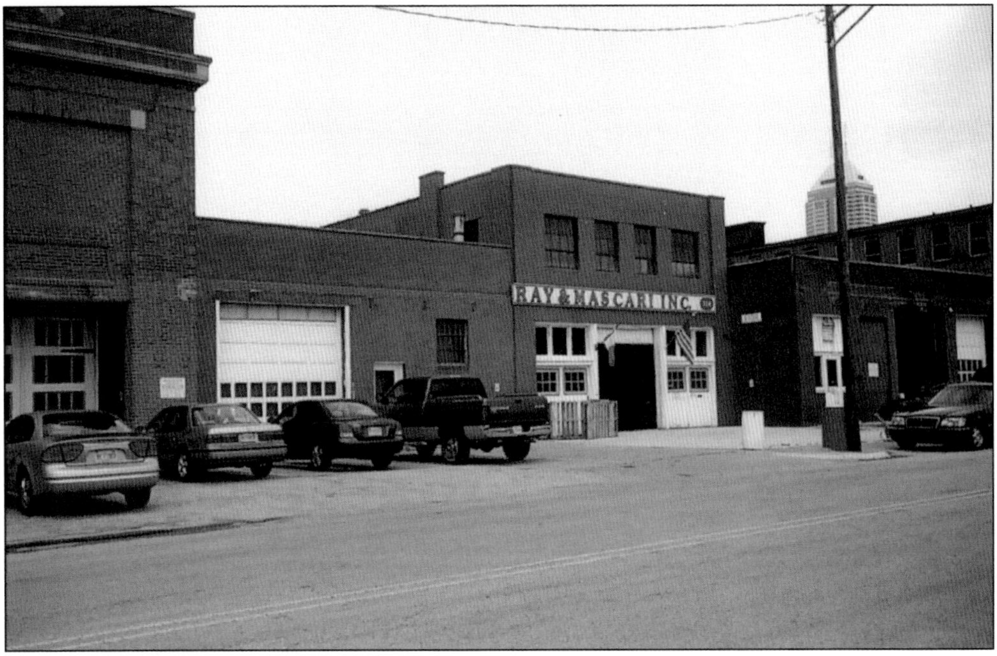

The City Market stand evolved into Ray and Mascari, Inc., produce merchants, near the corner of New Jersey and South Streets not far from Holy Rosary Church. Ray and Mascari flies both the American and Italian flags and was honored as the Italian firm of the year.

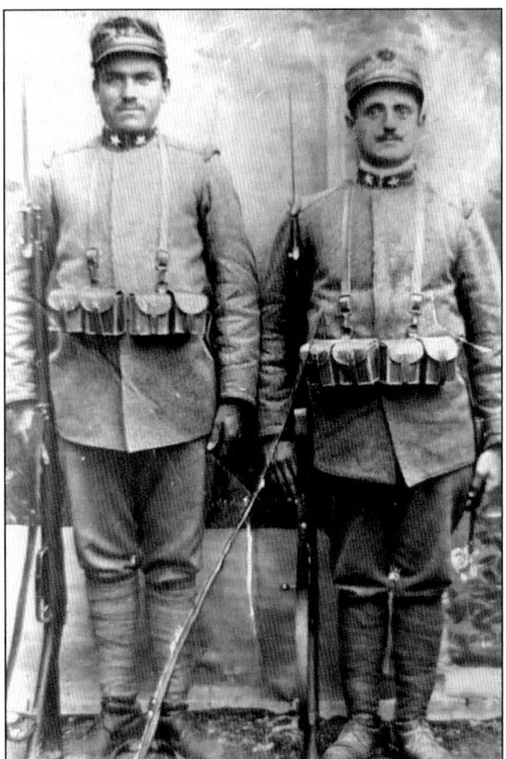

Michele De Fabis left Amaseno, provincia di Frosinone (Lazio), for Chicago Heights, Illinois, when he was 17 or 18 years old. Recalled to serve his military duty during World War I, he was held as a prisoner of Austria for 18 months. Here, Michele (right) and his comrade wear their Italian uniforms. (Courtesy Phil De Fabis.)

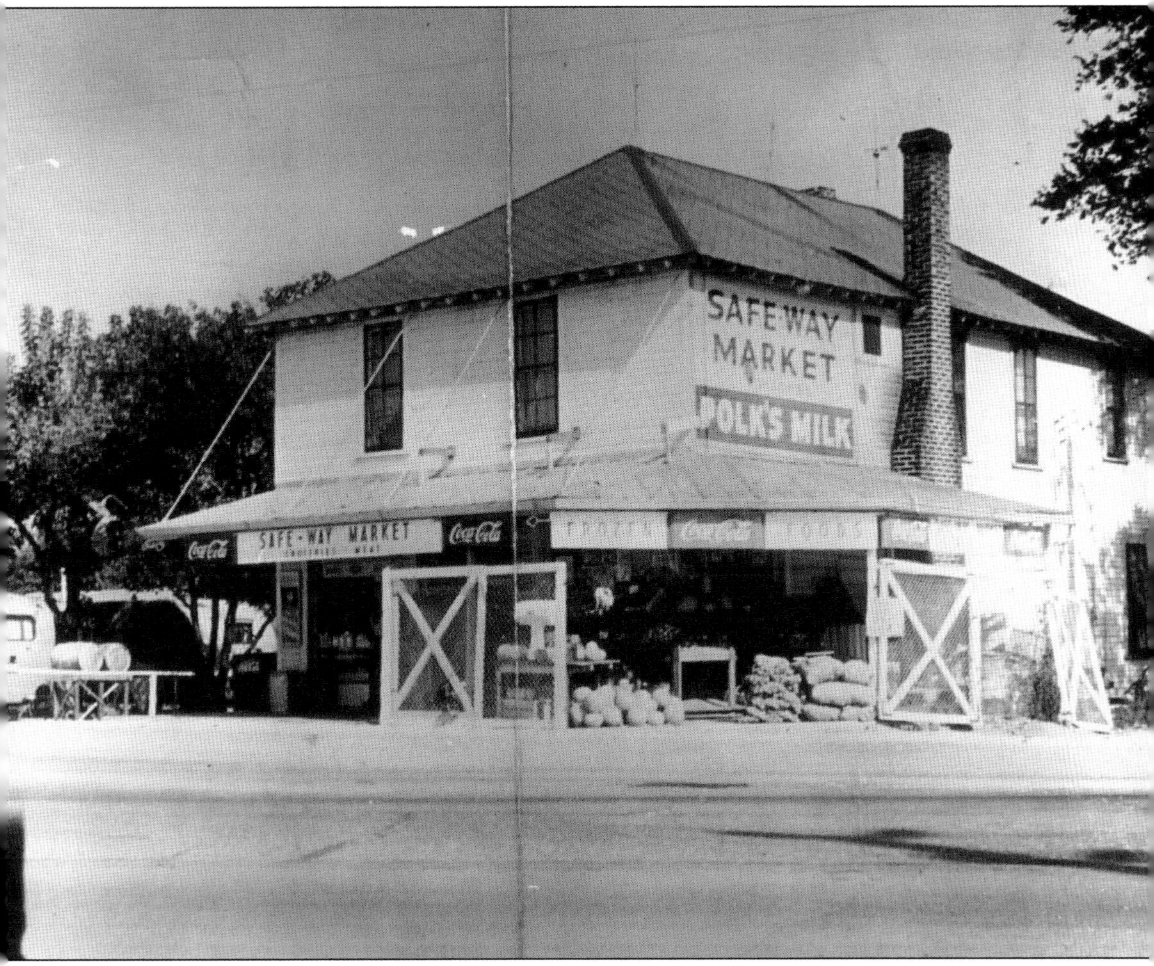

Michele was a sheet metal worker who made stills during Prohibition and ran hardware, paint, and grocery stores. When his sons returned from the Korean War in 1955, he bought a store on the west side, at Tibbs Avenue and Lafayette Road (above), for $50,000. Safeway stores grew into a chain of 18 supermarkets and a wholesale warehouse with 1,000 employees. It pioneered the deli-in-supermarket and the wholesale aisle. The Preston-Safeway supermarkets, as they were popularly called, were probably the largest Italian-owned business ever in Indianapolis. But by 1985, faced with strong competition from regional chains, their parents dead, Phil nearing retirement, and with an offer-to-buy before them, the De Fabis brothers decided to sell their chain and warehouse. Youngest brother Mike left the family business for a year and a half when he accepted Mayor Richard Lugar's appointment as deputy mayor in 1973. Then after the brothers closed out their interests in Safeway, Mike accepted a position as president and CEO of Associated Wholesale Grocers of Kansas City, Missouri, in 1993. After retiring in 1999, he returned to the Indianapolis area. (Courtesy Phil De Fabis.)

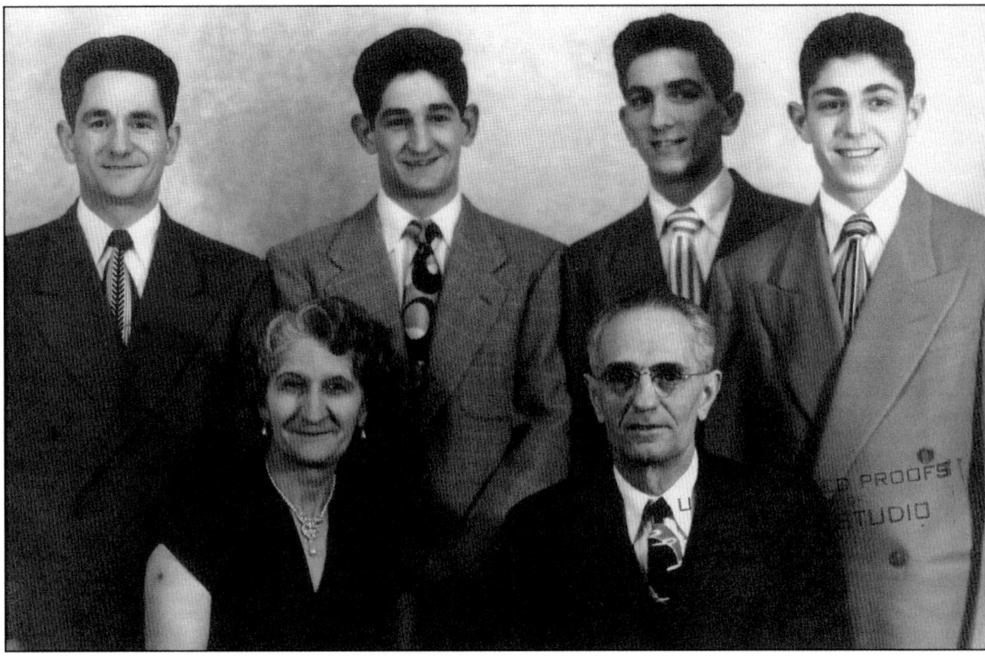

After World War I, Michele De Fabis headed for Chicago Heights and then Indianapolis. His wife, Domenica Seghetti De Fabis, and son Phil joined him in 1927, and they lived on Newton Avenue on the east side. Behind the parents, from left to right, are their four sons—Phil, Julius, Ernest, and Michael. (Courtesy Phil De Fabis.)

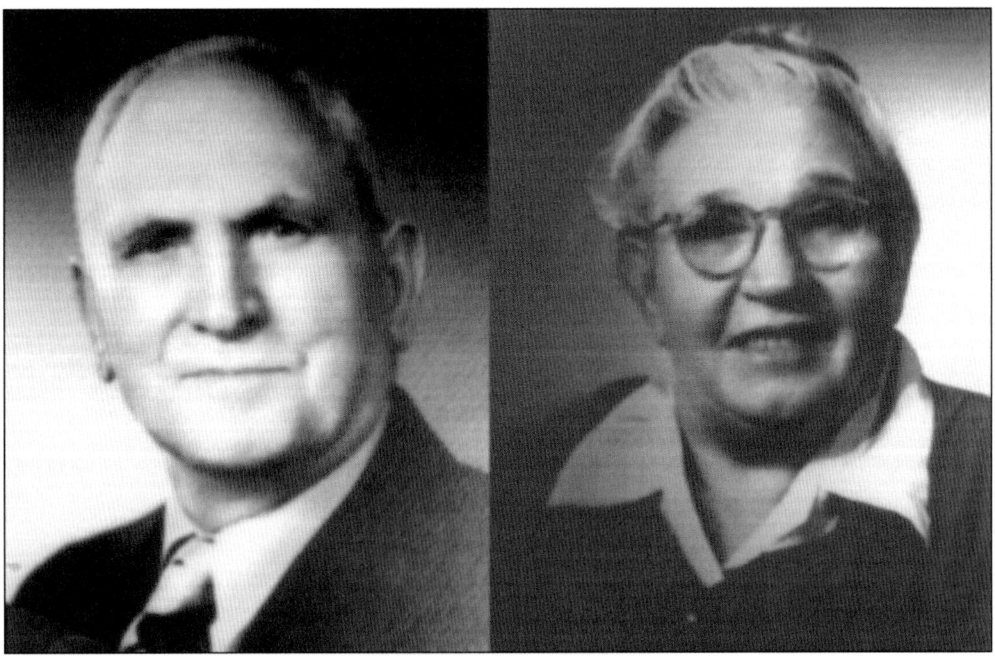

Giuseppe (left) and Maria Concetta Schipani Cortese (right) hailed from Mesoraca, provincia di Crotone (Calabria). Their son Thomas A. Cortese Sr. received his medical degree from Indiana University in 1933. A protégé of Vincent A. Lapenta, M.D., distinguished surgeon and scientist, Cortese practiced surgery with Lapenta at St. Francis Hospital after 1934.

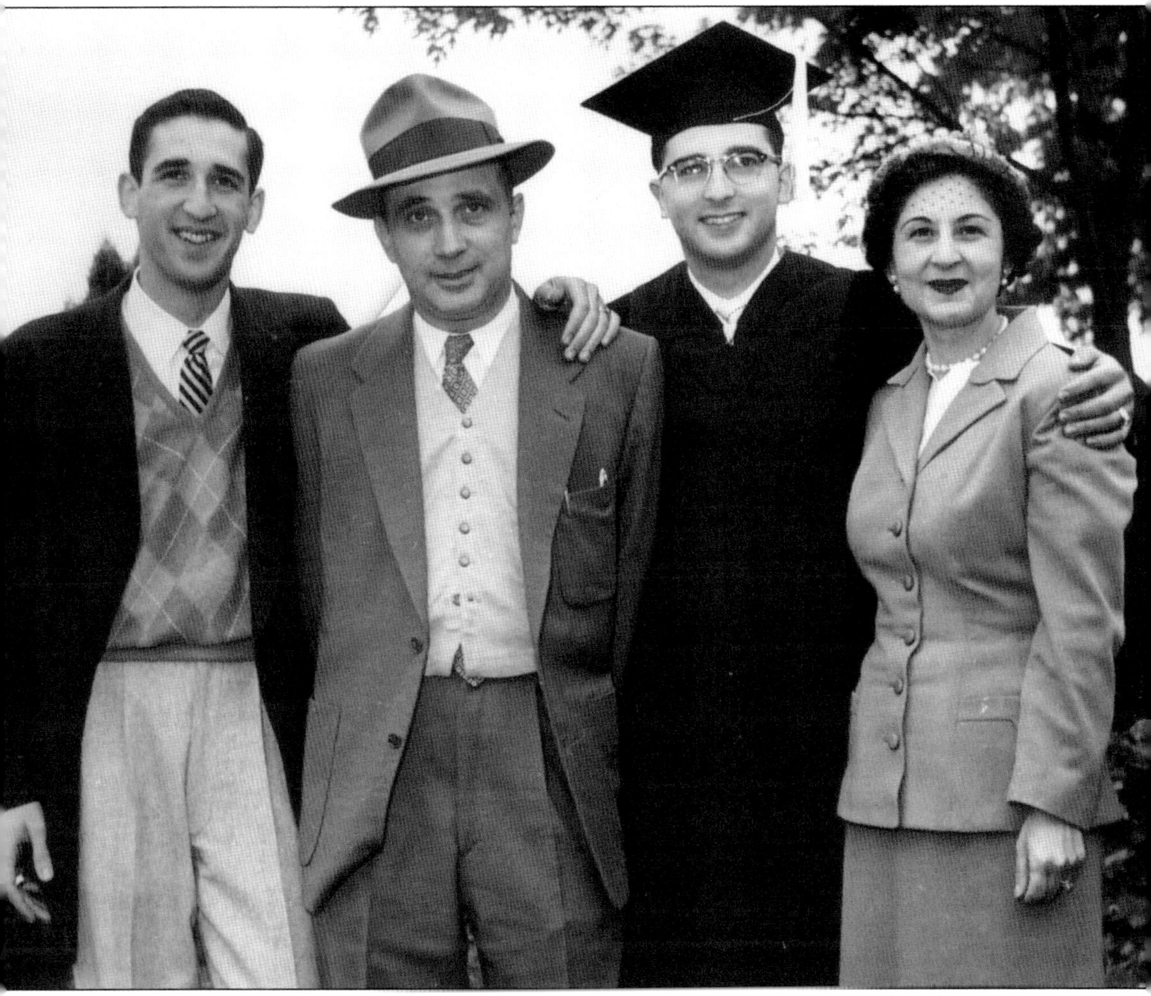

Dr. Thomas Cortese Sr. poses with his wife and sons at the college graduation of his older son in 1955. Shown here, from left to right, are Joe, Dr. Cortese, Tom Jr., and Thelma Donato Cortese.

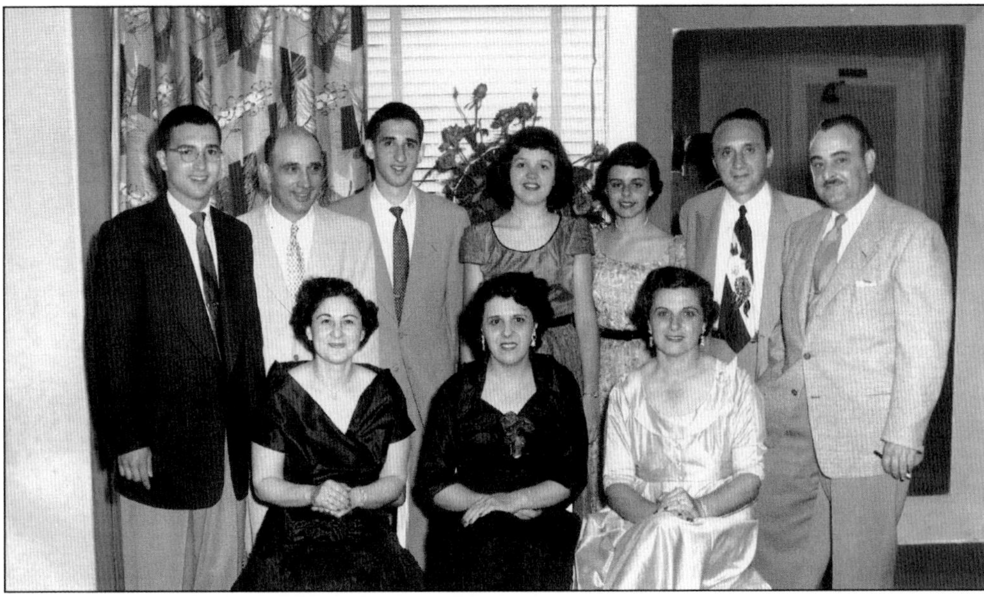

The Cortese family is unique for its great interest in health services. Pictured at this 1952 gathering of relatives are the following, from left to right: (first row) Thelma, Dr. Tom Sr.'s wife; Eleanore, brother Jim's wife; and Marie, Dr. Donato's wife; (second row) Tom Jr., future dermatologist; Dr. Tom Sr.; Joe, future dentist; niece Mary Ann, future radiologist; Elaine, future teacher; Dr. Tom Sr.'s brother Jim, general practitioner; and his brother-in-law Albert Donato Sr., obstetrician and general practitioner.

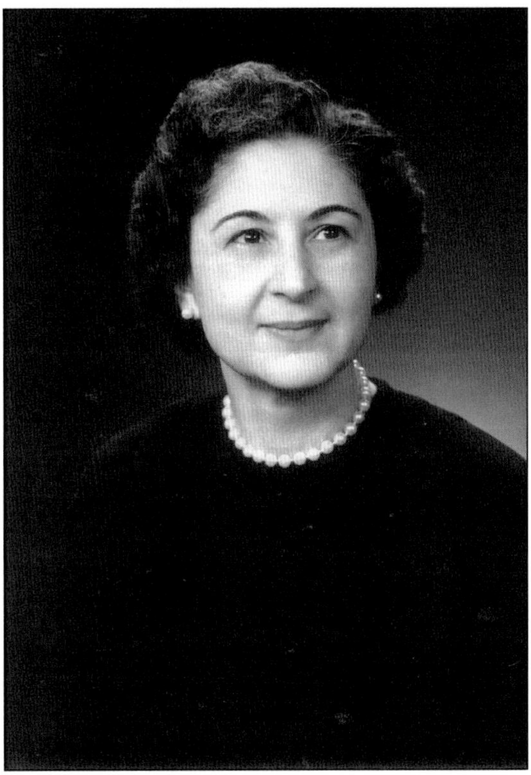

Thelma Donato Cortese should not be recognized only as the wife of Dr. Tom Sr. and the mother of Tom Jr. and Joe. Her father, Harry Donato, was a stone carver, as was her uncle Crescenzo Donato.

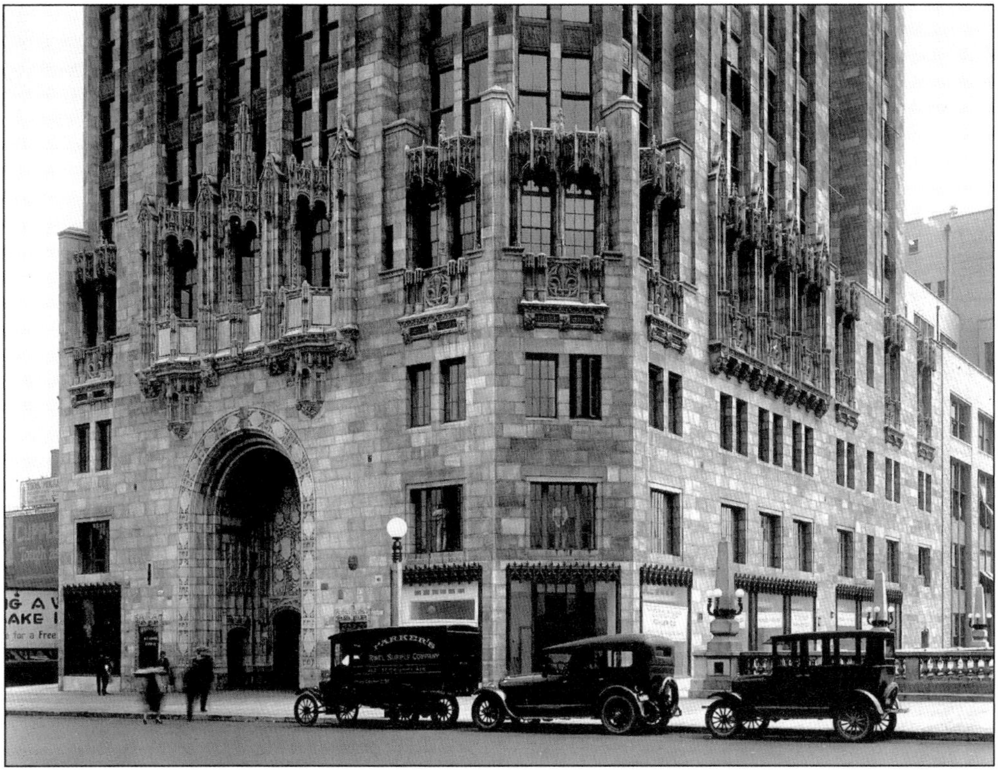

Crescenzo Donato, often called "C. D." or "Chris," worked as a stone carver and contractor in Bedford, Indiana, the site of the great Indiana limestone quarries. After retirement in Indianapolis, he became a painter. Out of these quarries came buildings in the nation's capital and the Empire State Building in New York. One of the most important Donato works is the Tribune Tower (above) in Chicago.

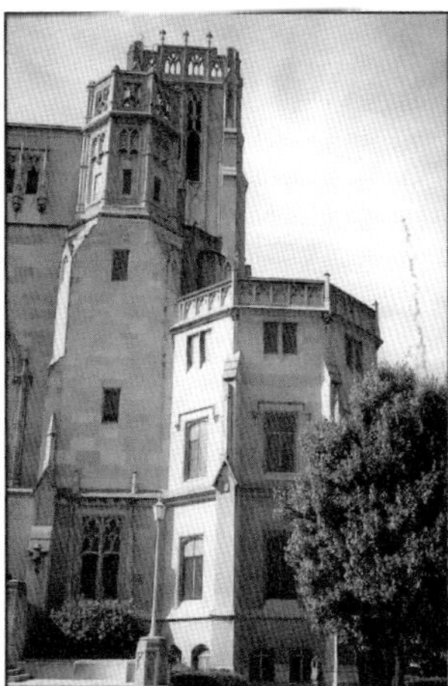
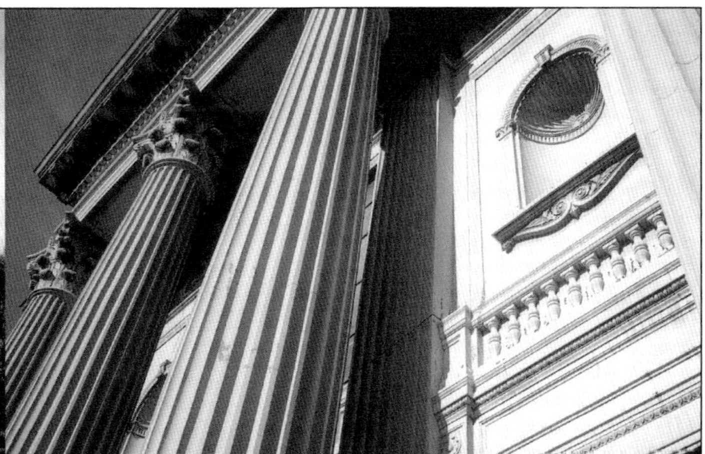

Donato works also include the Scottish Rite Cathedral (left) and SS. Peter and Paul Catholic Cathedral (right) in Indianapolis.

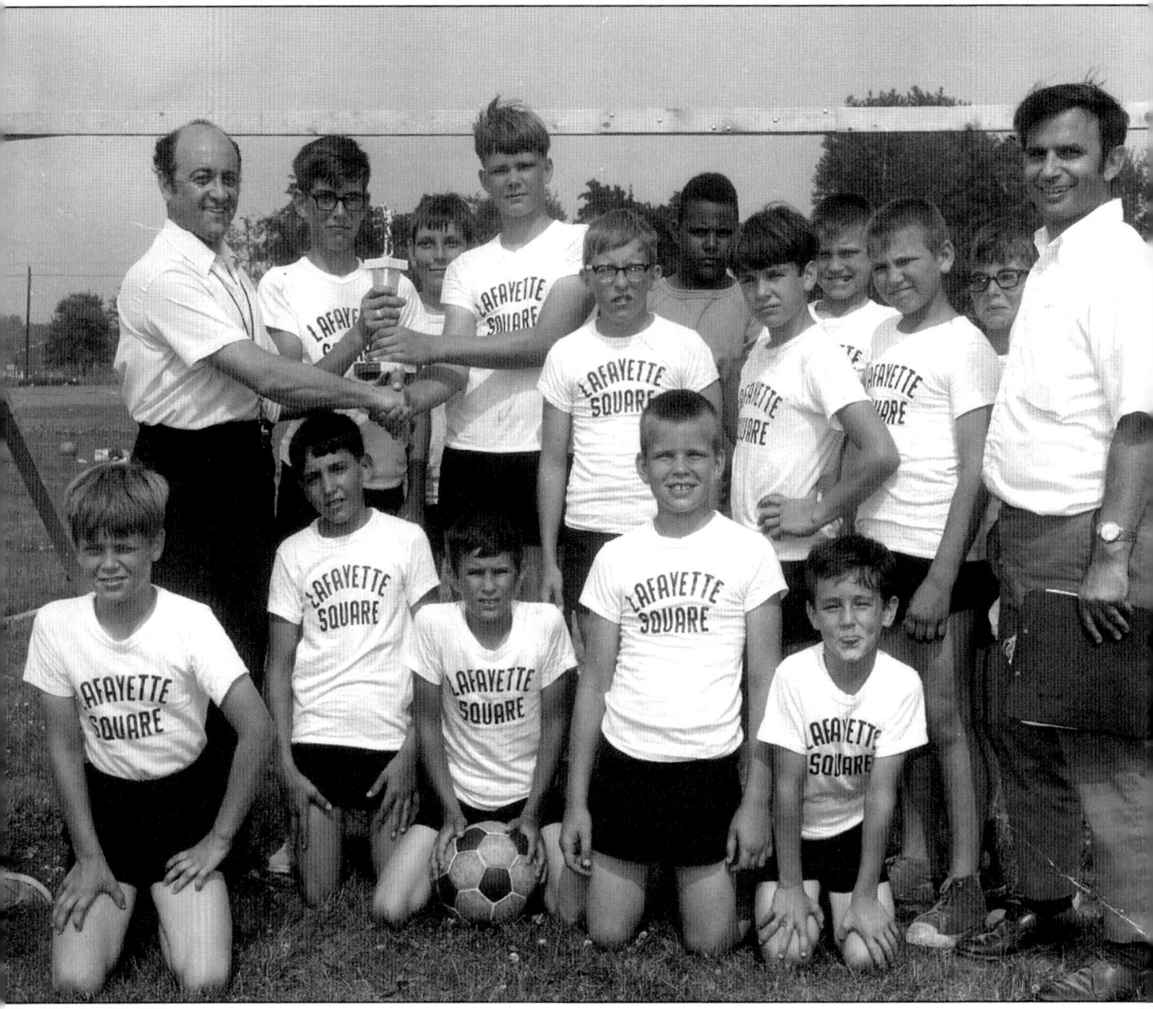

Italians may have brought bananas to Indianapolis, but they also founded a grammar school soccer league here. Italian-speaking Fr. Raymond Bosler, once a student at Rome's North American College and pastor of Little Flower Parish in 1969, met Italian immigrant Pietro Ferri at the rectory door. Pietro wanted to interest Little Flower pupils in soccer. "I know about soccer from my time in Rome," said the pastor. "Talk to the kids tomorrow at lunch time." Ferri, Italian immigrant Aldo Mina (St. Catherine's), and Herman Hartman (St. Simon/PS 102) established the Indianapolis Junior Soccer League. They obtained team sponsorships from a variety of businesses—from auto dealers to the Police Athletic League. As league president, Pietro (left) presents the trophy to St. Catherine soccer players, sponsored by Lafayette Square shopping mall. Aldo Mina, the winning coach, appears on the right, and his son Aldo Jr. in the center of the first row. (Courtesy Aldo Mina.)

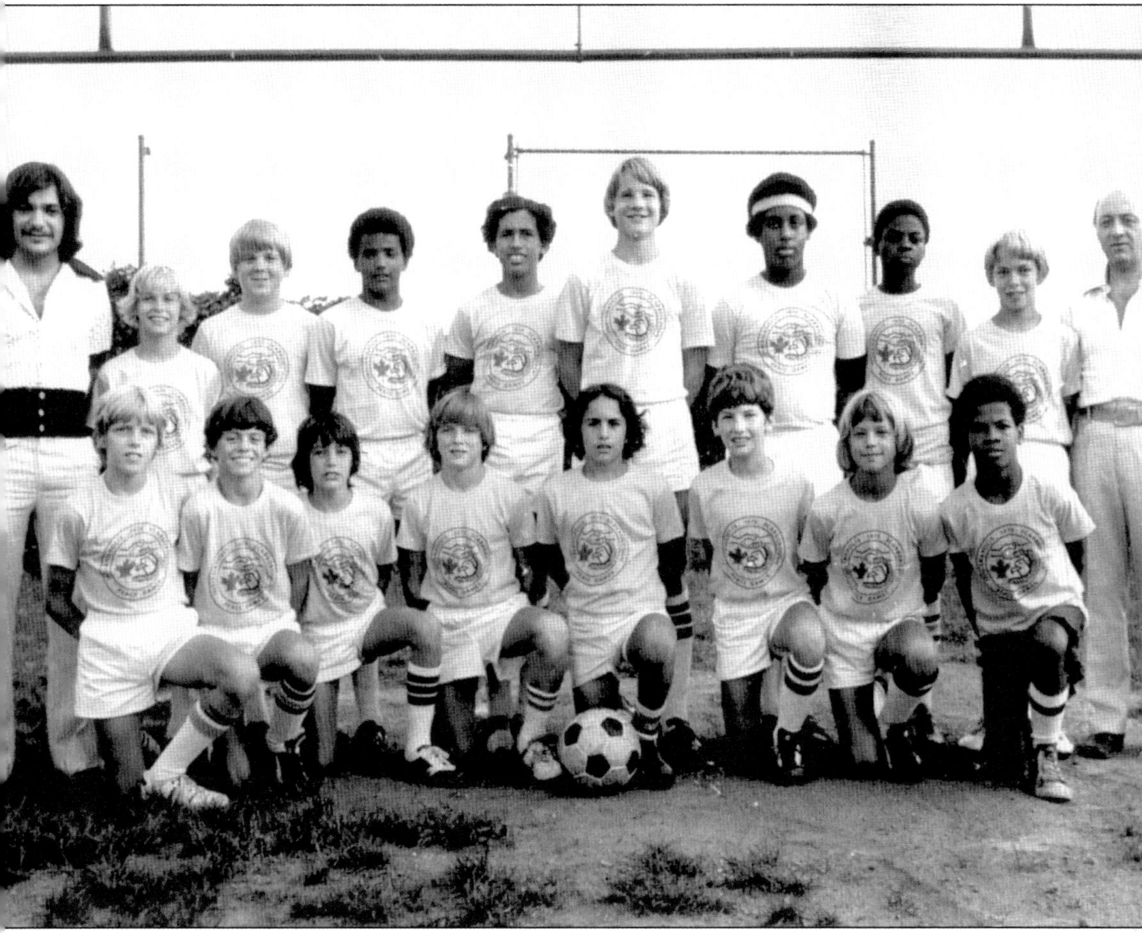

In 1971, the Indianapolis Junior All Stars played the Guelph, Ontario, Pee-Wees at German Park. Then in 1975, Pietro Ferri (right) and fellow coach Paul Cotter prepared the team for the Indianapolis-Scarborough Peace games. The team tied. When he congratulated the All Stars, Mayor Richard Lugar called Ferri a "missionary of soccer." (Courtesy Pietro Ferri.)

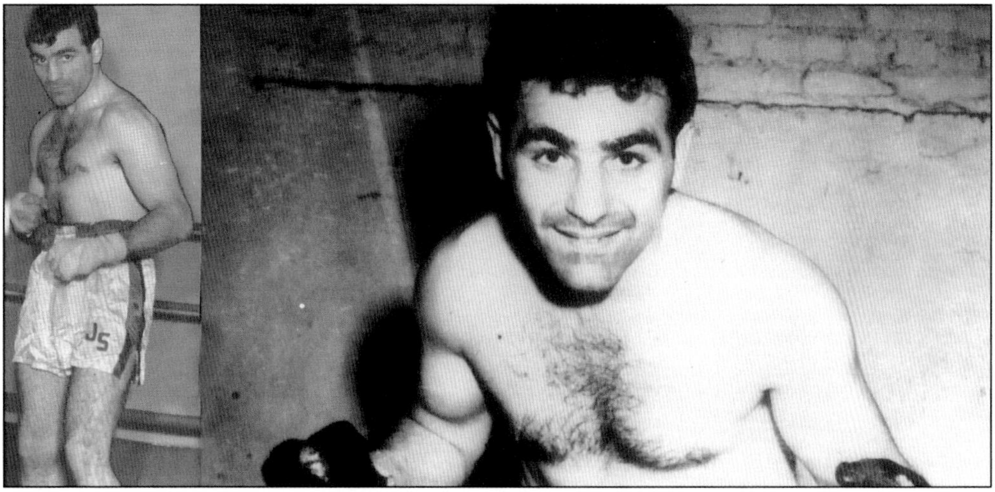

Joe Sgro, the son of Francesco (Ciccio) and Celestina Giordano Sgro from Roccaforte del Greco in Calabria, fought in 200 matches as an amateur boxer in the lightweight and welterweight divisions, winning many local golden glove titles. A member of the 1939 regional Golden Gloves team, he fought on the same card as the future great Sugar Ray Robinson in New York's Madison Square Garden. Joe never lost a bout while in the army during World War II. A professional after the war, he won the state welterweight title, compiling a record of around 66 wins and 12 losses. In 1949–1950 he fought world champions Joe Brown and Virgil Akins. He lost both bouts in close decisions. After one of Joe's many fights at Marigold Gardens in Chicago, promoter Doc Kearns invited him to join his stable of promising contenders in New York City. Joe declined, due to family obligations. Ciccio always climbed into the ring before a fight to give his son a good luck kiss. After his retirement in the 1960s, Joe worked as a referee and trainer, and even sparred for three, three-minute rounds at age 73. (Courtesy Michele Caporale.)

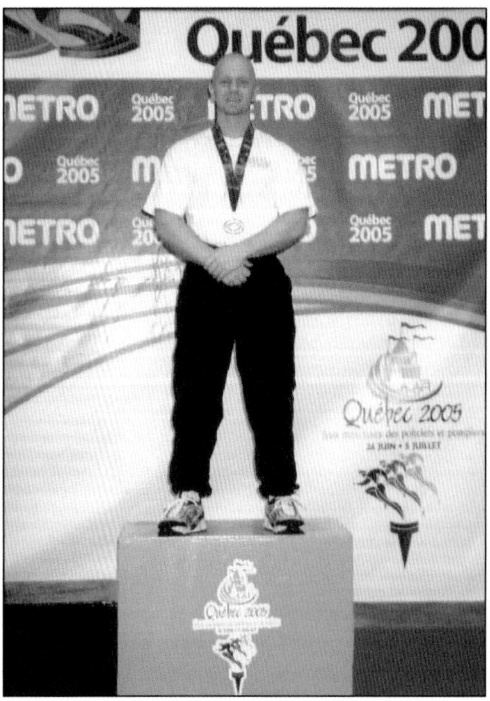

John Anthony "Tony" Burrello won a gold medal at the World Police and Fire Games held in Quebec in 2005. He bench pressed 325 pounds in the weightlifting competition where 352 pounds is the world record. An Indianapolis park ranger, he is the son of Salvatore (Sam) and Jacqueline Burrello, and the great-grandson of immigrants Francesco Paolo Dominici (Burrello) and Maria Concetta Giardina. She came to America from Termini to rejoin her husband in 1905.

No book dealing with Indianapolis can be silent about the annual Memorial Day race which attracts 300,000 fans. Run 500 miles since 1911, Italians or Italian-Americans who win the race become honorary members of the Italian community. They are Ralph de Palma (1915), Dario Resta (1916), Peter de Paolo (1925), Kelly Petillo (1935), and Mario Andretti (1969). Car owner and businessman Andy Granatelli embraced his driver Mario Andretti after his victory in the Indianapolis 500, on May 30, 1969. Andretti was born in Montona in Istria. His twin brother Aldo raced briefly and lives here. Son Michael and grandson Marco also appear on the track.

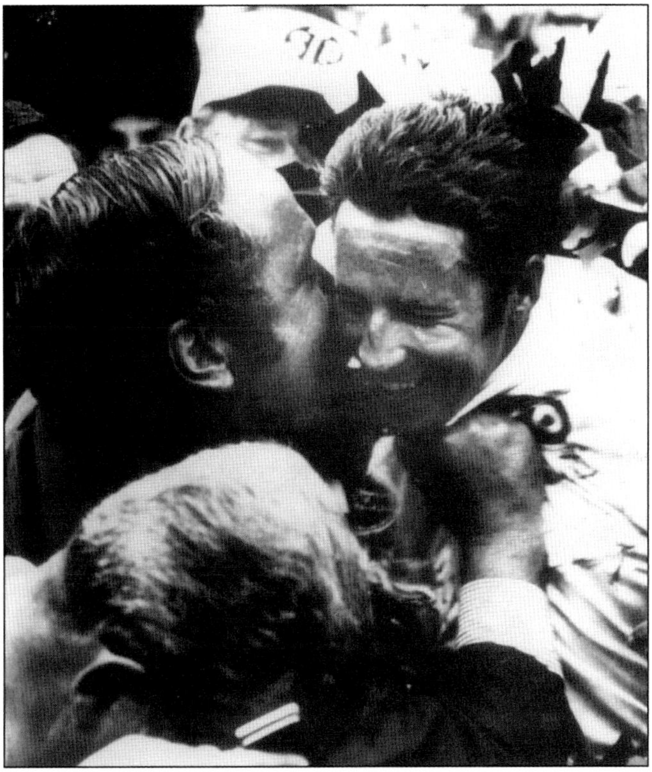

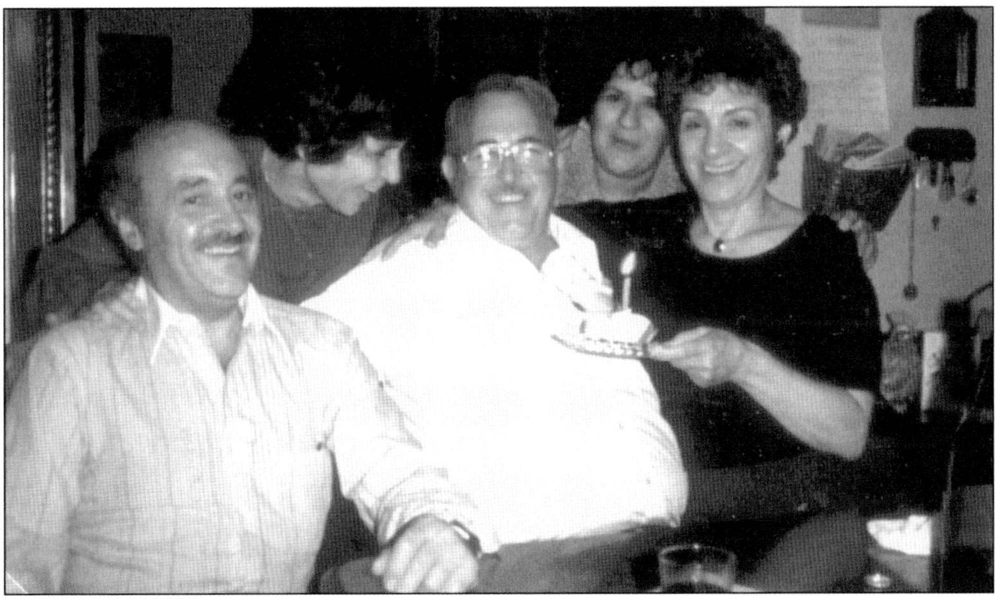

From Malden, Massachusetts, Ralph Forni served in the 82nd Airborne and was stationed at Fort Harrison outside Indianapolis during the Korean War. While here, he met Angela Morone and married her in 1954. He retired from the Chrysler foundry on the west side where he worked as a metallurgical engineer. Outside of work, he sang with the Knights of Columbus men's choir and served as Italian Heritage Society treasurer. In the photograph are, from left to right, Pietro and Silvana Ferri, Ralph Forni, Ada Mina, and Angela Forni. (Courtesy Aldo Mina.)

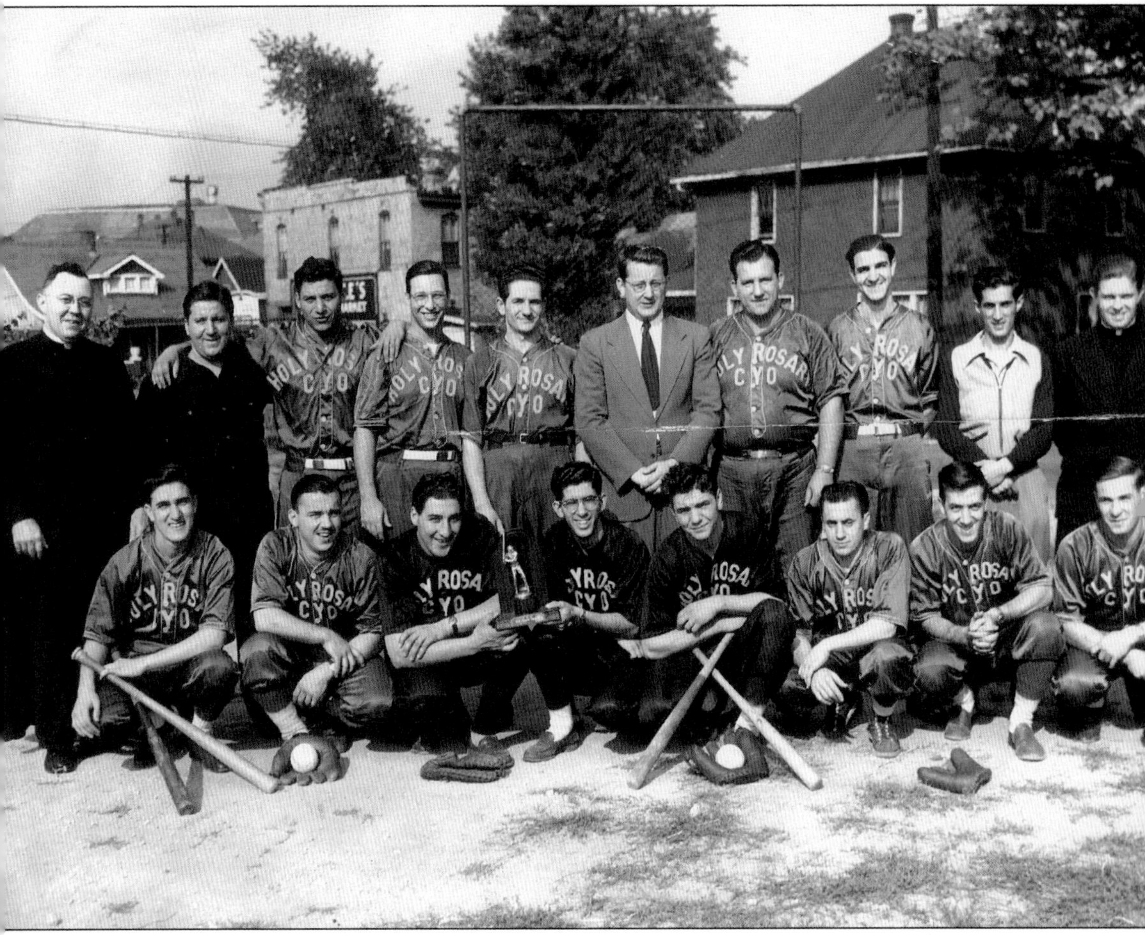

Members of the Holy Rosary CYO baseball team, with smiling faces, pose in what is now Lacy Park. Father William Knapp, pastor, is pictured at left, while Father Charles Noll, assistant, is at right. (Courtesy Phil De Fabis.)

Five

Politics
Local Political Participation

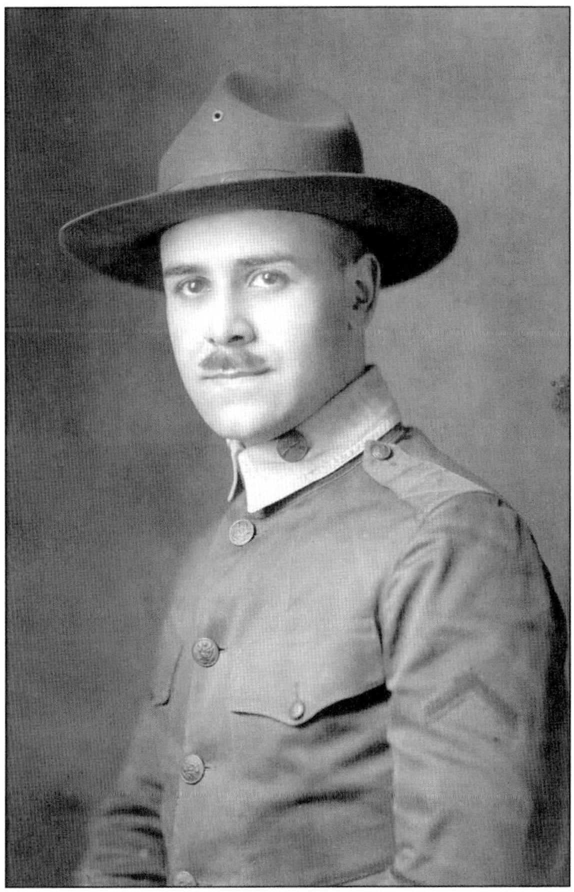

Ferdinand Montani was a son of musician Dominic Montani. Reputedly the city's first Italian lawyer, he wore the uniform of the American military during World War I. Freddie, as he was called by his large family, was interested in community service and had political ambitions, which relatives believe never reached fruition because of his Italian ancestry. Ferdinand headed an effort to raise funds in the Italian community to buy ambulances that would serve Italian wounded during World War I. He was also active in the Italian Relief Association. (Courtesy Steve Montani.)

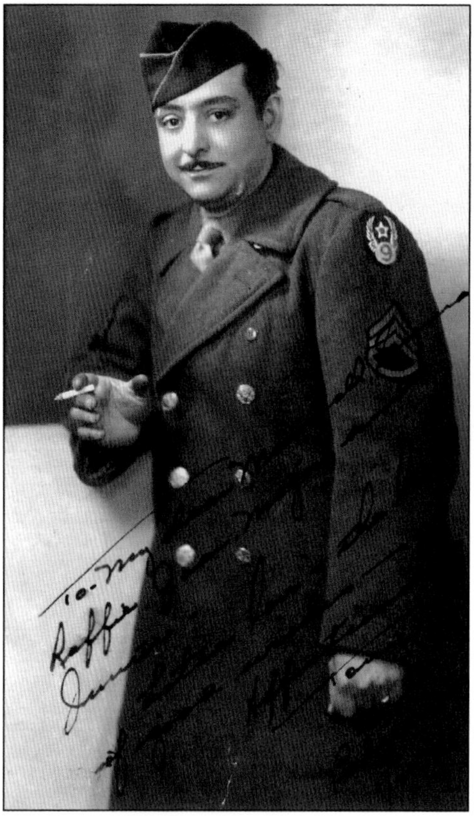

Anthony B. Montani, also a son of Dominic Montani, served his country in Belgium during World War II (left). He ran unsuccessfully for state senator from Marion County in the Republican primary, and may be the first Italian American to seek elective political office in this county (below).

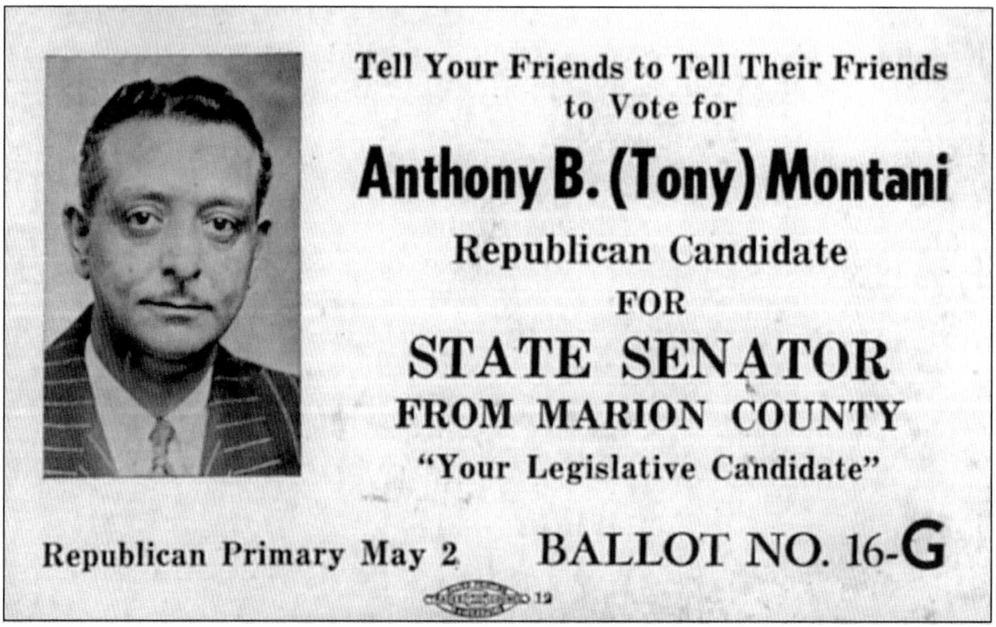

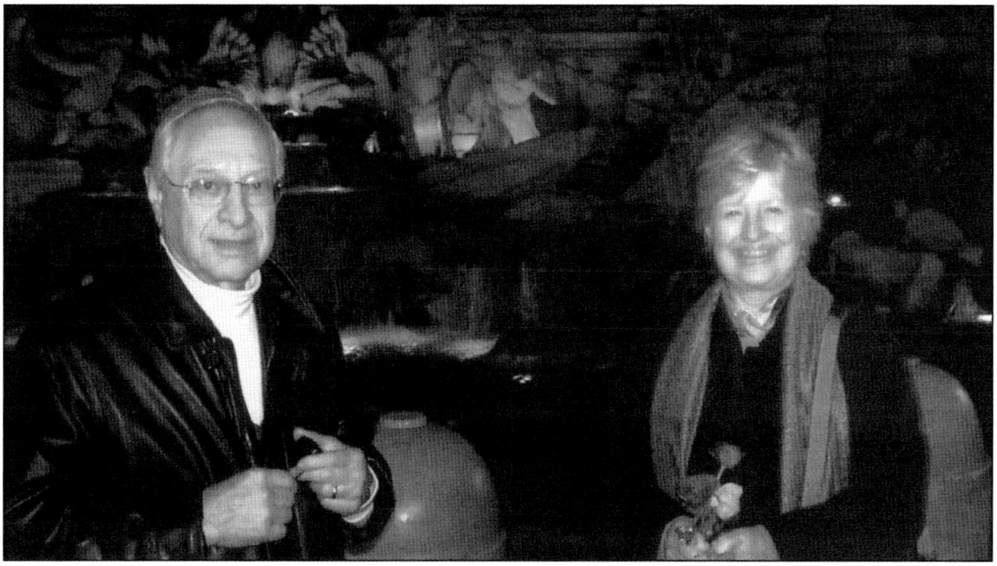

Paul Jerry Roland and his wife, Sarah, visited the Trevi Fountain in Rome during one of their many trips to Italy. Jerry is a native of New Jersey with family ties to Indianapolis. An attorney, he spent one term as a state representative and acted as honorary vice-consul of Italy for Indiana. He has been active in Italian societies for almost 50 years, a leader in the Italian-American Club, Columbus Commission '92, and the Italian Heritage Society of Indiana. Sarah has taught at Vicenza in the Veneto, and serves as docent for Italian art at the Indianapolis Museum of Art. (Courtesy of Paul Jerry Roland.)

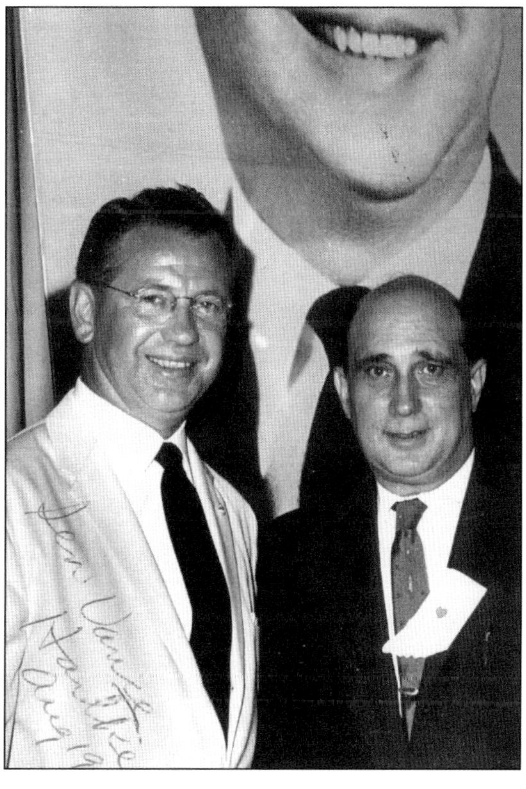

Dr. Tom Cortese Sr. (right) was active in the affairs of the Democratic Party. He was particularly interested in liberalization of immigration laws to permit the easy reuniting of family members living separately in Italy and the United States. Dr. Cortese received the Star of the Order of Solidarity from the Italian government in 1960. Here he wears his heart over Indianapolis and shares the spotlight with United States senator Vance Hartke (left) in August 1964. Dr. Cortese founded the Italian-American Club to maintain the unity of the Italian community. (Courtesy Dr. Thomas Cortese Jr.)

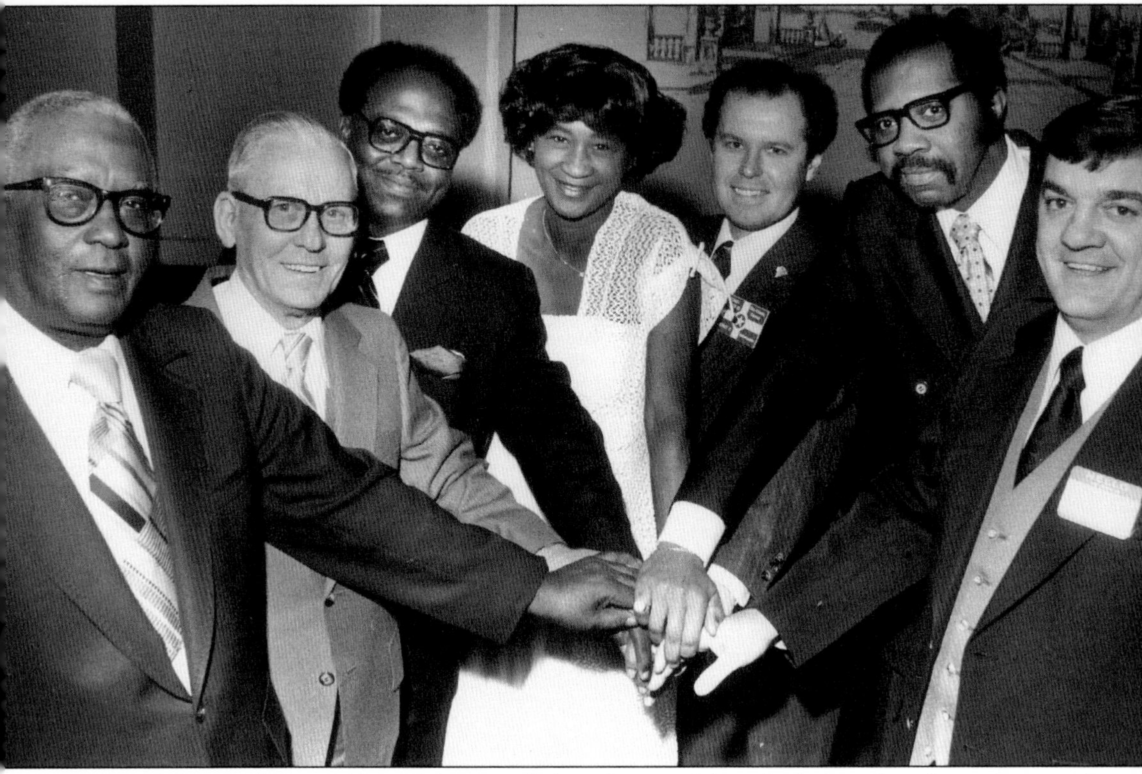

David Page is the son of Peter J. Page and Mary Corsaro. Mary died when David was three, and he was raised by her sister Antonia Constantino. He has run restaurants and banquet halls, invested in real estate, and built homes and condominiums. He has chaired Holy Rosary's annual Italian Street Festival for over 20 years. David (far right) was one of seven Democrats in the 28 member City-County Council. In 1979, he was appointed to fill one year of a term and then was elected to two consecutive terms, frustrated at every turn because Democrats were an impotent minority. Other Italian Americans who held political office in Marion County were Harry J. Gasper (Gaspari), a Democrat elected county clerk in 1958; Anthony M. Maio, county Democratic chairman; William Mercuri, Republican county assessor from 1967 to 1975, and then elected a judge; Italian-born Judge A. Toni Cordingsley; and City-County Councilman Frank Short. Short's mother's maiden name was Marturano, his maternal grandparents from Basilicata. (Courtesy Rosemary Page.)

Six

Religion
Community Church Life

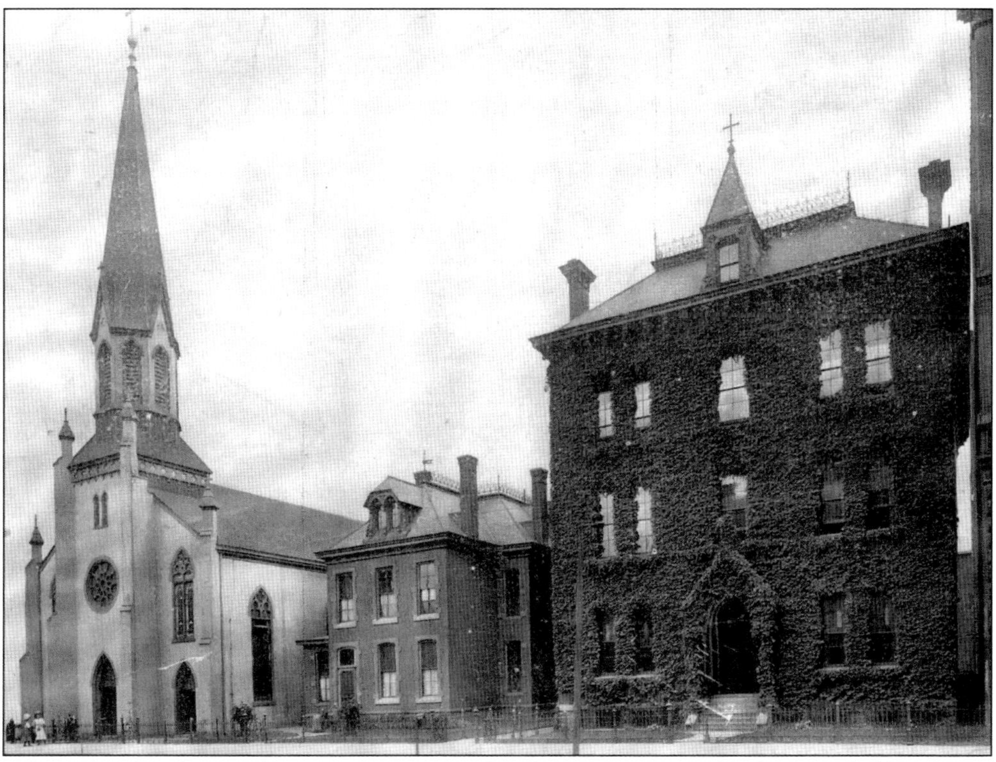

Italians first lived around Virginia Avenue and Delaware Street in the shadow of old St. Mary Church, on East Maryland Street between Delaware and Pennsylvania Streets. Although a German national parish, St. Mary's served the spiritual needs of hundreds of Italians who were baptized, married, and buried there between 1885 and 1909.

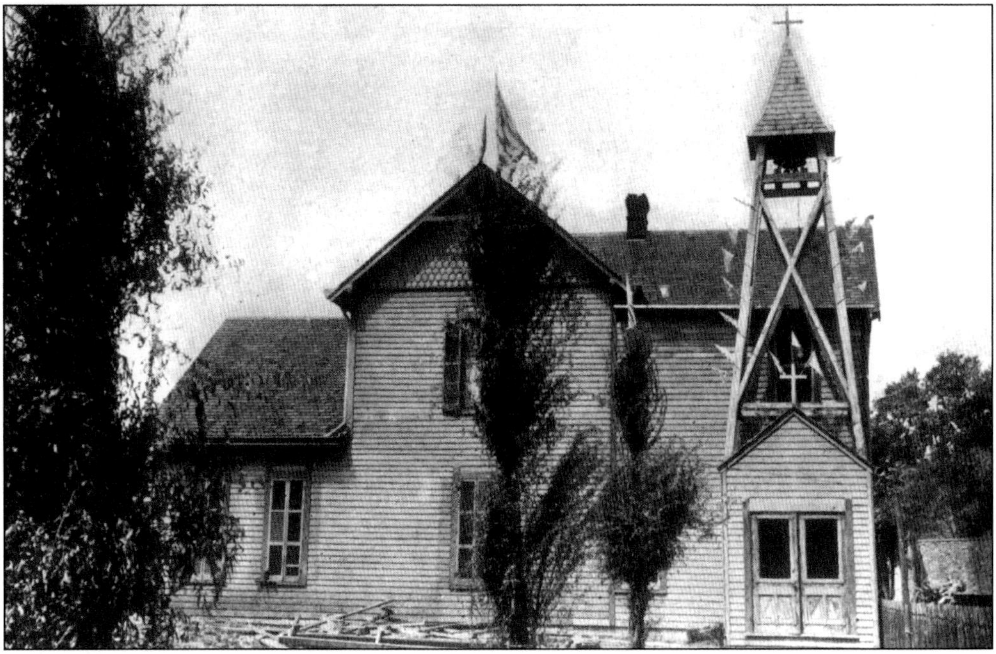

This frame residence on Stevens Street off of South East Street became the first church of the Italian national parish named for Our Lady of the Most Holy Rosary in 1909. Fr. Marino Priori organized Holy Rosary partially as a response to the efforts of the Methodist Episcopal Church to evangelize Indianapolis Italians.

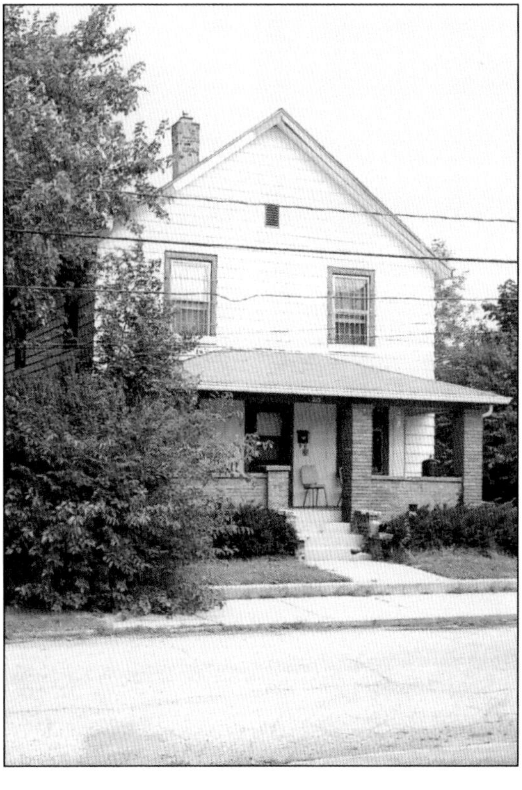

The first Methodist missionary was Nicolò Accomando, who came from Palermo in 1906. He served as federal census taker in the Italian neighborhood in 1910. Luigi Lops, born in San Giovanni Rotondo, provincia di Foggia (Apulia), succeeded Accomando. In 1912, Lops incorporated an Old Catholic diocese in Indianapolis to make his work more attractive among Italians. This new church could combine Catholic religious externals with a Protestant doctrinal approach. Ugo Crivelli, who migrated from Milan, and Methodist deaconesses succeeded Lops, working here until 1920. The mission provided English-language classes for adults, kindergarten-style supervision for children, and free bread for anyone who asked for it. Reverend Crivelli's mission was located at 903 East Bates Street; his parsonage, shown here, still stands at 215 South Davidson Street.

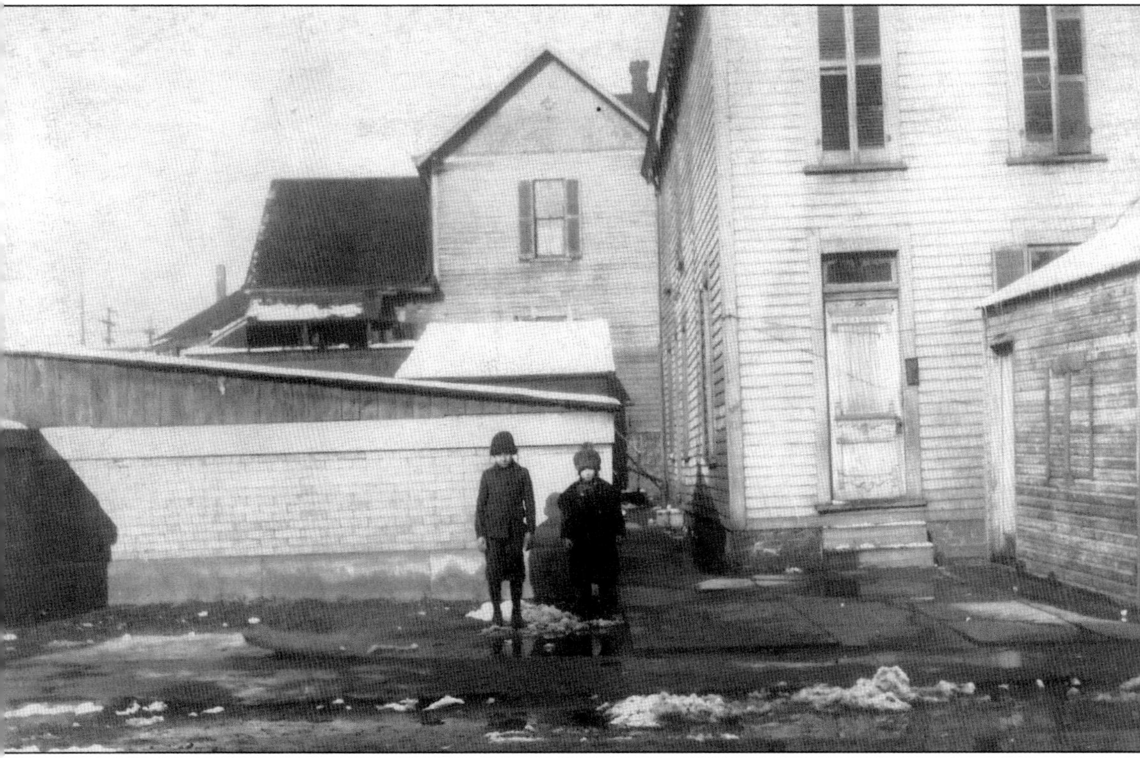

In 1911, Father Marino Priori was able to fund the excavation and building of the foundation to a new church, but lack of money forced him to cover over the foundation (left) and use the basement as a church.

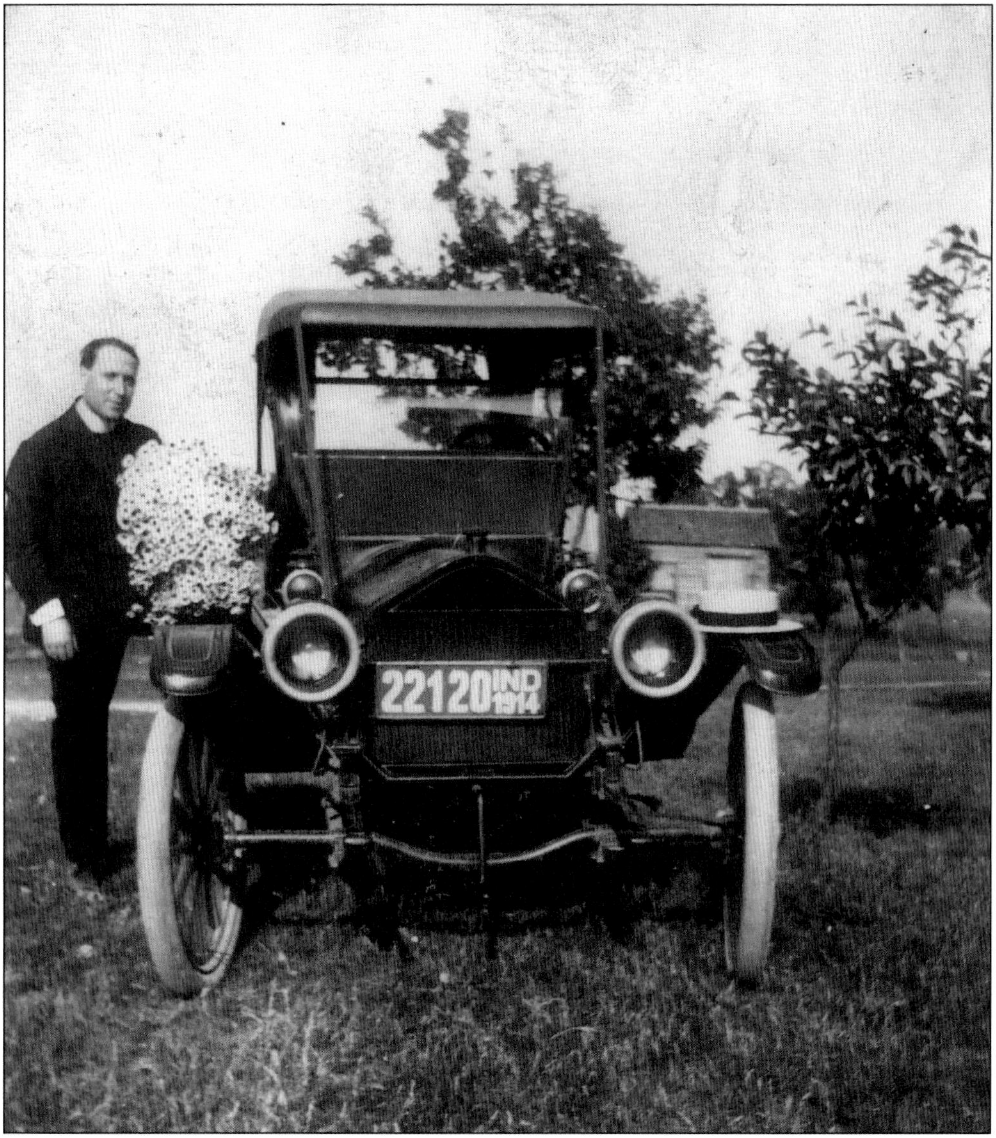

Father Priori is attentive to his new wheels in 1914. Priori was born in Montefalcone Appennino, provincia di Ascoli Piceno (Marches), in 1878. In 1895, at an early age, he joined the Franciscans and was ordained priest six years later. Since he was his family's sole male support, he requested permission to live outside his community and be a missionary to America. He arrived in 1908 and was assigned to Bedford, Indiana, to minister to Italian limestone quarry workers. Decline in their number—due to threats against foreigners and the beginning of Methodist evangelization—resulted in Priori's transfer to Indianapolis with the charge of founding a parish for Italians. The church basement was excavated in 1911 and a school started in 1912. Money problems delayed completion of the church and the building of a convent until 1925. Priori became a monsignor in the spring of 1933. After Bishop Joseph Chartrand's death in December 1933, Priori, because he was unable to raise sufficient donations from his parishioners even to pay the interest on the debt, was transferred from Holy Rosary to Troy, Indiana, on the Ohio River. He retired in 1941, died in a Louisville infirmary, and was buried in St. Joseph Cemetery, Indianapolis, in 1946. (Courtesy Freda Buennagel.)

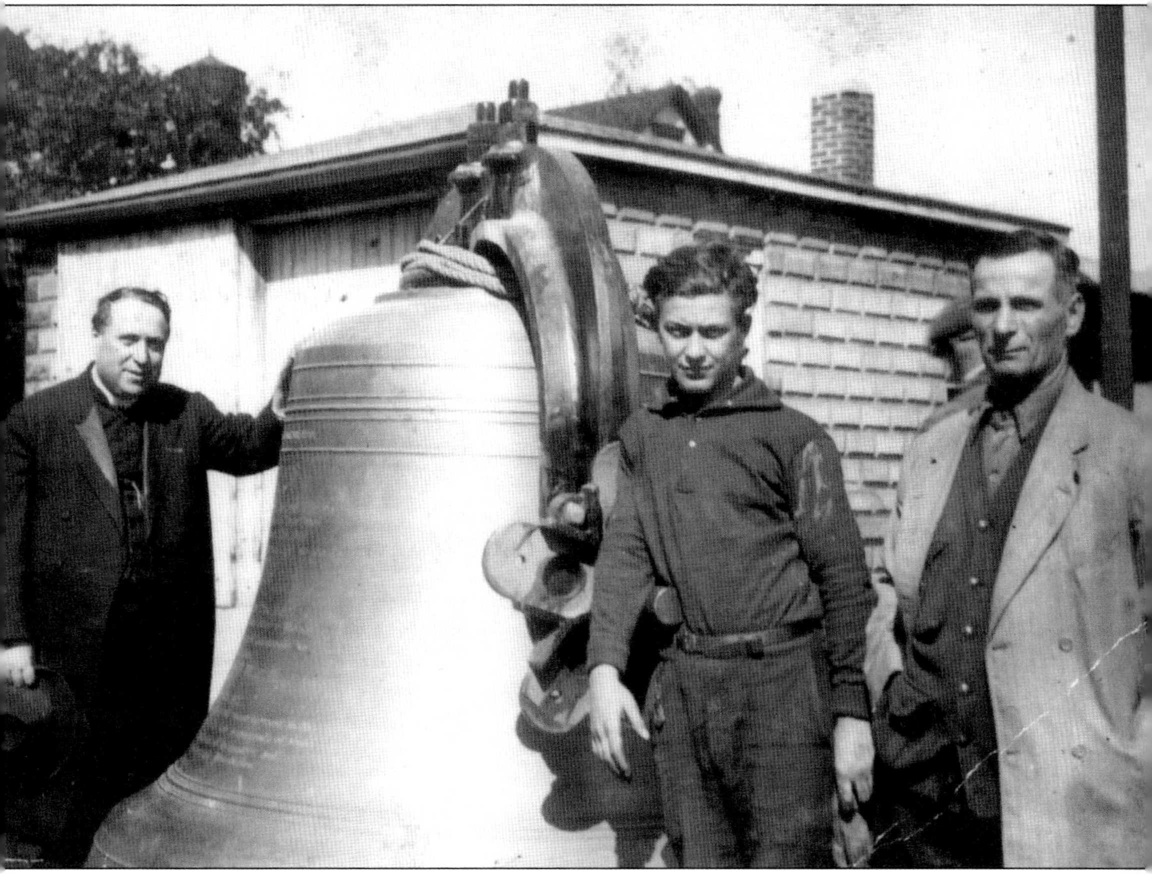

From left to right, Fr. Marino Priori, young Rosario Gatto, and Nicola Bondi flank the San Salvador bell in 1924. (Courtesy Matthew and Sandy Iaria.)

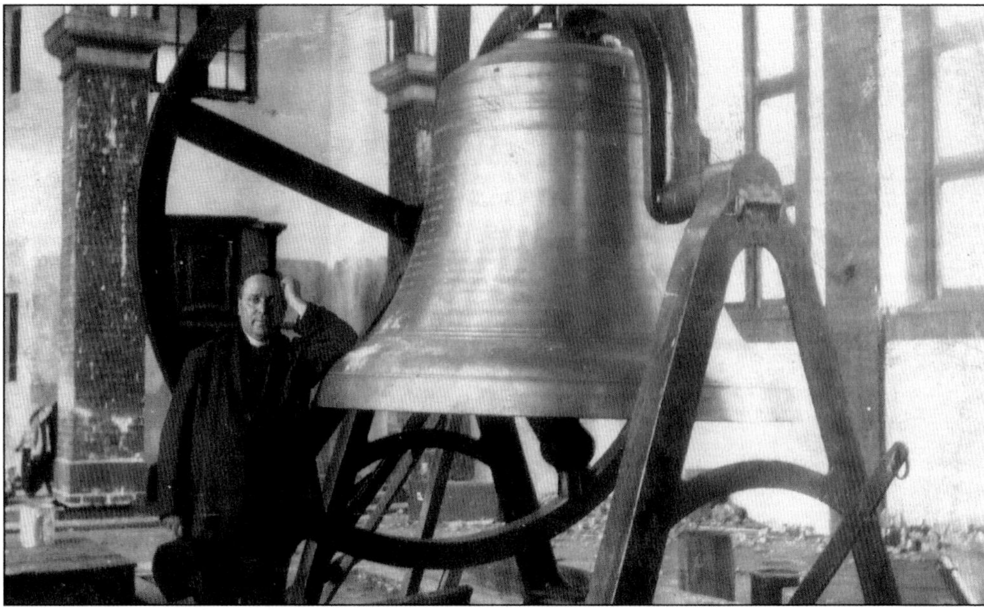

Holy Rosary's bells are the pride of the parish. At 7,000 pounds, the largest bell (above) was made by Buckeye foundry in Cincinnati and was the weightiest to be cast in the country. Named San Salvador in honor of Christopher Columbus, it was donated by the readers of *Eternal Light*, Priori's monthly magazine, and installed in the west tower in 1924. Five smaller bells (below), including the original bell of 1909, were placed in the east tower. Today, Holy Rosary bells would have a replacement cost of at least $300,000. Such a large expense is why no modern church has real bells, just recordings. Recordings were unsatisfactory and impractical in 1924, so Father Priori welcomed the real thing. Parishoner Josie Sigreto reported, "My father was very worried when he saw the church bells stored in the church. Surely the floor would give way and the bells and church would be ruined." (Courtesy Freda Buennagel.)

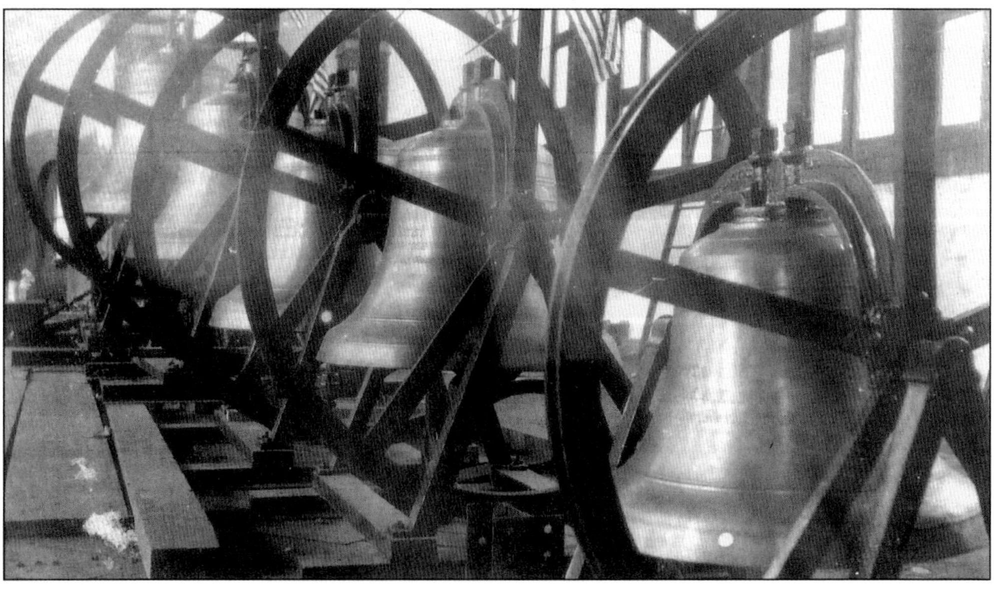

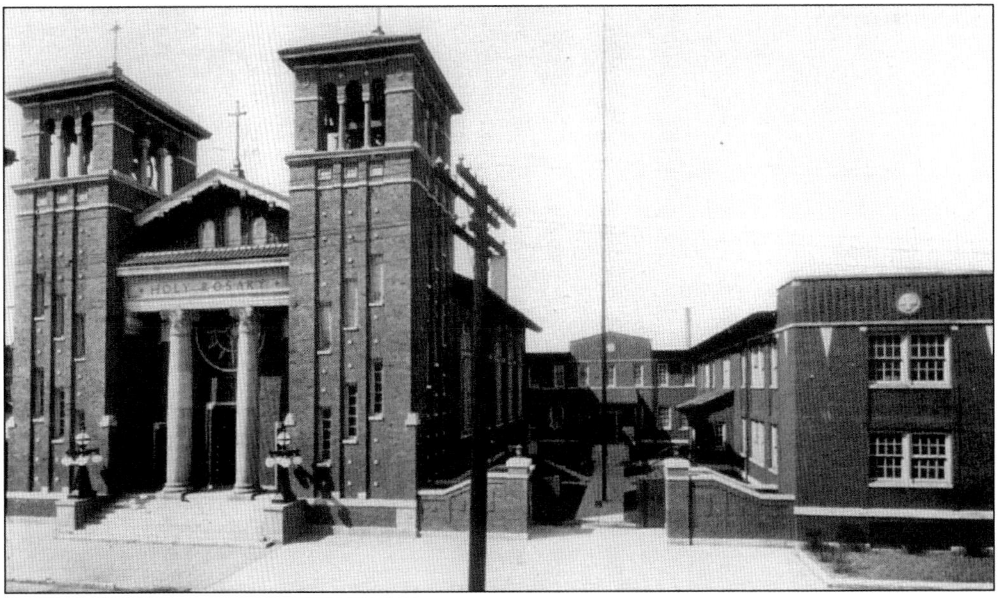

Holy Rosary Church, convent, and school were completed in 1925. Remembering the commitment behind the construction of the parish buildings, Msgr. Joseph D. Brokhage, Holy Rosary pastor 1956–1972, declared: "Father Priori and Holy Rosary saved the faith of the Italian people."

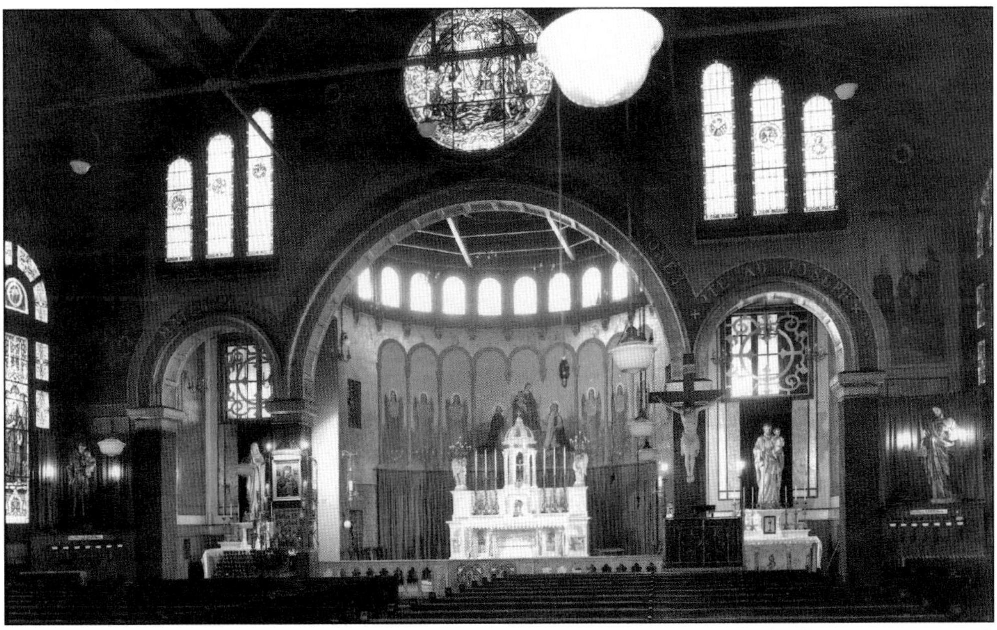

A native of Gallese, provincia di Viterbo (Lazio), where Father Priori had once ministered, Professor Marco Rigucci was a graduate of Rome's Academy of Fine Arts. When he departed Naples, he gave his friend Pietro Pacini, 610 Stevens Street, Indianapolis, as his destination. Father Priori invited him to decorate the recently-finished church interior. His major work was painting Our Lady of the Rosary on the wall of the apse above the altar. The original painting hangs in the chapel of an orphanage at Pompei outside Naples. The Madonna and child are flanked by St. Dominic and St. Catherine of Siena, two devotees of the Rosary. The side backgrounds are of Mount Vesuvius (left) and a country scene.

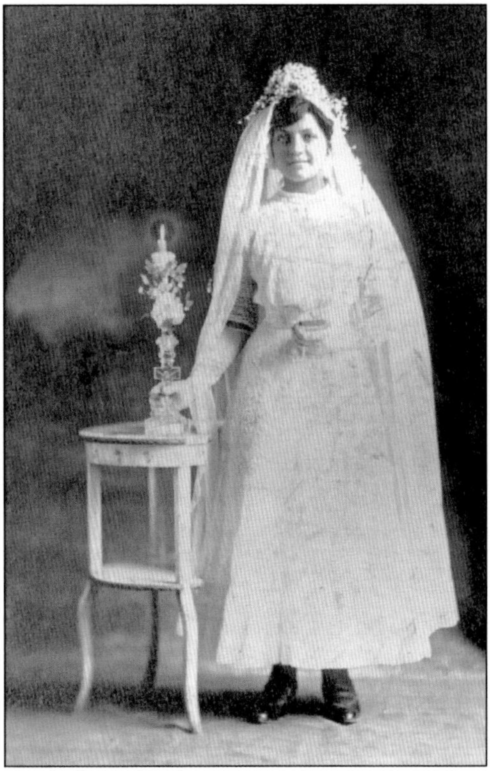

Rose Gatto holds a prayer book in her hand at solemn communion, always an important religious event in the life of a young person. (Courtesy Ninfa Gatto DeHilt.)

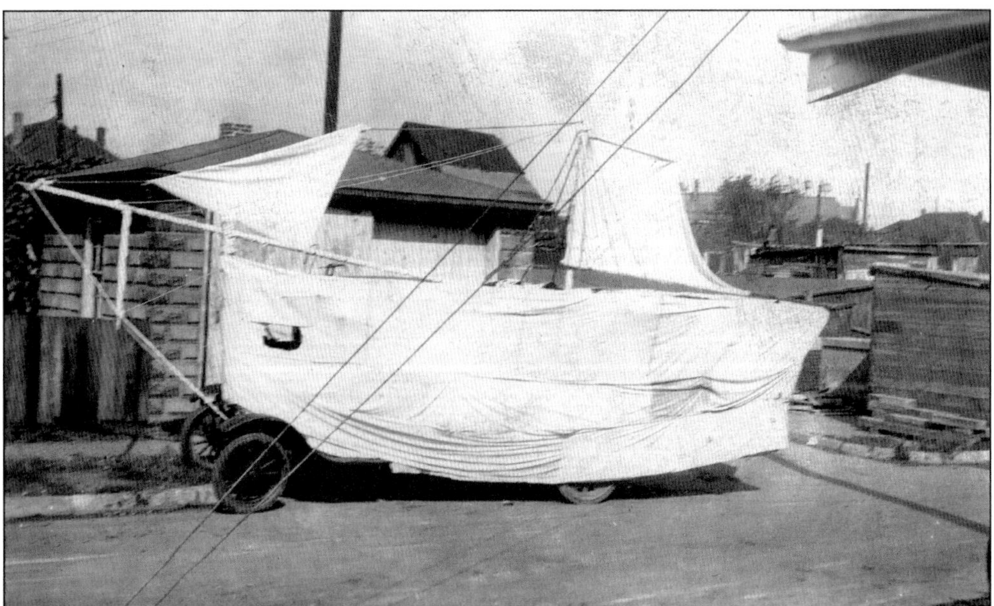

Holy Rosary pupils built a canvas *Santa Maria* float to mark Columbus Day in 1923. (Courtesy Freda Buennagel.)

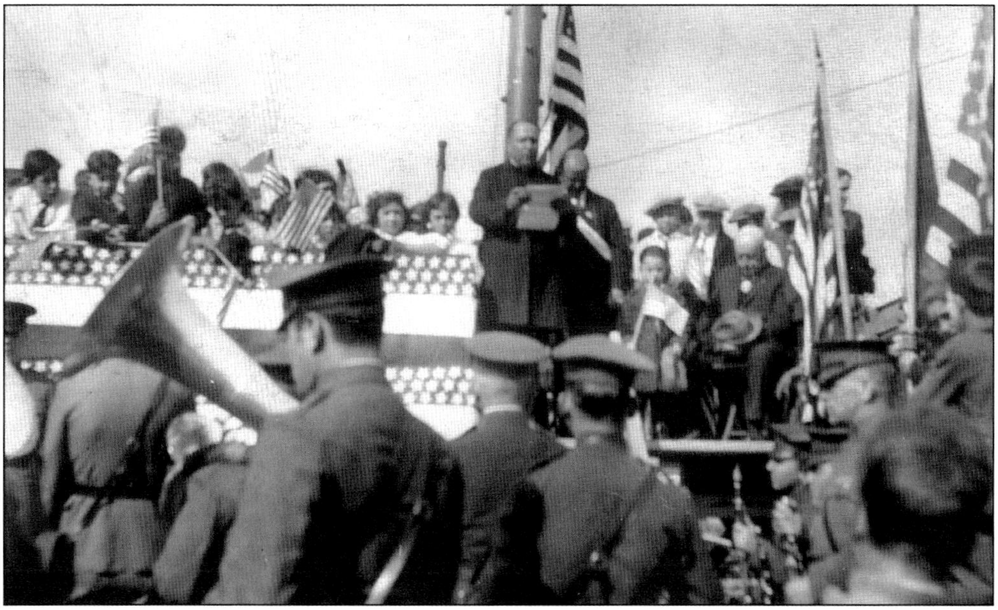

After World War I, patriotism created tension because of the rise of the anti-Catholic, anti-foreign Klan. A flagpole was erected in the courtyard (above) between the future Holy Rosary church and school as the focus of the Columbus Day celebration in 1923. Father Priori invited Mayor Lew Shank and Col. Russell B. Harrison to speak. Known to be anti-Klan, Shank would lose in the Republican primary election for governor in 1924. Harrison, son of Pres. Benjamin Harrison, was secretary of the nationalistic Marion County Defense Council during World War I. The high point of the celebration was the raising of the American flag (right). School kids attended, and a Fort Harrison band played. (Courtesy Freda Buennagel.)

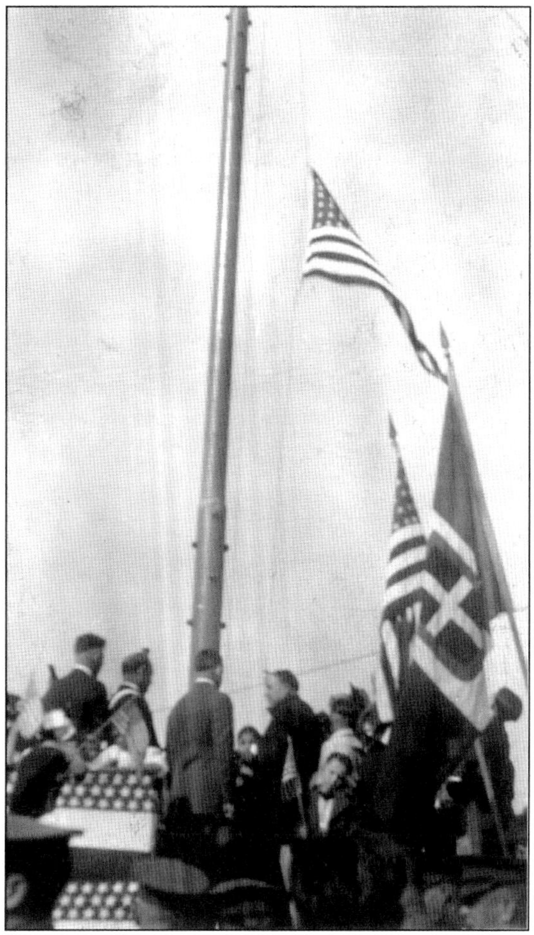

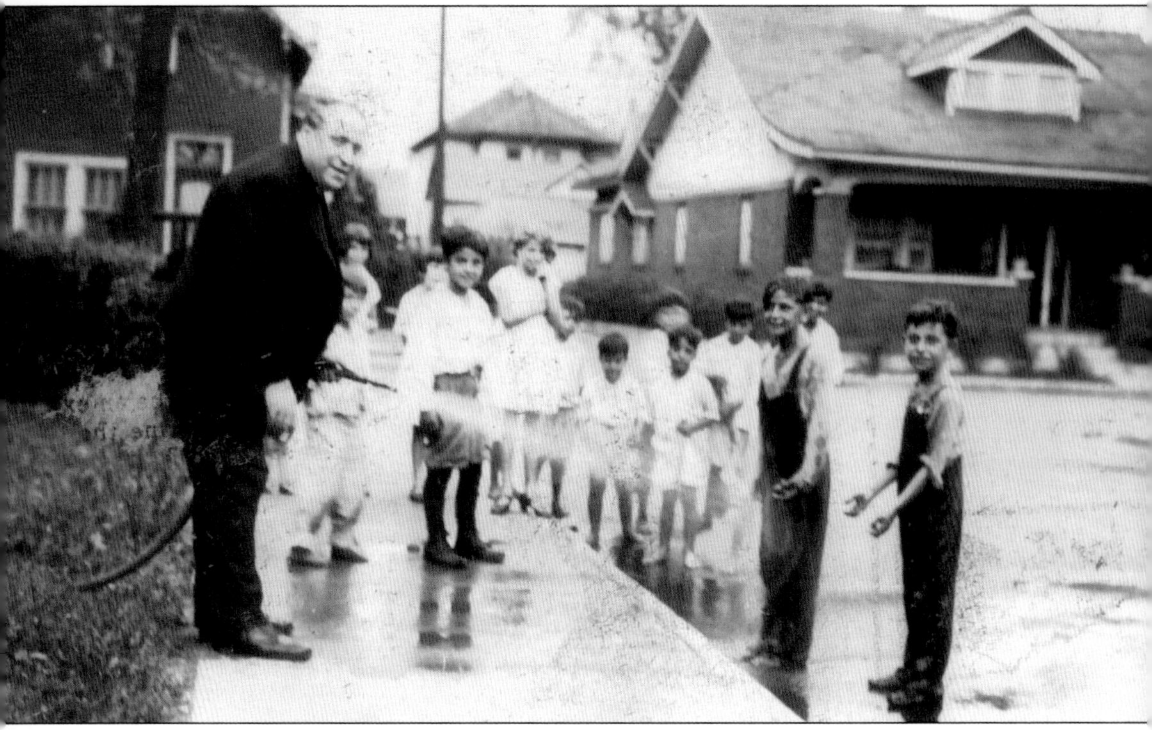

Father Priori takes a few minutes away from sprinkling the rectory lawn to water down the parish weeds who challenge him for a summer cool down. (Courtesy Freda Buennagel.)

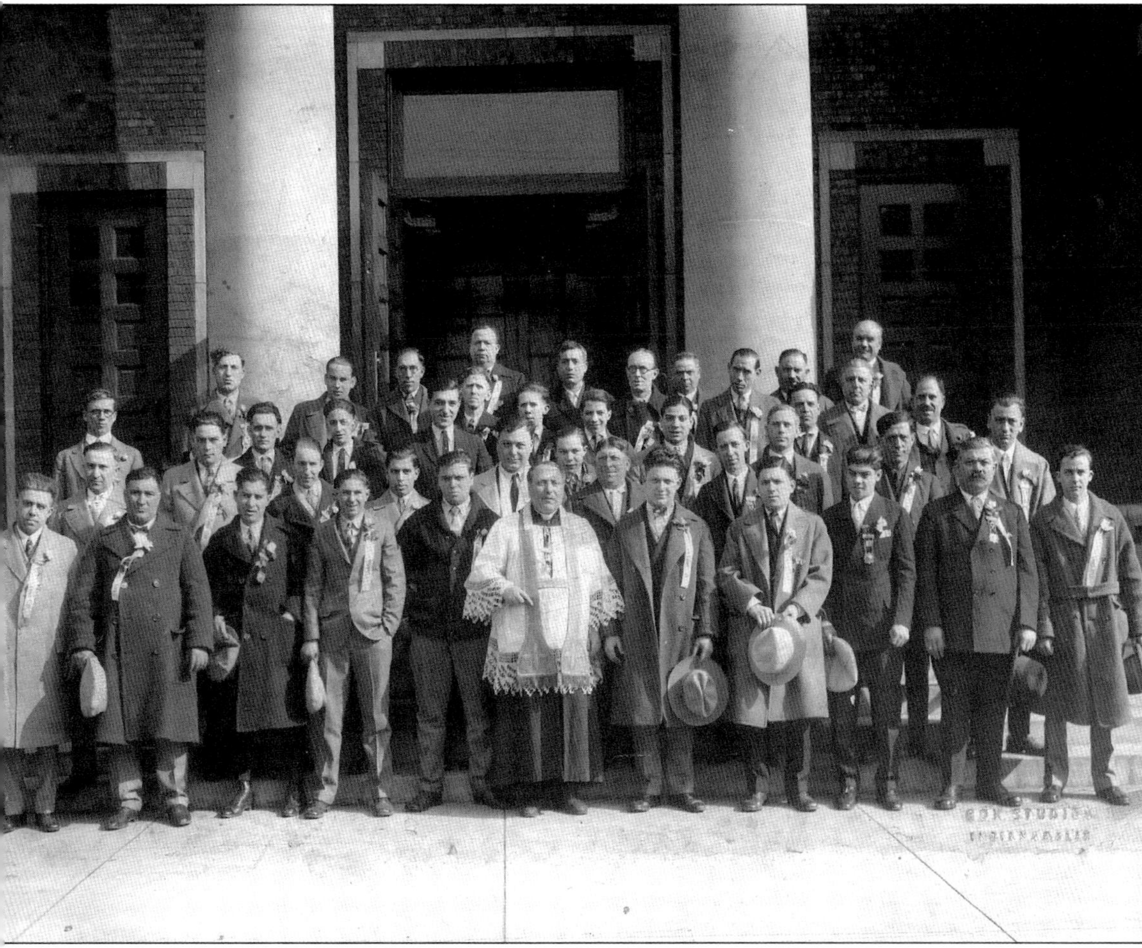

Holy Rosary men, members of Columbus Court 1715, Catholic Order of Foresters, stand on the steps of the church with their pastor, Father Priori, around 1929. (Courtesy Charles Farah.)

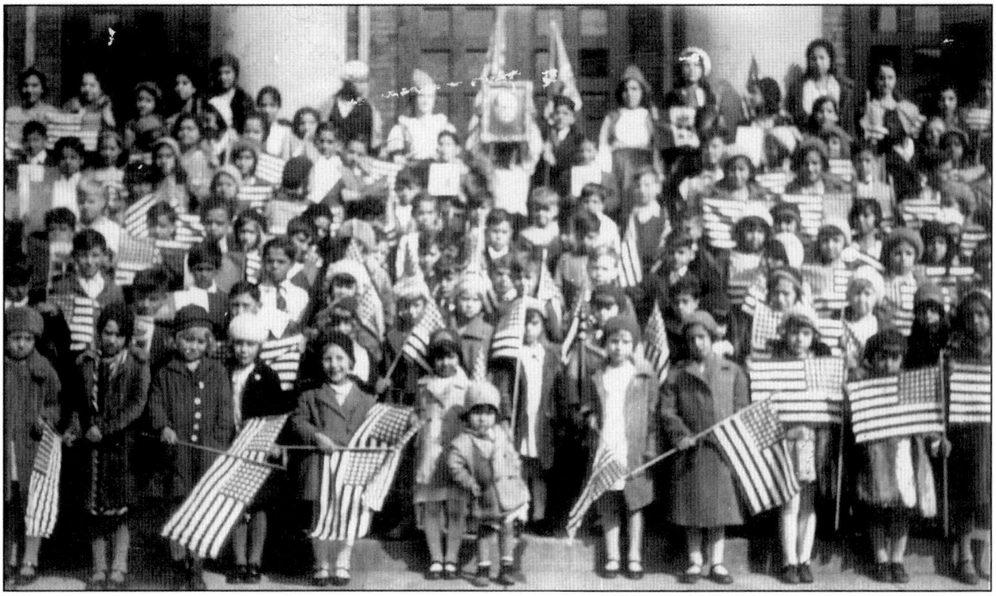

The Lateran Pacts of 1929, which solved the 60-year Roman Question between the papacy and Italy and established the Vatican as an independent country, made the Fascist dictator Benito Mussolini a hero among Italian Catholics in America. For Columbus Day, Holy Rosary schoolchildren gathered to wave American flags and show Mussolini's photograph (above). In the church courtyard (below), children pointed at the United States and Italy on a globe, waved both countries' flags, and displayed Mussolini's portrait. The priest at left is the newly ordained Fr. Augustine Sansone. Father Priori wrote, "The Roman Question would have been settled a long time ago if Italy would have had a premier like the great genius Mussolini."

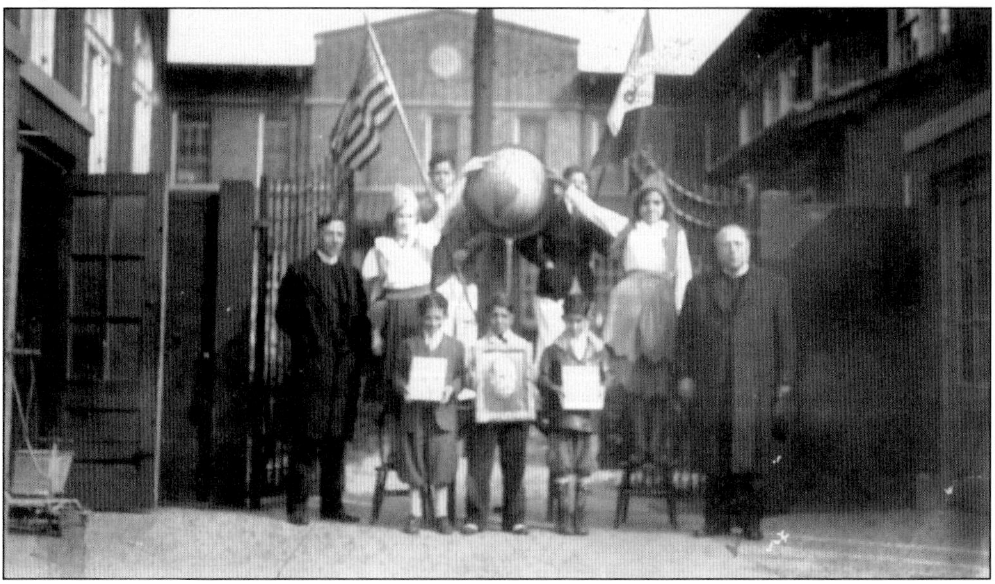

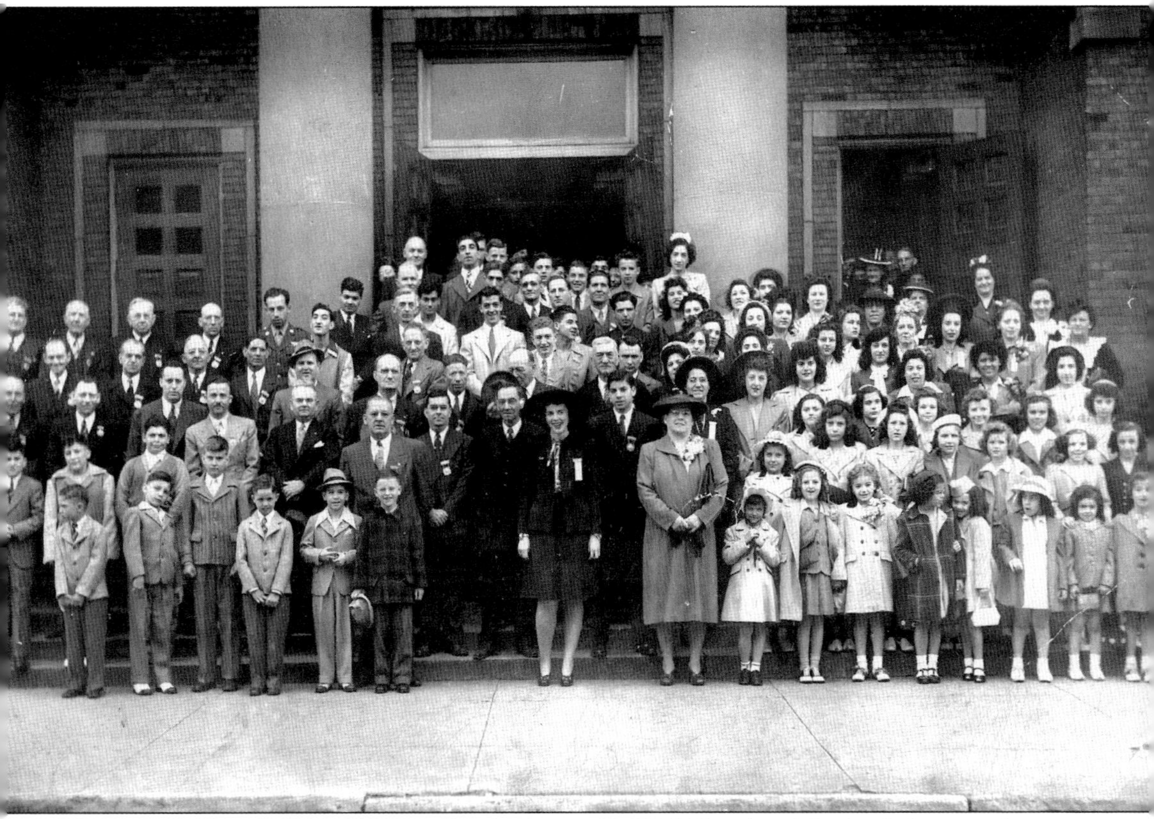

The Holy Rosary crowd attends Easter Sunday services in 1945. The church had an Italian-speaking priest available until the late 1970s. Whenever the pastor did not know the language, an Italian-speaking former student at the North American College in Rome was appointed assistant to the pastor. Thus, the Holy Rosary staff was composed of some of the brightest and most intelligent clergy available in the archdiocese. (Courtesy Joanna Milto-Bergin.)

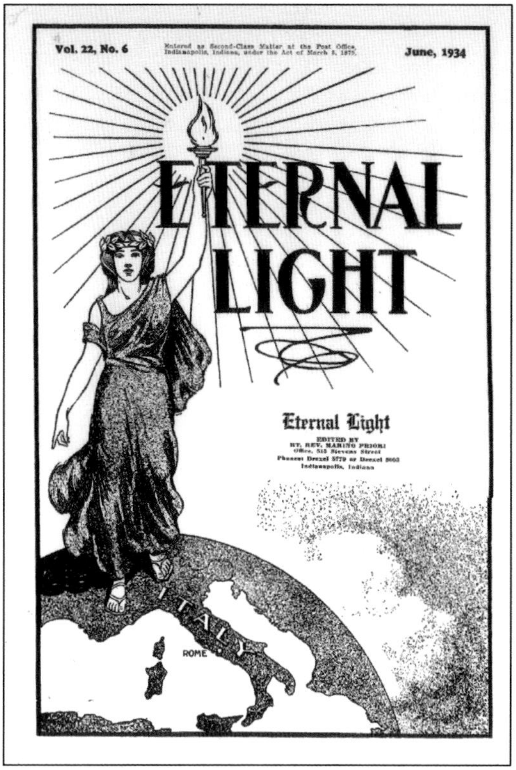

Although Holy Rosary was their national church, Italian immigrant families were anti-clerical and seldom monetarily generous. They were always willing to contribute time to some fund-raising activity, but the biggest financial supporters of the parish through its dinners, raffles, and feste were actually Americans (non-Italians). From 1913 to 1934, *Eternal Light* was published to supplement the income received from Sunday collections. Large photographs, spiritual articles, and pastor reflections filled its pages. Libraries and subscribers preserved the commemorative issues. Most subscribers were non-parishioner Americans.

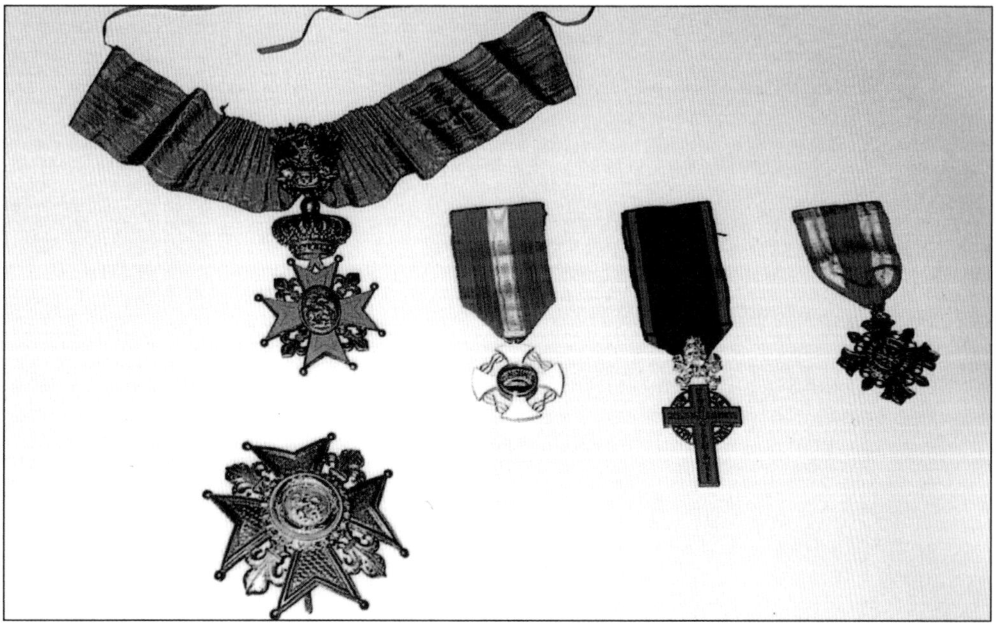

Monsignor Priori continued to be presented with honors even after he departed Holy Rosary. The awards he received were, from left to right, the blue ribbon, medal, and star, commander of the Order of St. George de Bourgogne (1934); knight of the Royal Crown of Italy, awarded by King Victor Emmanuel III (1932); and *Benemerenti* (1938) and *Pro Ecclesia et Pontifice* (1924), church honors awarded by Pope Pius XI.

Priori pets his two dogs in his rectory at Troy, his birds and paintings nearby. Priori returned to Italy annually to visit family and conduct diocesan business. He also brought back art objects and paintings, many of which were hung in parish buildings, especially the convent. When the Sisters of St. Francis took charge of the parish school in 1927, they felt they were moving into an art museum rather than a convent. (Courtesy Freda Buennagel.)

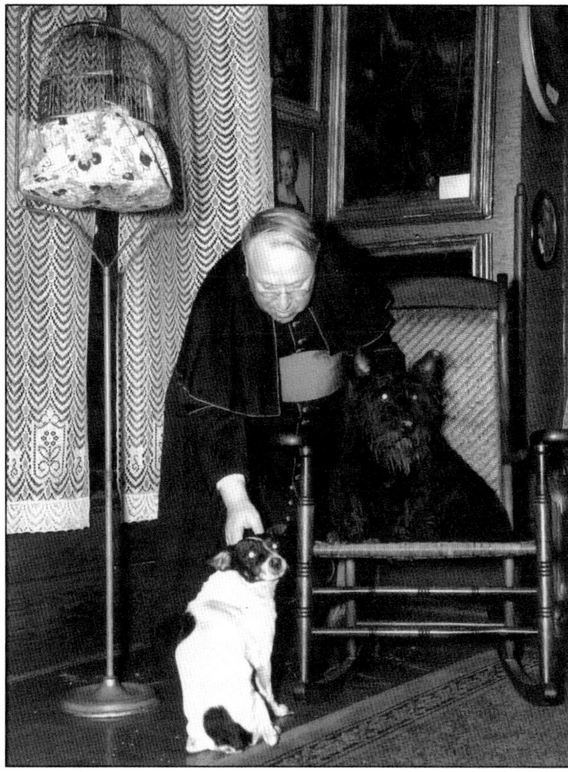

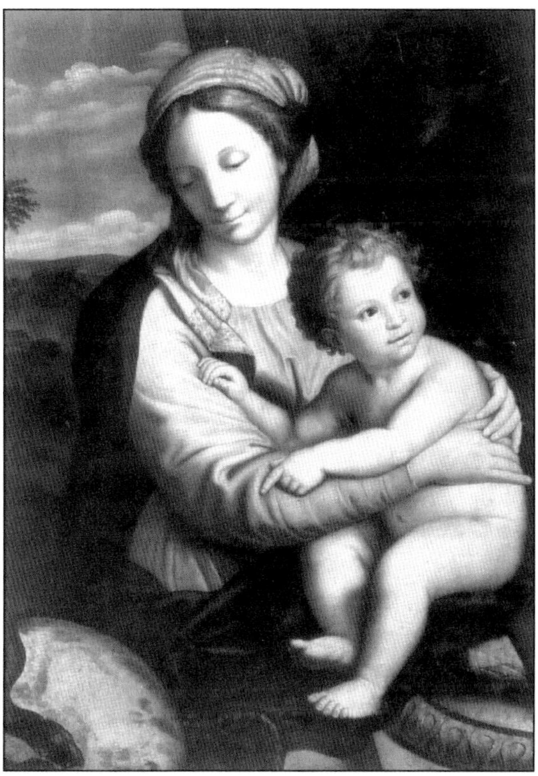

After the death of Monsignor Priori, his paintings passed to his housekeeper and Fr. Augustine Sansone, who donated them to Marian College. Although most pieces have now been sold, one of Priori's jewels was a Sassoferrato (1590–1645) canvas of 29 by 40 inches. It remained at Marian and presently hangs in the foyer of the college's Allison Mansion. (Courtesy Freda Buennagel.)

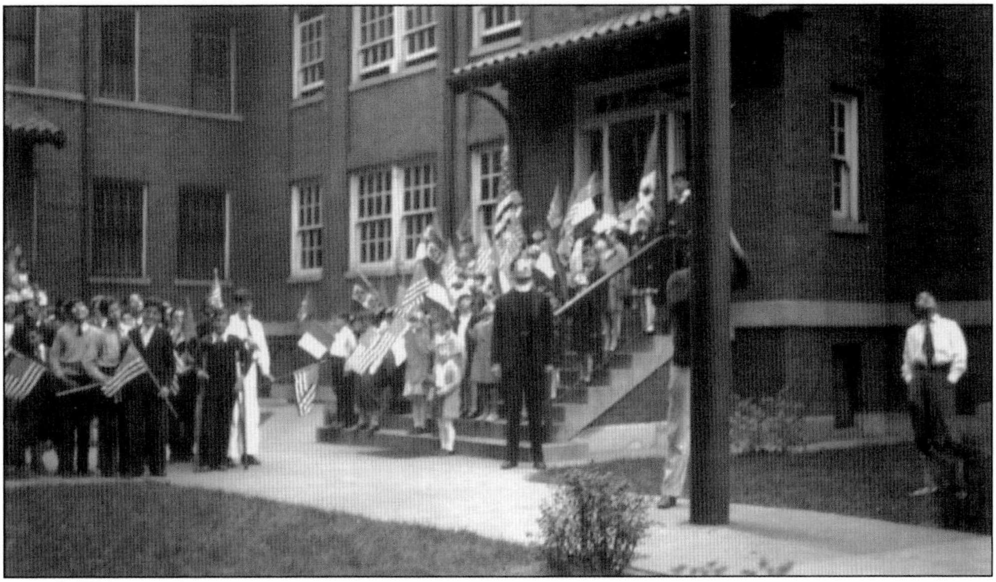

Fr. Augustine Sansone and the Holy Rosary children look skyward to observe the raising of the American flag. Father Gus was the first son of Holy Rosary parish to be ordained. Born at Indianapolis in 1904, he was named priest at Holy Rosary upon ordination in 1929. He served as fourth pastor of Holy Rosary, from 1951 to 1956, while the parish enjoyed a financial surplus, but its membership soon began to decline because of the change in generations. Father Gus also was assigned to churches in Osgood and Terre Haute, retired in 1970, and died in 1991.

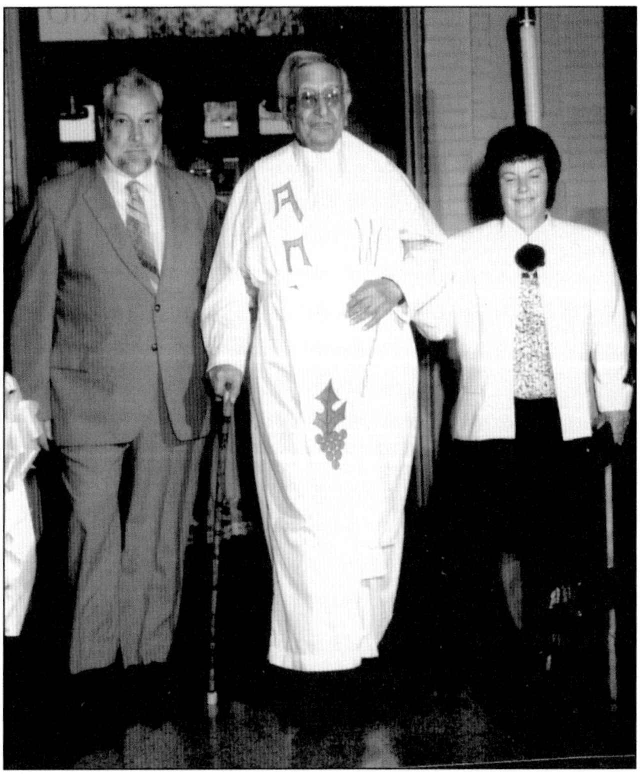

Father Gus enters Holy Rosary Church to mark his 60th anniversary of ordination in 1989. He is accompanied by his nephew Gus Stinnett and Gus's wife, Ruth. (Courtesy Gus Stinnett.)

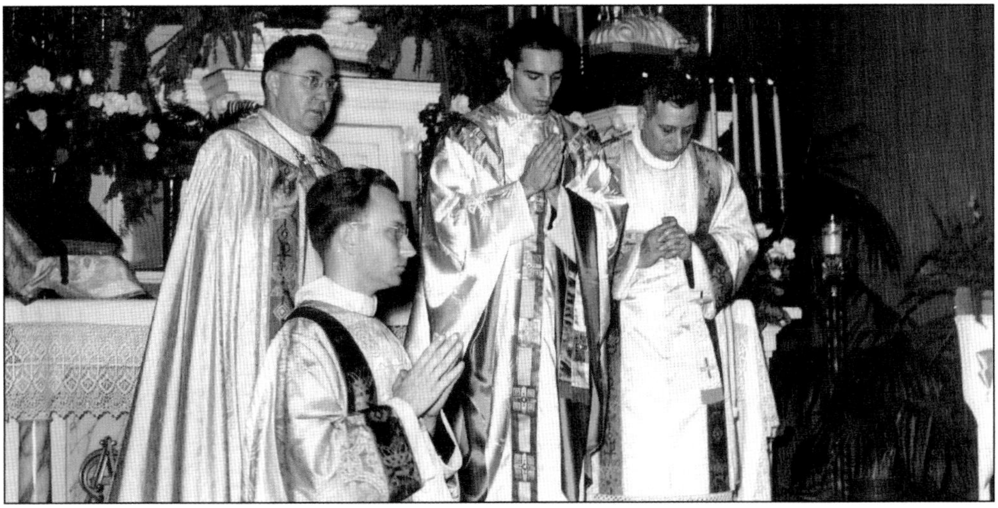

Fr. Anthony Spicuzza, a native of Indianapolis, celebrated his first mass in Holy Rosary Church in 1946. Pictured here, from left to right, are Fr. William Knapp, third pastor of Holy Rosary; Fr. Joseph Brokhage, assistant priest and later fifth Holy Rosary pastor; Father Spicuzza; and Father Gus. Father Tony was a longtime pastor of Annunciation Parish in Brazil, Indiana (1961–2001). His ordination is an occasion to salute the Benedict brothers. Msgr. James F. Benedict and Msgr. Michael J. Benedict both celebrated their first masses at Holy Rosary (1939 and 1943, respectively) and ministered in Louisiana. Their siblings were Sr. Angela Benedict, OSF, and Tom Benedict, whose barbershop provided a social center for Holy Rosary Parish. (Courtesy Rosemary Page.)

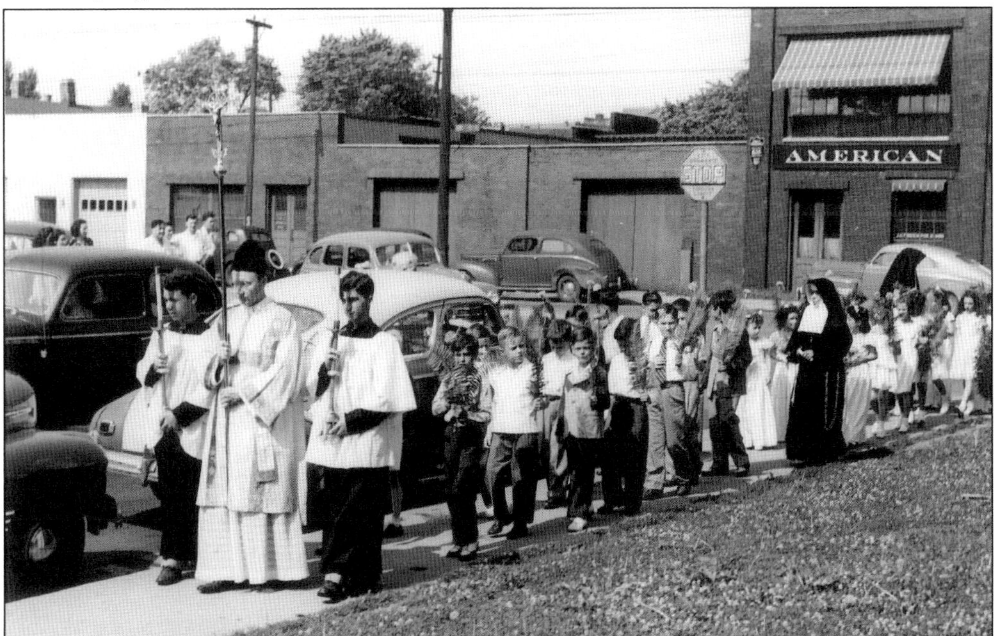

The Palm Sunday children's procession rounds the corner of Stevens and South East Streets. Note the buildings on the west side of the street, now occupied by Eli Lilly and Company. Fr. Joseph Brokhage carried the cross to lead the procession, and two Franciscan sisters from Oldenburg, Indiana, ordered the children. (Courtesy Matthew and Sandy Iaria.)

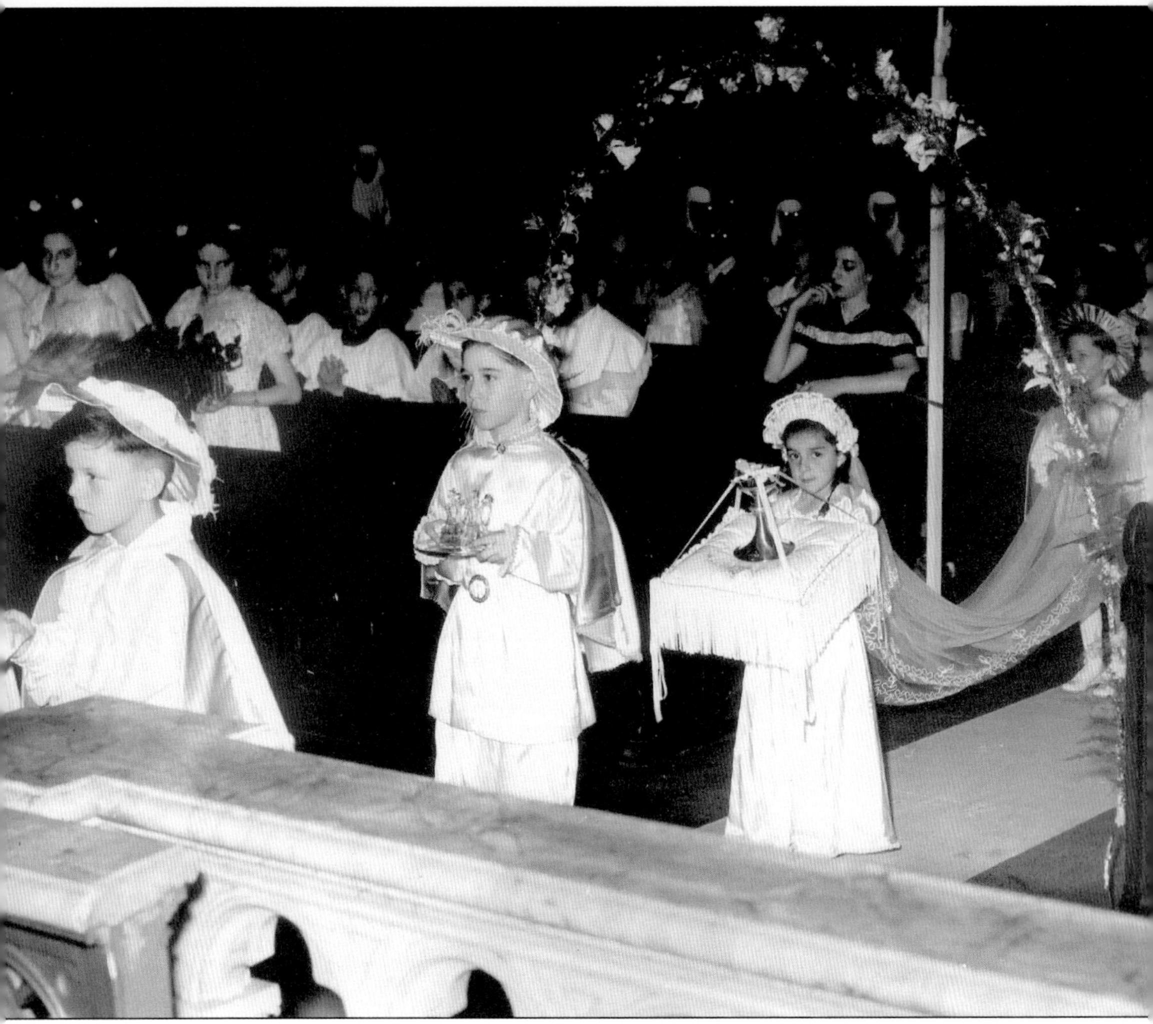

The children who participated in the procession during the first mass of Fr. Anthony Spicuzza at Holy Rosary were, from left to right, Pete Piazza, Charles Quattrocchi, and Rosemary Spicuzza (Father Tony's sister), followed by Paul Page and Pete Iaria. (Courtesy Rosemary Page.)

Holy Rosary graduates are joined by their pastor and sister in 1949. (Courtesy Margaret LaGrotto.)

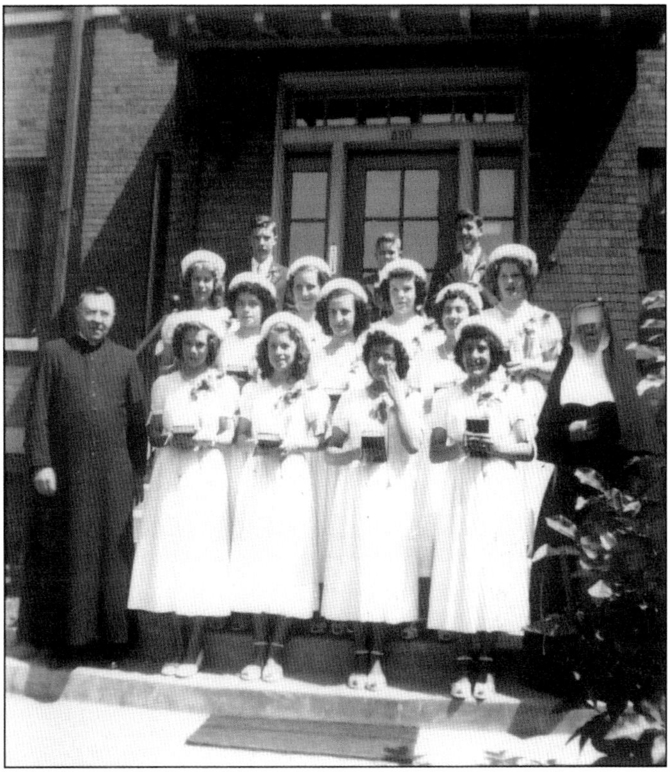

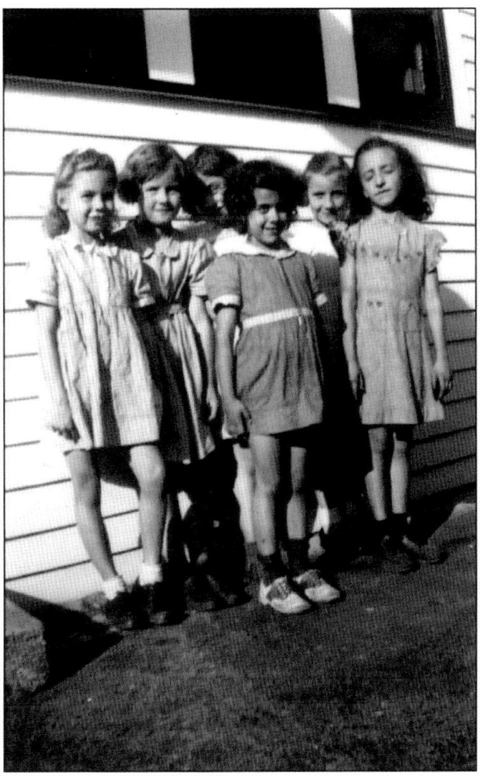

The camera caught these little girls in the neighborhood. Shown from left to right are Dixie Hoyt, Coleen Byrne, unidentified, Mary Catherine Ardizzone, Jo Anne Murello, and Anne Marie Spicuzza. (Courtesy Margaret LaGrotto.)

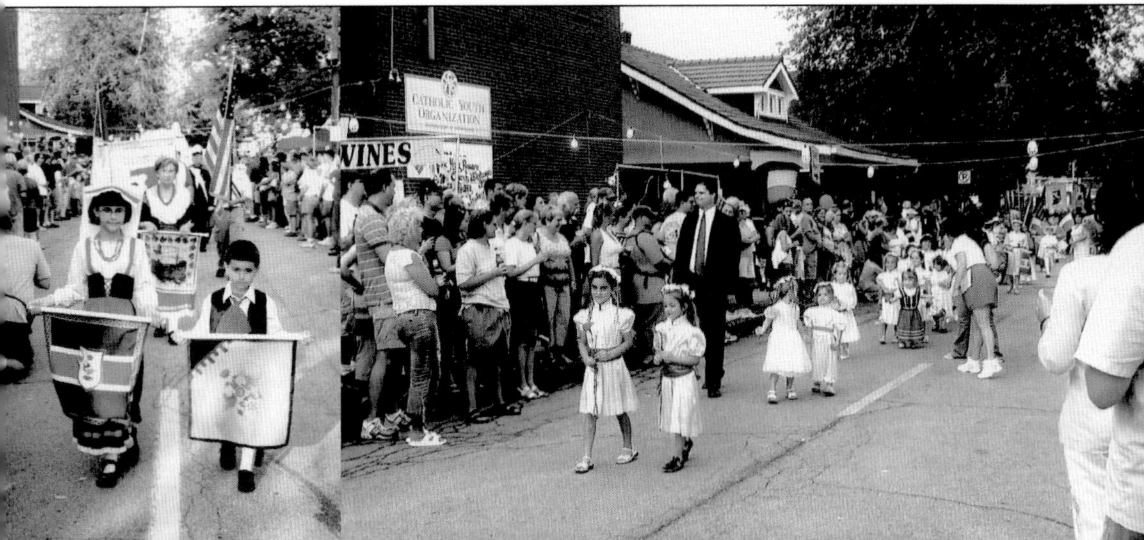

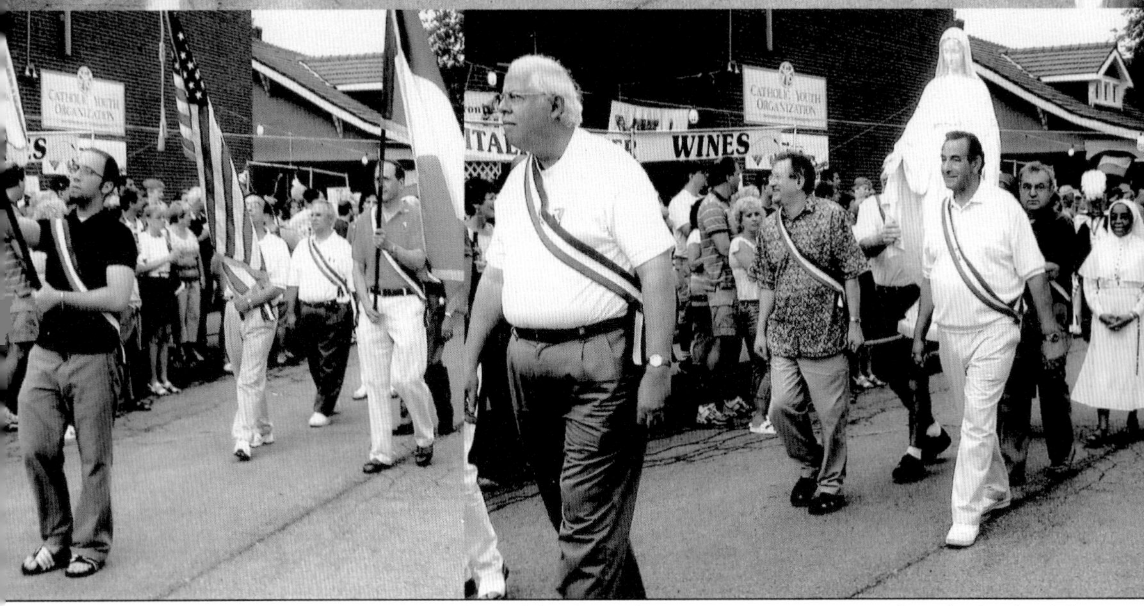

When the frame residence was purchased for the Italian mission, it was moved to the back of the lot to make room for a lawn fete. Within a few years, the fund-raising festivities spilled out onto Stevens Street. By the 1930s it became the largest parish carnival held in the city; thereafter bingo and raffles became major sources of parish income. In the mid-1980s, the Italian Street Festival was revived and featured a religious procession. Small children in native dress (upper), Italian Heritage members, and Fourth Degree, Knights of Columbus (lower) accompany the statue of the Virgin Mary. Food stands feature Italian sausage, caponata, meatballs, cannoli, fried ravioli, pizza, antipasto salad, fettucine, and various wines. This festa is the largest summer ethnic event in the city.

Seven

Monuments
Material Culture

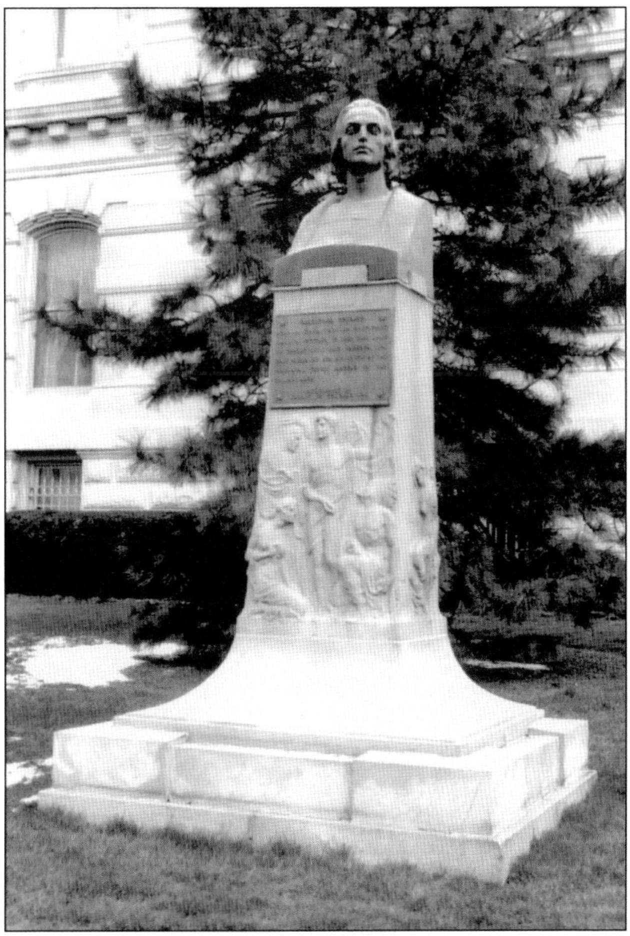

The Columbus bust, dedicated in 1920, continues to remind passersby of the great Italian discoverer. The Knights of Columbus laid a wreath here in 1955, and then returned with the Italian Heritage Society on October 12, 1992, to rededicate the monument on the quincentenary.

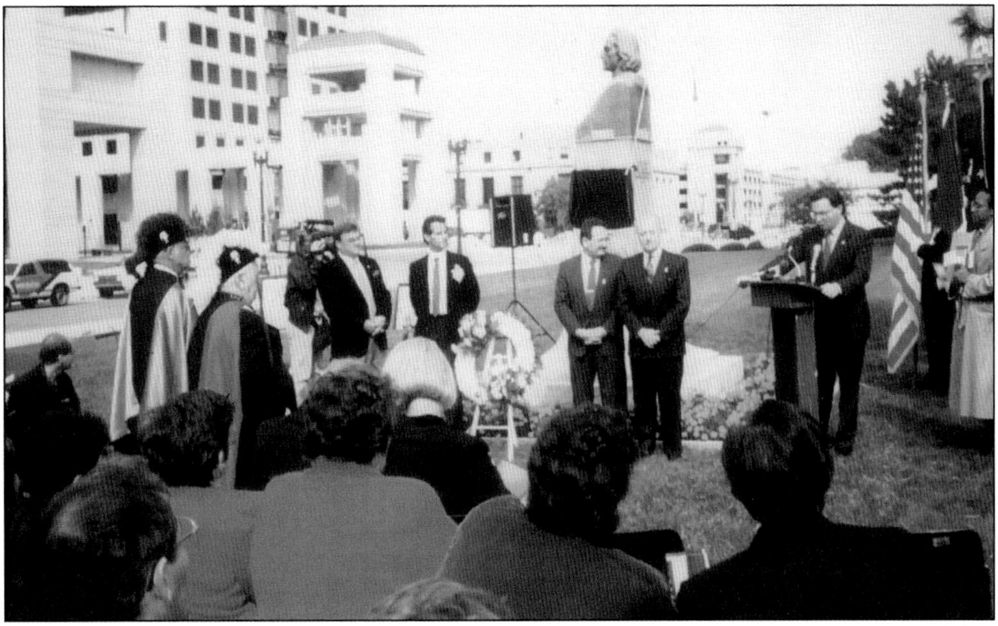

Marking the quincentenary of Columbus's discovery of 1492, Susan Bayh represented her husband, Gov. Evan Bayh. Facing the audience, from left to right, are former councilman David Page; scholarship chairman Matthew Iaria; Michael Agostino, M.D., representing the honorary Italian vice-consul; Columbus Commission '92 president Pietro Ferri; councilman Frank Short at podium; and deputy mayor Nancy Silvers.

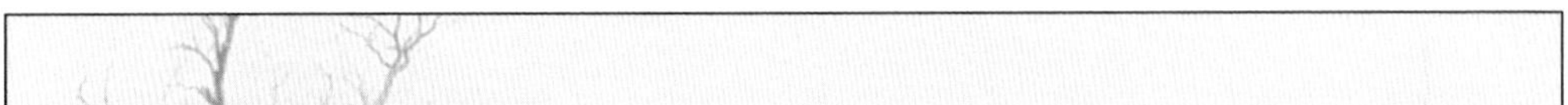

During World War II, about 3,000 Italian prisoners of war were captured in North Africa and transported to Camp Atterbury, 30 miles south of Indianapolis. Their permanent mark on the camp was a carved rock at the entrance and a chapel dedicated to the Madonna, which was built and decorated from surplus materials. The apostolic delegate, Archbishop Amleto Cicognani, dedicated the chapel on October 17, 1943. When the Italians left, German POWs replaced them.

All prison buildings but the chapel were dismantled after the war. The chapel interior deteriorated rapidly, and the building fell into disrepair over the next 20 years. Public schoolchildren and interested local people sought to publicize the chapel's condition with the hope that renovations could take place. Finally, the Indiana National Guard began repairs, and the camp commandant's wife redecorated the chapel.

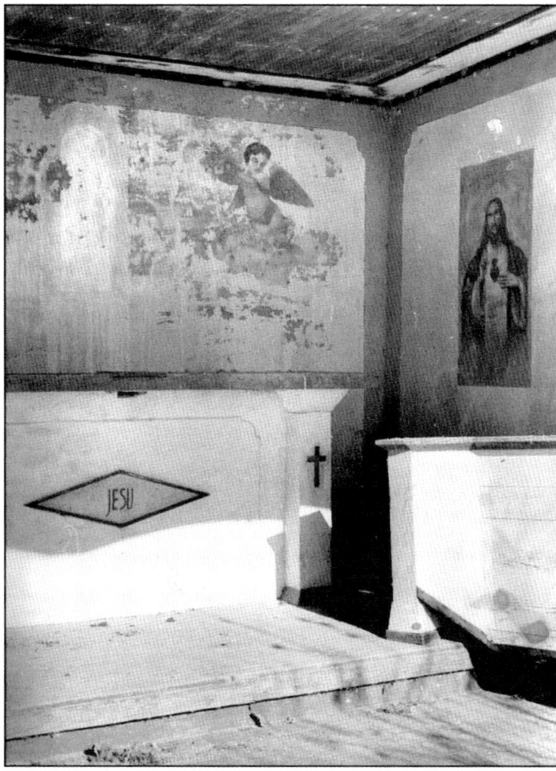

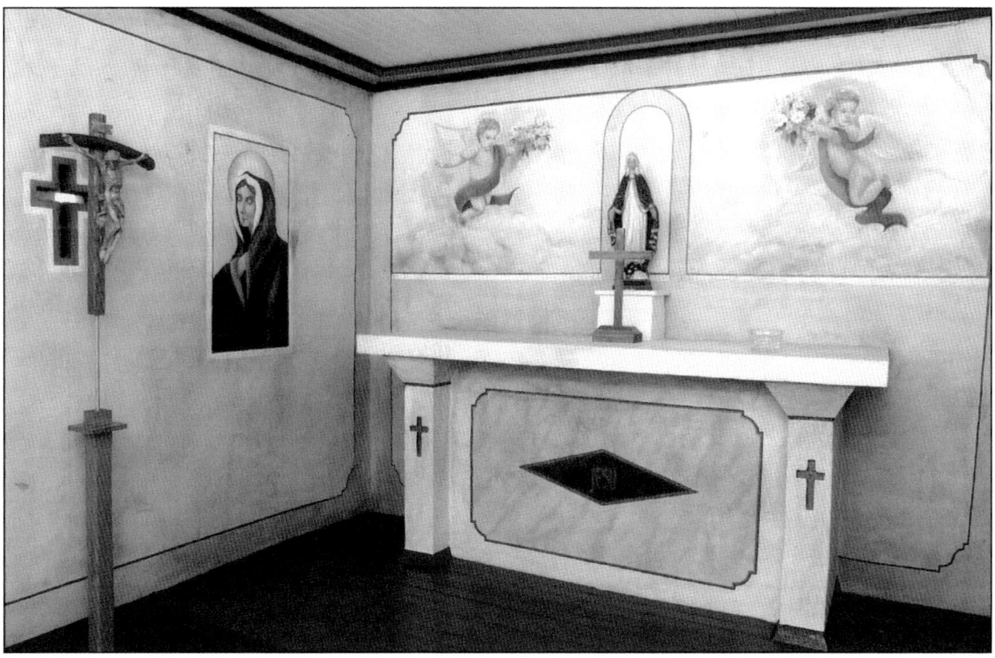

Since 1989, the Italian Heritage Society, in conjunction with the National Guard, sponsors an annual POW reunion, mass, and picnic in late summer at the chapel. About 300 attend each year, including former POW Libero Puccini of suburban Cleveland and his family, and Teresa Tedesco of Jeffersonville, Indiana, the widow of a POW, and many of her seven sons.

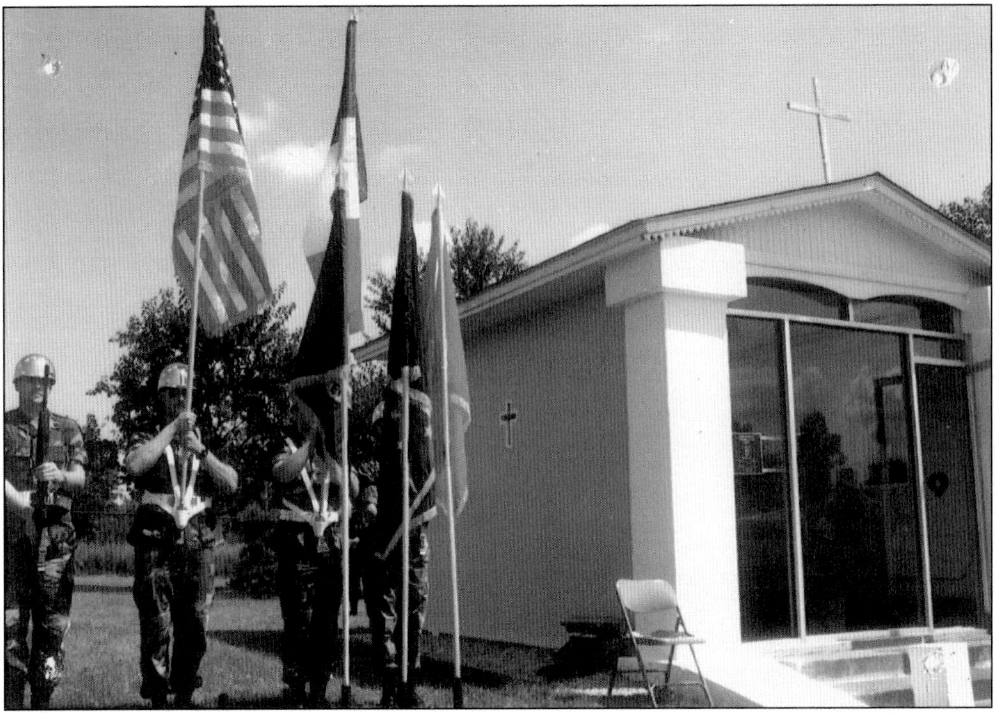

The Indiana National Guard honor guard posts colors at the Italian POW Chapel to open the annual reunion, Mass, and picnic.

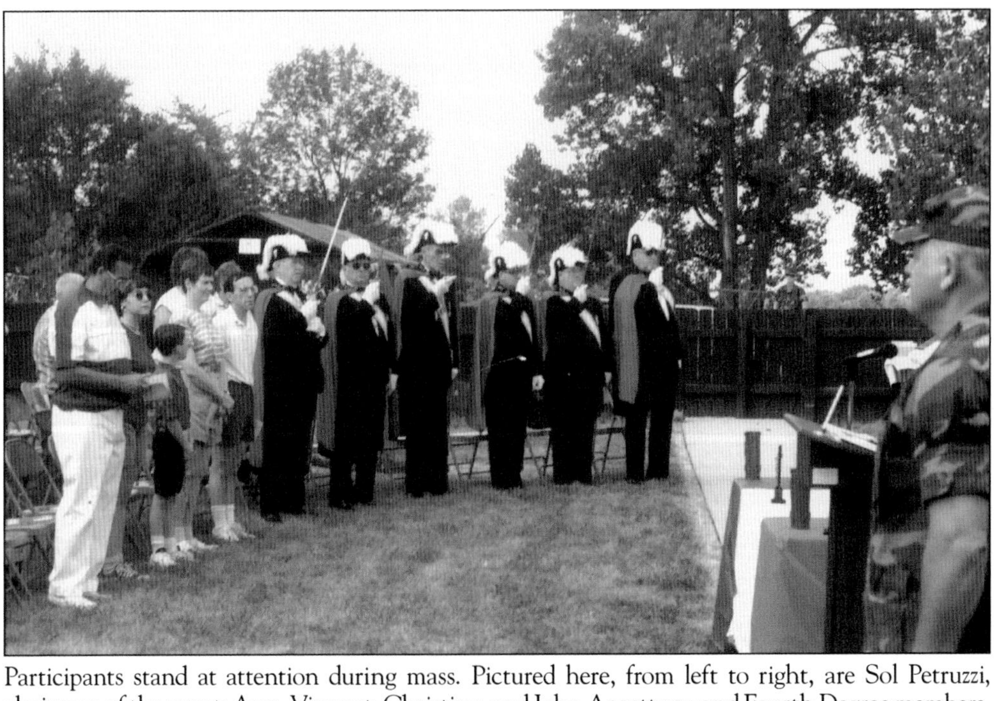

Participants stand at attention during mass. Pictured here, from left to right, are Sol Petruzzi, chairman of the event; Ann, Vincent, Christine, and John Accetturo; and Fourth Degree members, Knights of Columbus. On the right is Sgt. Maj. Pete Iaria of the Indiana National Guard.

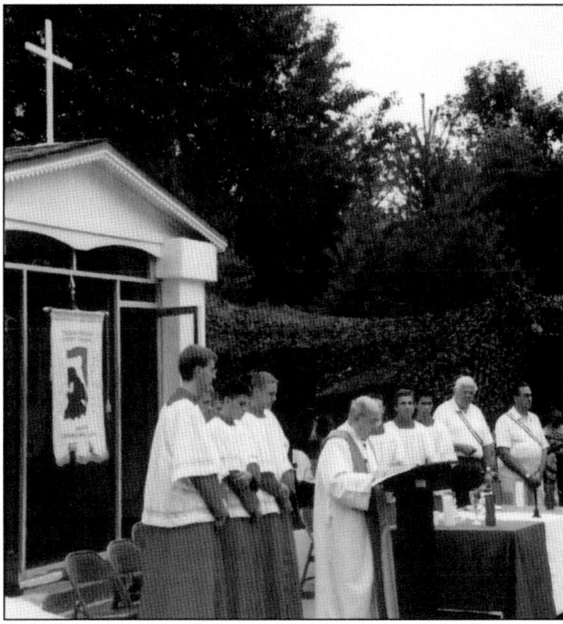

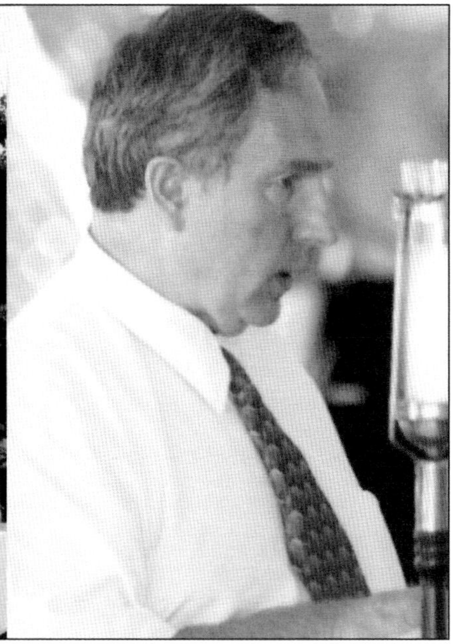

At left, Fr. John Sciarra, founding pastor of St. Barnabas Parish on Indianapolis's south side, reads the Gospel at the POW mass. Father Sciarra was born in Seymour, Indiana, the son of an immigrant from Chiáuci, provincia di Isernia (Molise). His father was traveling from Cincinnati to St. Louis in 1908. Since he did not want to eat lunch on a moving train, he got off in Seymour to eat, liked the looks of the town, and settled there. At right, Paul Burns, Italian Heritage board member, presents scriptural readings at mass.

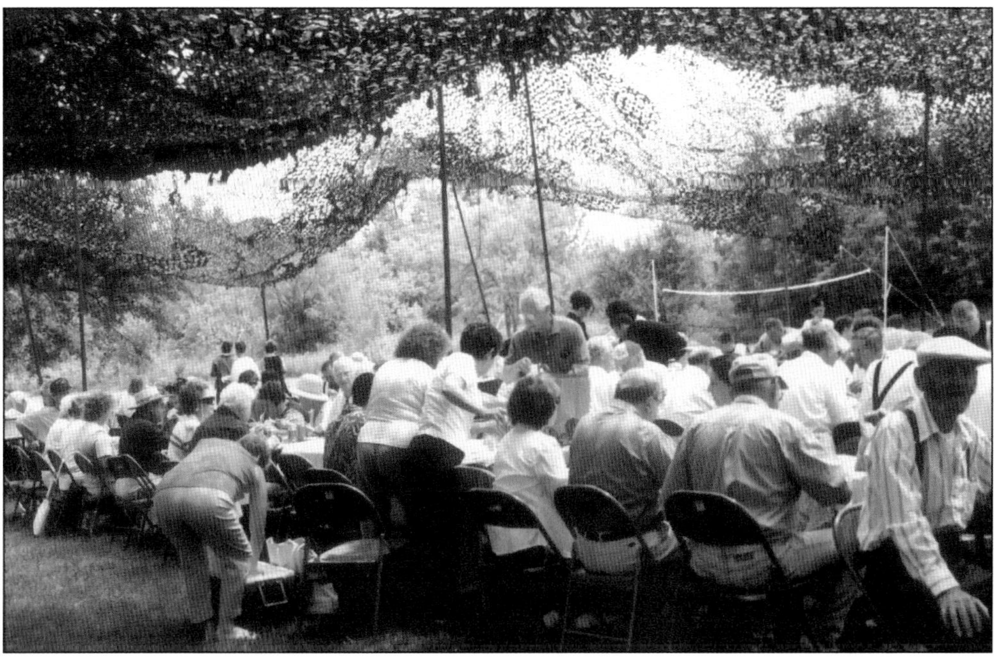

The event concludes with *mangiare*. Although a pitch-in dinner, both locally owned and chain restaurants respond enthusiastically. Generally around 31 eateries donate lasagna, fried chicken, pizza, Italian sausage in tomato sauce, antipasto trays, bruschetta, and more.

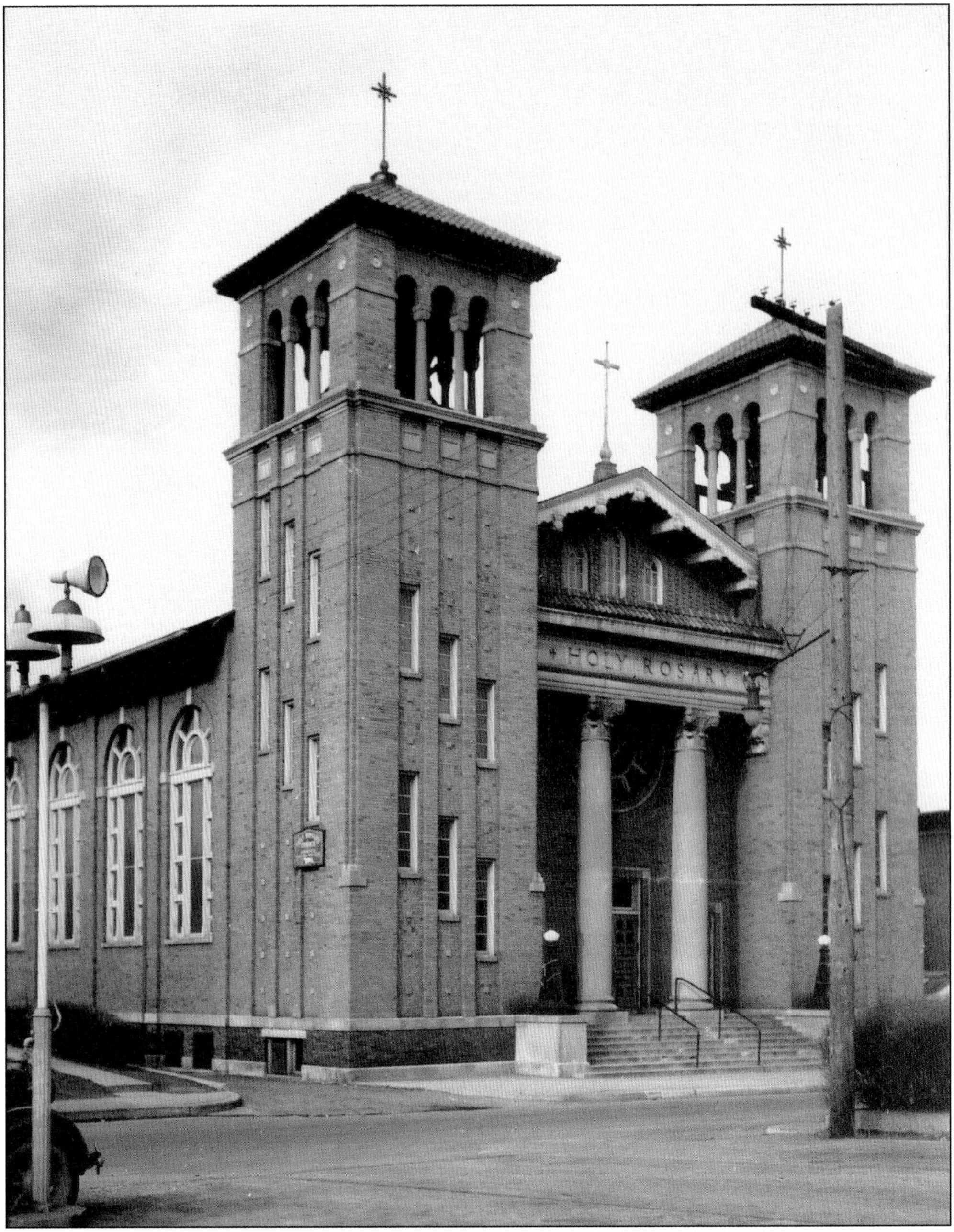

Perhaps the most imposing contribution by Italians to the Indianapolis landscape, Holy Rosary Church was designed by architects J. Edwin Kopf and Kenneth K. Woolling after the church of San Giorgio on Via Velabro in Rome. Father Priori was an acquaintance of San Giorgio's titular pastor, Cardinal Luigi Sincero, in the 1920s.

Eight

ORGANIZATIONS
PRESERVING HERITAGE

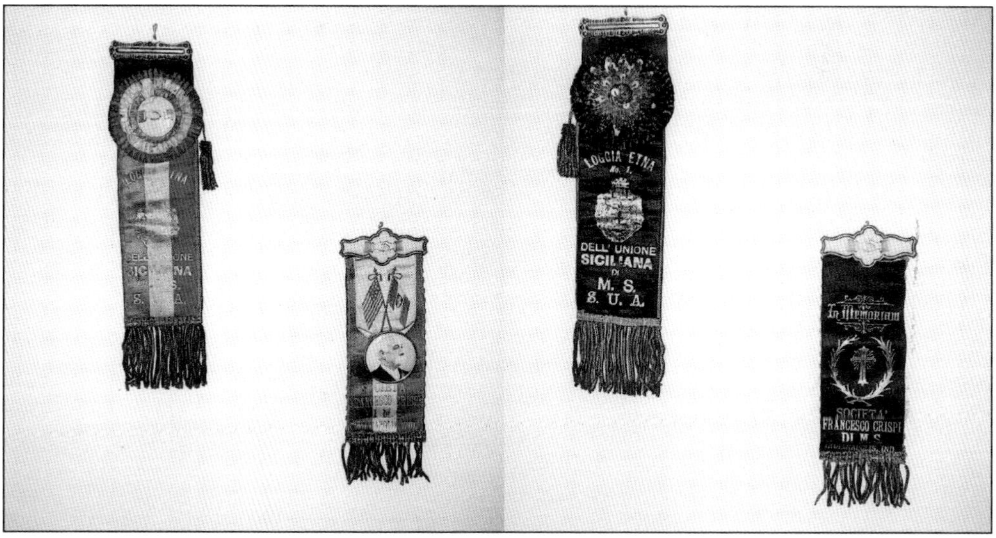

Mutual aid societies were important before Social Security and unemployment compensation. Immigrants joined together to provide assistance in case of death and sickness. Society members wore sashes, medals, or ribbons to exhibit pride in membership. The first Italian fraternal association in Indianapolis was Umberto Primo Mutual Aid Society, founded in 1891. Named for the second king of united Italy, Humbert I (1878–1901), it had 70 members in 1908. It became Sons of Italy Lodge No. 1040, when Sicilian members seceded to form their own Francesco Crispi Society in 1920. The ribbon second from left is inscribed "Società Francesco Crispi di M.S. Indianapolis, Ind." (Francesco Crispi Mutual Aid Society). In the Italian national colors (green, white, red), the ribbon is headed by a fraternal handshake and the crossed flags of the United States and Royal Italy. In the center is an image of Crispi, Sicilian politician and Italian prime minister. The reverse side of the Crispi ribbon, at far right, is black with silver print, bearing the Latin inscription "In Memoriam" with a cross and the society name; this side faced out at members' funerals. The reversible ribbon of Loggia Etna No. 1 of the Unione Siciliana is pictured at far left and second from right. This controversial mutual aid society was founded in Chicago in 1895 to aid Sicilian immigrants. (Courtesy Rosemary Page and Matthew Iaria.)

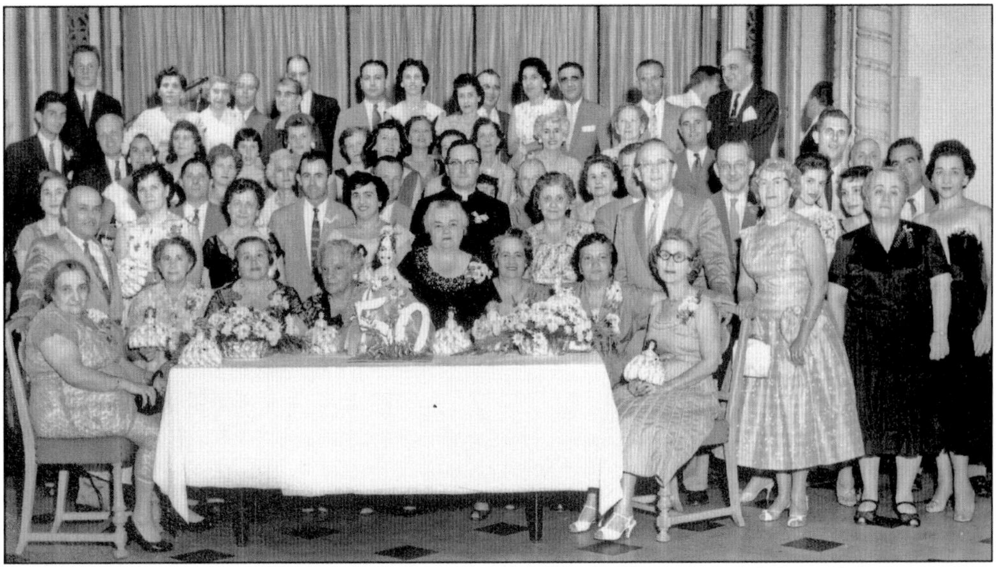

The Regina Margherita Society for women, founded in 1908, was one of the Italian immigrant societies. Queen Margherita was the popular wife of King Humbert I. Members sponsored a dance to mark their 50th year, in 1958. In the center is Fr. Raymond Bosler, archdiocesan newspaper editor. Ann DeHilt, sitting with a purse on her lap at the right end of the table, contributed this photograph to the Indiana Historical Society.

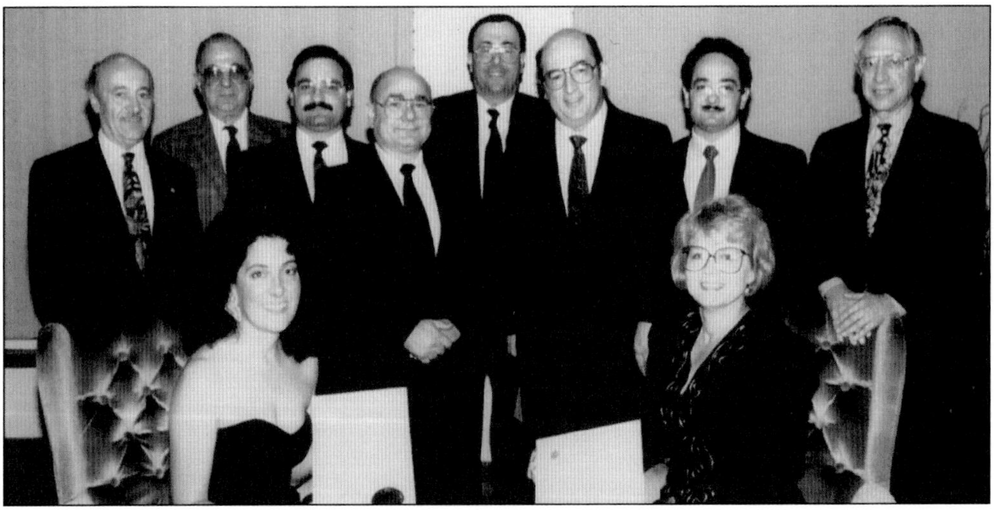

Replacing defunct immigrant societies, Dr. Thomas Cortese Sr. founded the Italian-American Club in the late 1950s. Presidents included Gino P. Sgro, George F. De Fabis, and Joseph F. Macri. The group purchased a clubhouse at 3850 South Meridian Street and sponsored an annual Columbus Day dinner, and various sports and social events. After it and a new Sons of Italy disbanded, Pietro Ferri called the first meeting of the Columbus Commission '92 in April 1989, to plan events marking the 500th anniversary of Christopher Columbus's transatlantic voyages. Discussing various governmental proclamations honoring the Columbus quincentenary were, from left to right: (first row) attorney Judy Cannavo and Linda Sereno of the Mayor's office; (second row) Columbus Commission president Pietro Ferri, unidentified, attorney Peter J. Agostino, honorary Italian consul Pietro Agostino, Pres. Daniel Felicetti of Marian College, dermatologist Thomas Cortese Jr., surgeon Michael Agostino, and attorney Paul Jerry Roland.

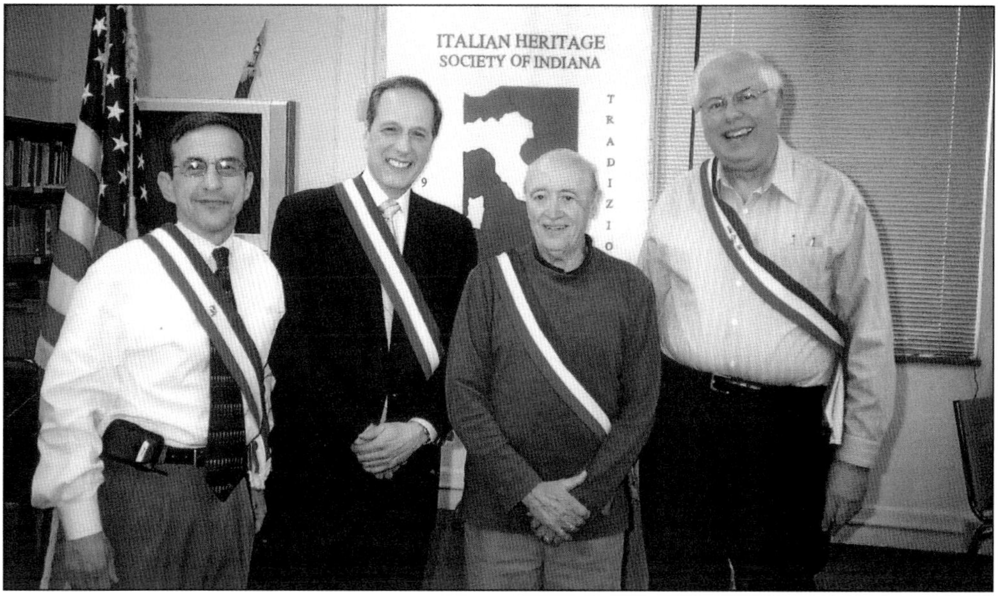

The Italian Heritage Society of Indiana was founded in 1993 as a successor to the Columbus Commission '92, which completed its work with the passing of the celebration year. Pietro Ferri served as both Columbus Commission president and second Italian Heritage president. Shown here, from left to right, are John Accetturo, fourth president; Ralph Tambasco, third and fifth president; Ferri; and James J. Divita, current president. The first president, Michael Agostino, M.D., now lives in South Bend, Indiana.

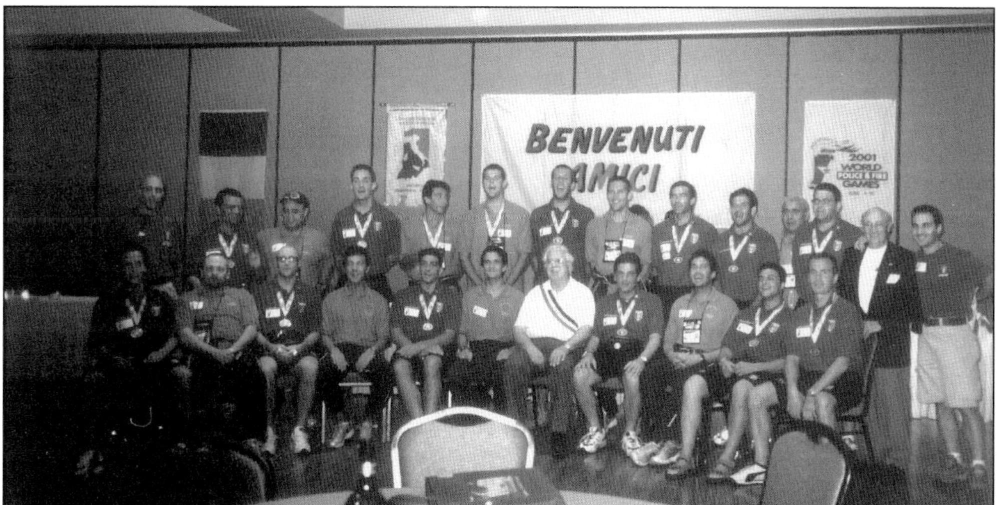

Italian Heritage sponsors a variety of events: for the sporty, golf and bocce tournaments; for the social, the Christmas party, Carnevale, and Columbus Day dinner dance; for the culturally minded, video discussions and the International Festival; for the religious, Italian mass and mass at the Italian POW Chapel. The club hosted a dinner for the Italian team participating in the 2001 World Police and Fire Games, with policemen and firefighters from Ferrara and Padua. It also hosted a pilgrimage group accompanying the torch of St. Benedict, patron of Europe, when it passed through Indianapolis. The group stopped in New York and Rome on its return to Norcia (Nursia), provincia di Perugia (Umbria), Benedict's birthplace.

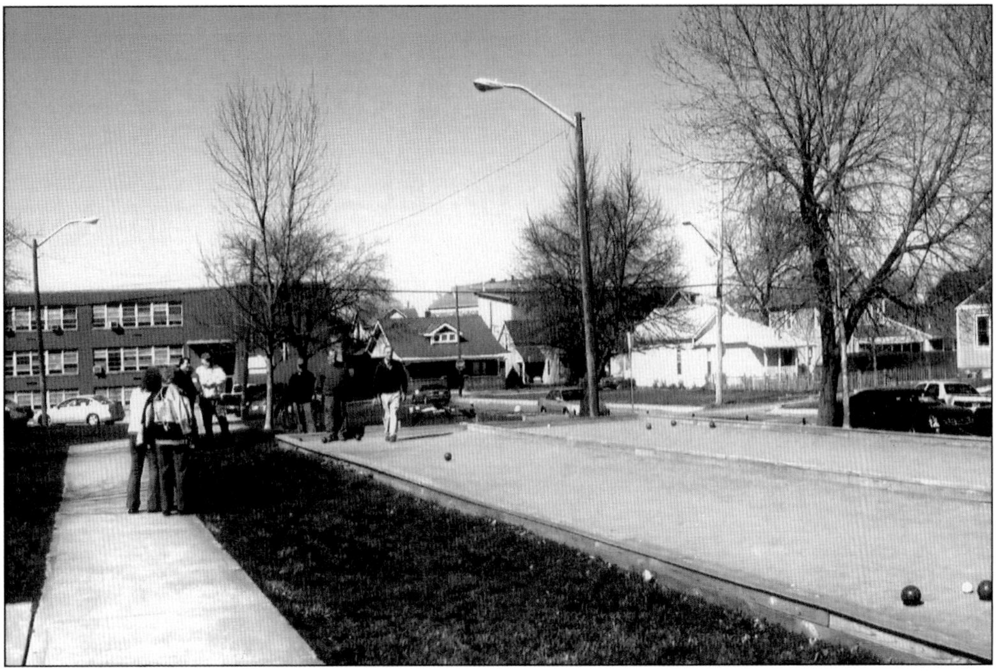

Bocce is such a popular game that these courts across from Holy Rosary Church will soon be expanded.

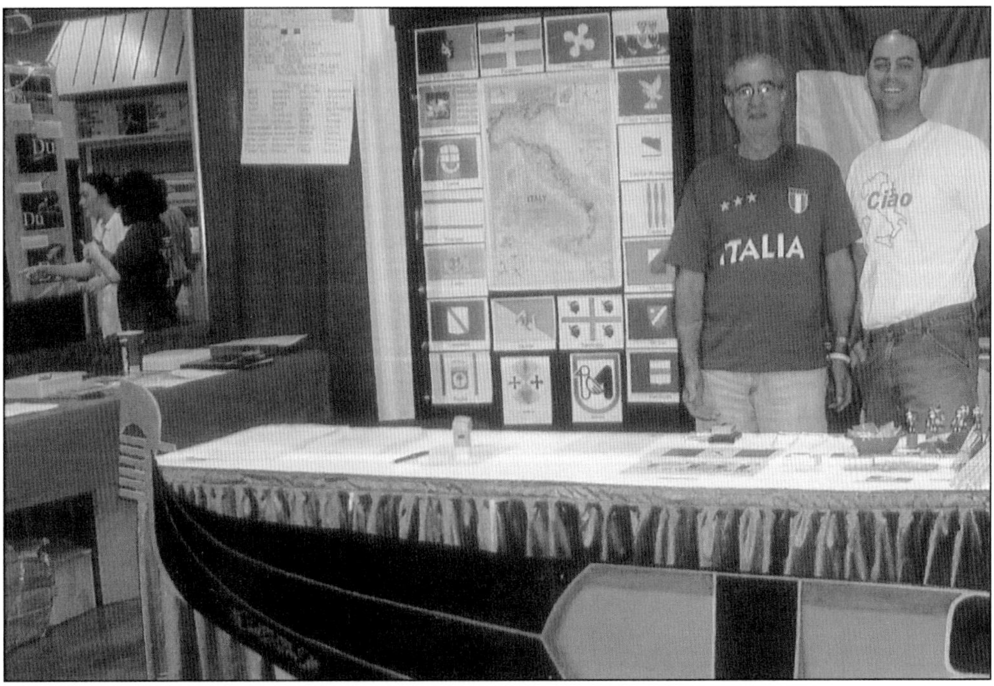

Italian speakers man a booth at the annual International Festival, begun to exhibit the city's cultural diversity. Here, Angelo Piga (left), creator of the Venetian gondola model (foreground), and Eric McElroy proudly survey the Italy booth with all its informational material.

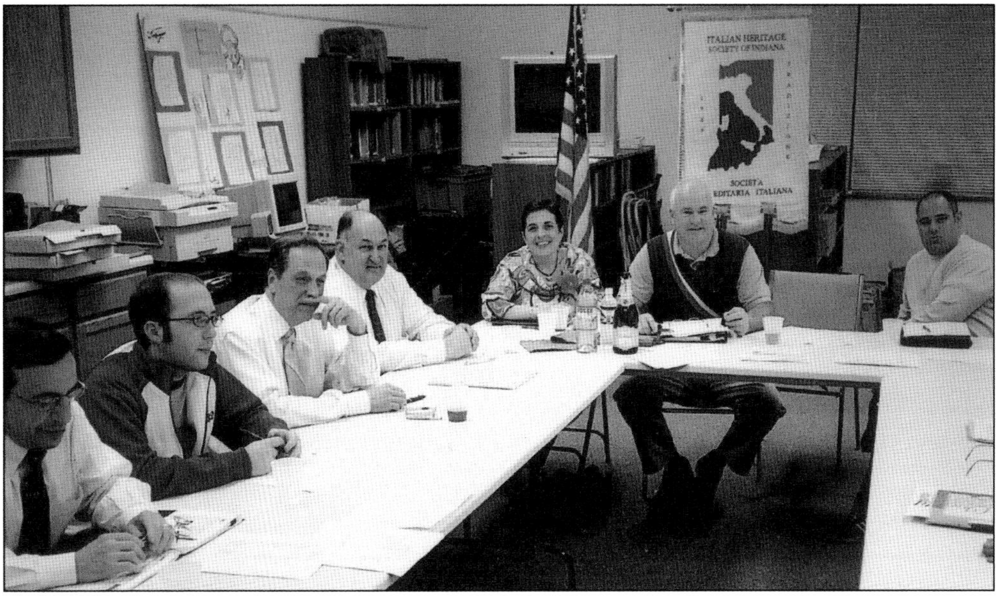

The Italian Heritage Society Board socializes before meeting in May 2006. Pictured from left to right are John Accetturo, Vincent Accetturo, Ralph Tambasco, Anthony Campo, Mary Grace Pennella, Joe Giacoletti, and Gino Sgro.

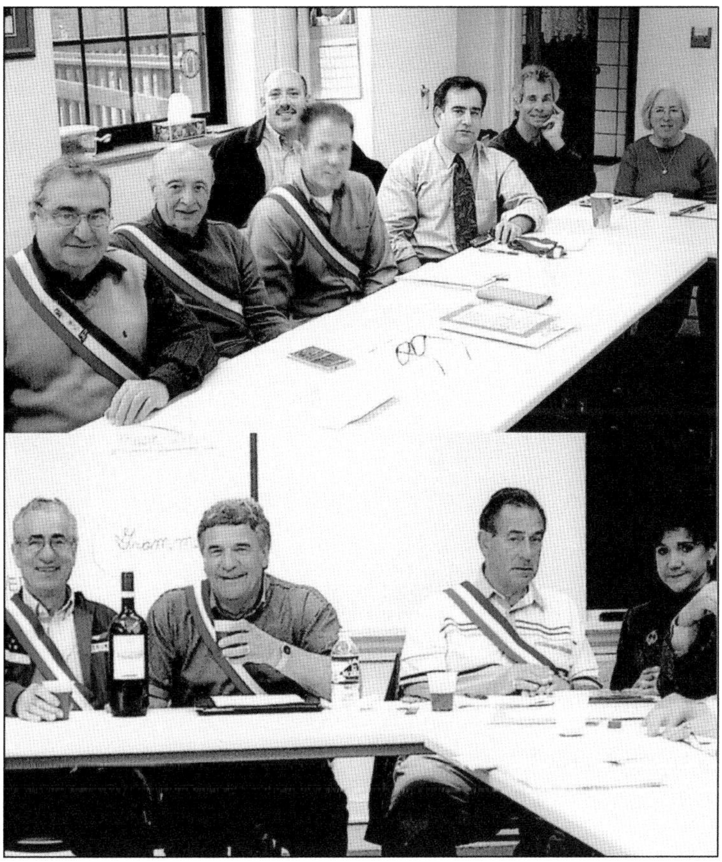

The top photograph is a sampling of old and new Italian Heritage members. Seen here, from left to right, are Nino Morone, Pietro Ferri, Thomas Cortese III, Tom Burke, Joseph Caito, Matthew Iaria, and newsletter editor Rina Piga. In the bottom photograph, emptying half-full wine bottles are, from left to right, Angelo Piga, Henry Cole, Sol Petruzzi, and Joanna Milto-Bergin.

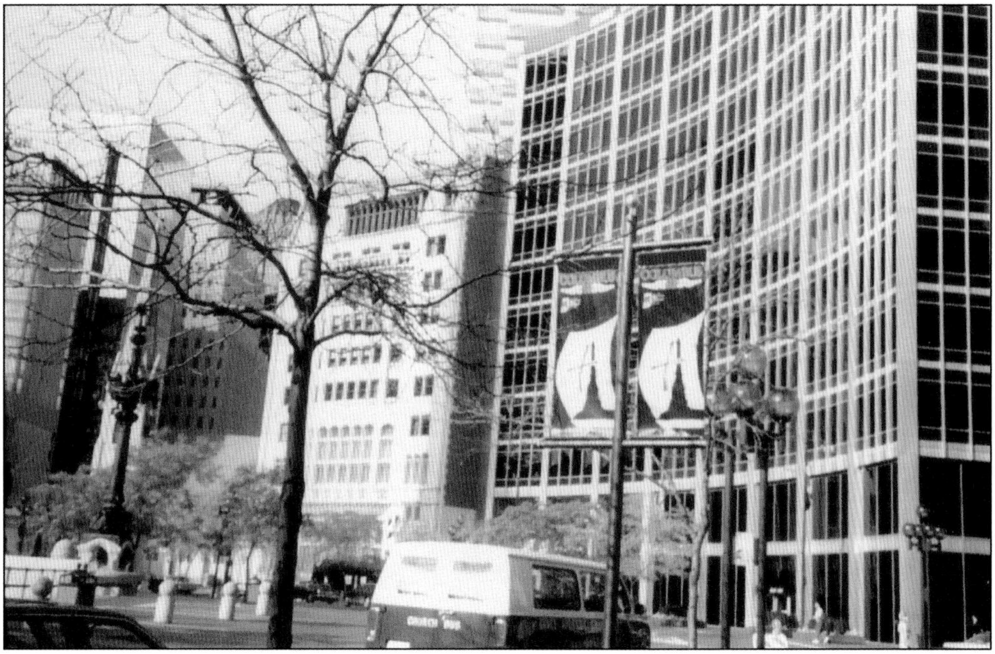

Columbus Commission '92 arranged for the design of a Columbus quincentenary banner to be displayed on the circle and downtown in October 1992. It featured the sail of Columbus's ship, the *Santa Maria*, with the silhouette of Indianapolis's Soldiers and Sailors Monument. (Courtesy Pietro Ferri.)

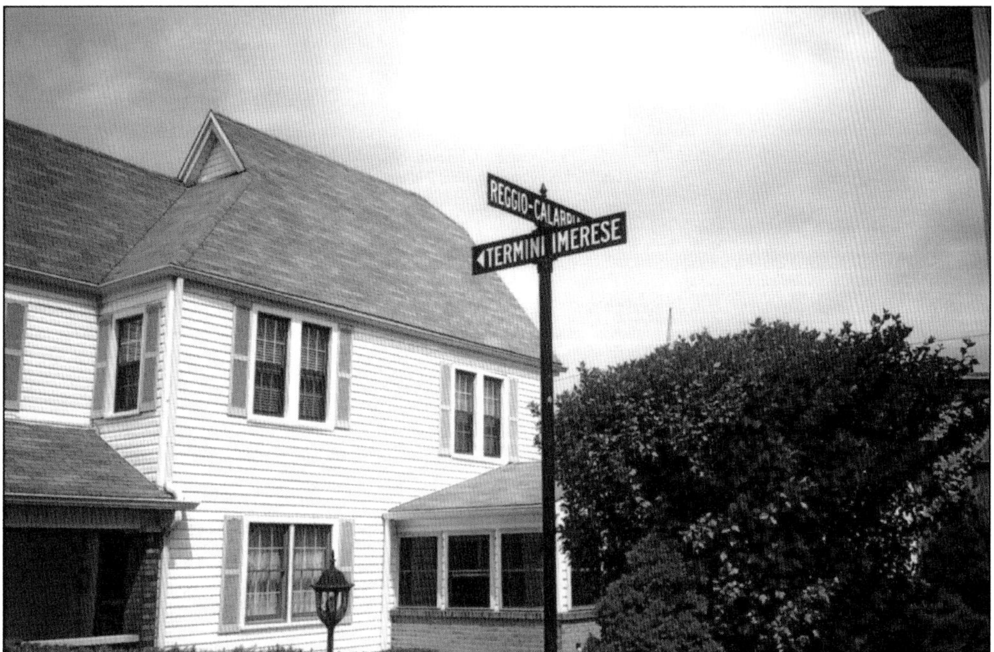

In memory of their ancestors in the Spicuzza, Mascari, and Corsaro families, David and Rosemary Page erected a sign next to their house on Stevens Street pointing back to Termini Imerese and Reggio Calabria.

EPILOGUE

Never has Indianapolis had a high percentage of immigrants in its population. Indeed, Italians in this city nowhere equal the percentage of Italians who moved into Chicago, Detroit, or New York. After a few pages, one realizes that a majority must have been Sicilian (about 60 percent, many from one town: Termini Imerese) and in the produce business. As one reads on, the diversity of origin becomes clearer, for other places in the "Boot" are reported—from Lombardy to Calabria. Yet as Jerry Roland points out in the introduction, many opened businesses as the next generation began to move into professional careers. Sicilian dominance also declined after World War II, though the island is still the origin of the majority. Almost all Italians and Italian Americans moving into the city come from the Boot and are making their mark.

Do not think that this is a complete history of the Italian community in images. Some noteworthy citizens, restaurants, and organizations were not available for contributions. Still others were simply not documented visually. This was the best the author could do with the available resources in the time allotted following the guidelines of Arcadia Publishing.

The author concludes with a plea for preservation. Many people think historians have great imaginations and just make up what they write. The truth is he or she spends long hours researching the topic at hand—that is, reading and evaluating the sources of information. Ethnic historians are handicapped by the scarcity of information and are forced to rely heavily on official documents, newspaper articles, some artifacts, and photographs.

As you know from the acknowledgments, this book exists because of the willingness of descendants to share their ancestors' lives, and the willingness of organizations like the Indiana Historical Society to share their archives. Do not think that your old photograph albums are worthless, or nobody is interested in that old stuff. If you get the urge to destroy old artifacts or memories, hold on! Phone the right archives or library. Your ancestors—and future historians—will greatly appreciate it.

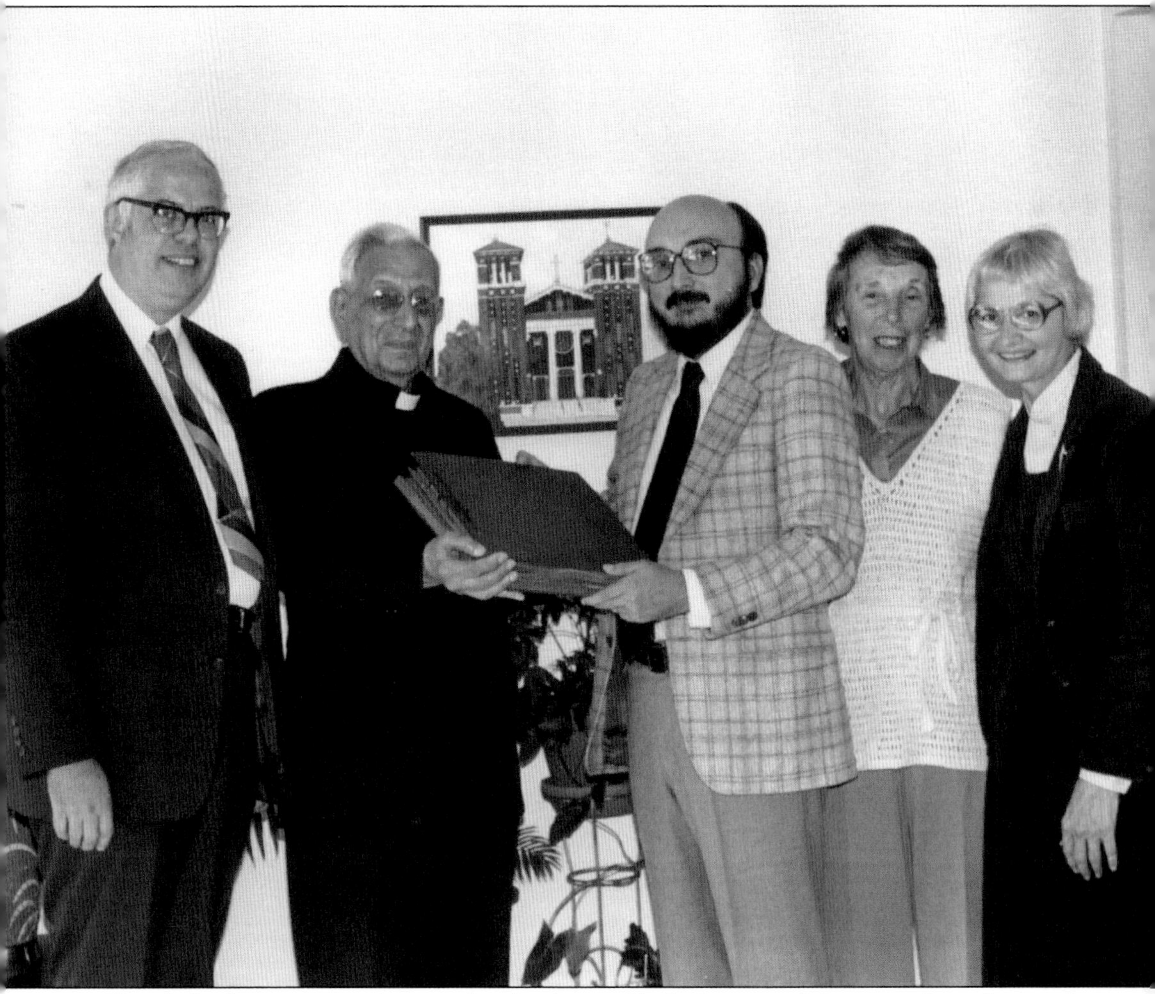

They helped us preserve the past for the future. Freda Buennagel, longtime housekeeper for both Msgr. Marino Priori and Fr. Augustine Sansone, organized a scrapbook of letters from high ranking Vatican officials and Italian bishops to Msgr. Priori over the years. Standing before a photograph of Holy Rosary Church, Father Gus presented the scrapbook to Eric Pumroy, Indiana Historical Society library. Witnessing the presentation were, from left to right, James J. Divita, history professor at Marian College, Freda's niece Mrs. Elmer Marien, and Sr. Charles Van Hoy, S.P., pastoral associate at Holy Rosary.

BIBLIOGRAPHY

Divita, James J. "The Indiana Churches and the Italian Immigrant 1890–1935." *US Catholic Historian*. Fall 1987.

———. *The Italians of Indianapolis: The Story of Holy Rosary Catholic Parish 1909–1984*. Indianapolis: Holy Rosary Parish, 1984.

———. *L'Italia on White River: Introducing the Italian Presence in Indianapolis by Tracing Its History and Describing Its Material Culture*. Indianapolis: Holy Rosary Pastoral Council and Italian Heritage Society of Indiana, 1995.

Taylor, Robert M. and Connie A. McBirney, eds. *Peopling Indiana: The Ethnic Experience*. Indianapolis: Indiana Historical Society, 1996.

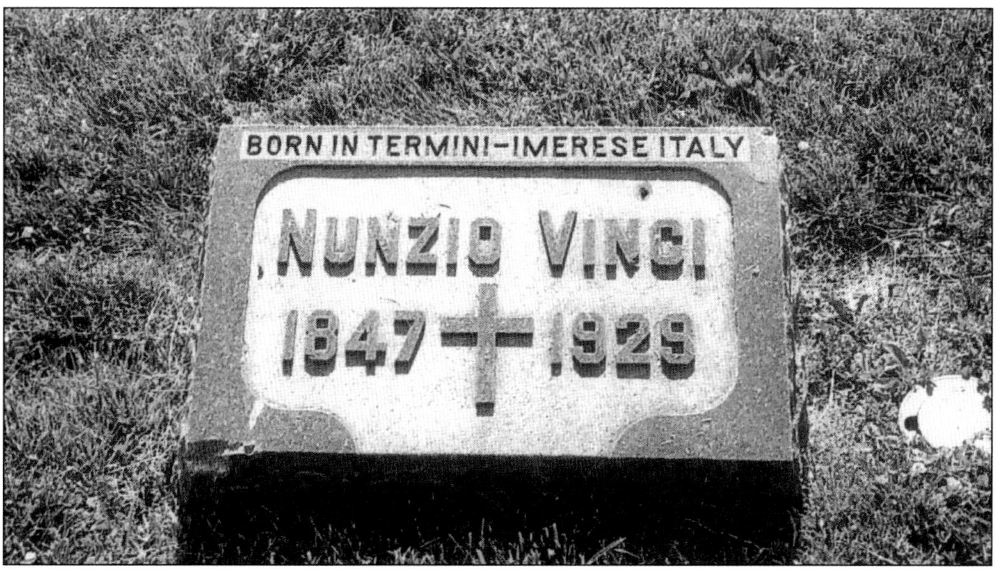

Nunzio Vinci (pronounced by Americans "Vin-sigh") was the father of Michael J. Vinci, a highly successful grocer, importer, and realtor. Although reputedly the city's first Italian millionaire, Vinci cemetery markers are small because the Depression hit Michael hard. Nonetheless, his father's marker reminds us that one little Sicilian town with an ancient past and an economically ambitious population contributed much to the Italian community, and helped the Italian community to contribute to the broader society of Indianapolis.

INDEX

Accetturo, John, 114, 119, 121
Accetturo, Vincent, 121
Accomando, Nicolò, 92
Agostino, Michael, 112, 118, 119
Agostino, Peter J., 118
Agostino, Pietro, 118
Annarino, Anthony, 40
Annarino, Rose, 40
Ardizzone, Mary Catherine, 109
Benedict family, 107
Bondi, Nicholas (Nicola), 72, 95
Bondi, Santina, 72
Bova Conti, John, 7, 70, 74
Bova, Giuseppina, 33
Bova, Salvatore, 33
Buennagel, Freda, 124
Burke, Tom, 121
Burns, Paul, 115
Burrello, Tony, 84
Caito brothers, 75
Caito, Filippo, 15
Caito, Joseph, 121
Caito, Josephine, 34, 35, 61
Caito, Mary Ann, 16
Caito, Michelina, 15, 16, 75
Caito, Philip H., 34, 35, 61
Caldarone, Charles, 36
Caldarone, Ninfa Gatto (see DeHilt, Ann), 36
Campo, Anthony, 121
Cannavo, Judy, 118
Catalano, Nicholas, 12
Cavallaro, Anthony J., 46
Cavallaro, Christina, 43
Cavallaro, Orlando, 43
Cavallaro, Pietro, 43, 44, 45, 47
Cavallaro, Tony, 43
Cento, Lisa, 64
Cento, Paul, 64
Cole, Henry, 121
Columbus bust at state house, 37, 111
Comado, Sam, 73
Constantino, Antonia, 17, 90
Cordingsley, A. Toni, 90
Corsaro, Concetta, 17
Corsaro, Danny, 17
Corsaro, Joe, 17
Corsaro, Paolo, 17
Corsaro, Paul, 17
Corsaro, Peter, 17, 71
Corsaro, Tony, 17
Corsi, Peter, 12
Cortese, Giuseppe, 78
Cortese, Joe, 79, 80
Cortese, Maria Concetta, 78
Cortese, Thelma, 79, 80
Cortese, Thomas A. Sr., 7, 78, 79, 80, 89, 118
Cortese, Thomas Jr., 79, 80, 118
Cortese, Tom III, 121
Crivelli, Ugo, 92
Dagro, Salvatore, 32
De Cecco, Carlo, 31, 62
De Cecco, Erna, 62
De Fabis, Domenica, 78
De Fabis, Ernest, 78
De Fabis, Julius, 78
De Fabis, Michael, 77, 78
De Fabis, Michele, 76, 77, 78
De Fabis, Phil, 77, 78
DeHilt, Ann, 118 (see Caldarone, Ninfa Gatto)
DeJulio, Frank, 37
Della Penna, Dominic, 37
Divita, James J., 7, 119, 124
Donato, Albert Sr., 80
Donato, Crescenzo (Chris), 80, 81
Donato, Harry, 80
Eternal Light, 104
Faenzi, Carol, 19, 55
Faenzi, Olga, 19
Faenzi, Otto (Ottavio), 55
Feld, Lucile (Nunzia), 17
Felicetti, Daniel, 118
Ferri, Pietro, 7, 68, 82, 83, 85, 112, 118, 119, 121
Ferri, Silvana, 63, 68, 85
Foppiano, John, 12
Forni, Angela, 85
Forni, Ralph, 85
Furlan family names, 31
Gasper, Harry, 7, 90
Gatto, Rosario, 32, 95
Gatto, Rose, 98
Giacoletti, Joe, 7, 8, 121
Gioscio, Dominic, 50
Gioscio, Fred, 50
Gioscio, Giovanni, 27, 28, 50
Gioscio, Maria, 27
Giuliano, Joseph, 12, 15
Guedelhoefer, Loretta, 73
Holy Rosary Catholic Church, 7, 71, 92, 96, 116

Iacobazzi, Jeff, 71
Iaria, Antonia, 17
Iaria, Mate, 18
Iaria, Matthew, 7, 18, 112, 121
Iaria, Pete, 108
Iaria, Sgt. Maj. Pete, 114
Iaria, Pietro, 17
Indianapolis 500 Italian winners, 85
Indianapolis Fruit Company, 17, 75
Indianapolis Italian Band, 47, 48
Indianapolis Produce Terminal officers, 75
Indianapolis Statuary Company, 38
Iozzo, Dominic, 20
Iozzo, Fred (Santoro), 19, 20, 47, 48
Iozzo, Rosaria, 19
Iozzo, Vincent, 20
Italian immigrant class of 1955, 63
LaGrotte, Leo family, 65
Lapenta, Vincent A., 37, 49, 50, 78
Lombardo, Gus, 24
Lops, Luigi, and Old Catholic diocese, 92
Maestri, Gabriele, 55, 56
Maestri, Rudy, 55, 58
Maio, Anthony, 7, 90
Mascari, Frank, 75
Mascari, Frank (first Sicilian), 7, 12, 13, 70
Mascari, Gus, 75
Mascari, Joseph, 32
Mascari, Mary Sansone, 70, 71
Mascari, Mike, 17
Mascari, Salvatore (Harpo), 70
McElroy, Eric, 120
McPherson, Allen, 69
McPherson, Evi, 69
Mercuri, William, 7, 90
Miceli, Annie, 14
Miceli, Josephine, 14
Miceli, Ninfa, 14
Miceli, Philip, 14
Miceli, Salvatore, 24
Miceli, Salvatore (Tudie), 49
Milto, Anna, 33, 62
Milto, Antonio, 33, 62
Milto, Philip and family, 62
Milto-Bergin, Joanna, 121
Mina, Ada, 67, 85
Mina, Aldo, 67, 82
Mina children, 67
Minà (Mina), Salvatore, 66
Modaffari, Joe, 65
Modaffari, Mary, 65
Modaffari, Paul, 65
Montani, Anthony (violinist), 26
Montani, Anthony B., 88
Montani, Dominic, 25, 26, 38, 87, 88
Montani, Ferdinand (lawyer), 87
Montani, Ferdinando, 13, 25, 26
Montani, Gaetano (Guy), 26, 38, 39
Montani, Nicola, 26
Montani, Pasquale, 26
Morone, Antone (Nino), 47, 121
Morone, Joseph Peter, 47
Morone, Margaret, 47
Murello, Christine, 54
Murello, Helen, 53, 70
Murello, Jo Anne, 109
Murello, Joe, 51, 52, 53, 54, 70
Murello, Margaret, 52
Murello, Margaret Catalano, 52
Murello, Tony, 51, 52, 54
Navarra, Michele, 32
Odorico, Maria, 69
Page, David, 7, 90, 112, 122
Page, Paul, 108
Page, Rosemary, 30, 108, 122
Pennella, Mary Grace, 121
Petruzzi, Sol, 114, 121
Piazza, Pete, 108
Piccione, Giacomo, 29
Piccione, Joe, 28
Piccione, Josephine, 28
Piccione, Mary, 29
Piccione, Sandra, 29
Piga, Angelo, 7, 68, 120, 121
Piga, Caterina, 68, 69, 121
Pizzi, Antonietta, 63, 64
Pizzi, Frederico, 64
Povinelli, Anselmo (Sam), 56
Povinelli, George, 56
Povinelli, Narcisso, 56
Povinelli, Pete, 56
Povinelli, Vito, 55, 56, 59
Priori, Marino, 7, 32, 92, 93–96, 97, 100–102, 104, 105, 124
Quattrocchi, Charles, 108
Ratti, Francis Anthony and sons, 11
Ray and Mascari, Inc., 30, 75, 76
Ray, Diana, 21
Ray, Joe, 21
Rigucci, Marco, 97
Roland, Frank (Corsaro), 17
Roland, Paul Jerry, 7, 17, 71, 89, 118, 123
Roland, Sarah, 89
Romano, Roy, 46
Rosasco, Angelo, 13
Rosasco, John, 13, 37
Safeway supermarket chain, 77
Sansone, Augustine, 23, 102, 105, 106, 107 124
Sansone, Joe, 22, 23
Scarpone, August (Augusto), 41, 42, 47
Scarpone, Francesca, 41
Scarpone, Pat, 41, 46
Sciarra, John, 115
Sereno, Linda, 118
Sergi, Anthony, 46
Sgro, Gino, 121
Sgro, Joe (boxer), 84
Sgro, Joe (war casualty), 46
Short, Frank, 7, 71, 90, 112
Sigreto, Josephine, 70, 96
Spicuzza, Anne Marie, 109
Spicuzza, Anthony, 107, 108
Spicuzza, Gus, 30, 75
Spicuzza, Rosa, 30
Stinnett, Gus, 106
Stinnett, Ruth, 106
Straffa, Jacob, 40
Straffa, Josephine, 40
Tambasco, Ralph, 119, 121
Uberta, Pasquale, 60
Vespo, Antonette, 60, 61
Vespo, Antonio, 60, 61
Vespo, Paolina, 60
Vinci, Michael, 125
Vinci, Nunzio, 125
Vittori, Enrico (Harry), 38

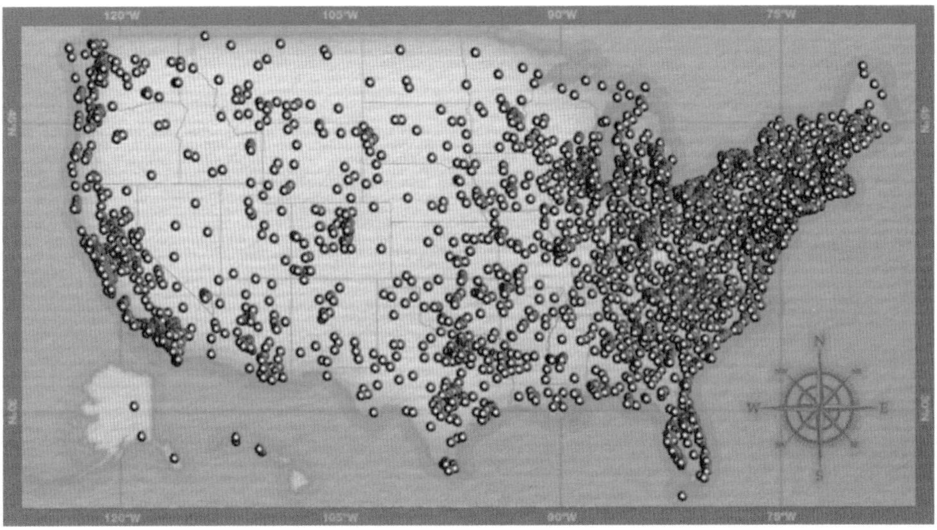

Consistent with our mission to preserve history on a local level, this book was printed in South Carolina on American-made paper and manufactured entirely in the United States. Products carrying the accredited Forest Stewardship Council (FSC) label are printed on 100 percent FSC-certified paper.

MADE IN THE USA